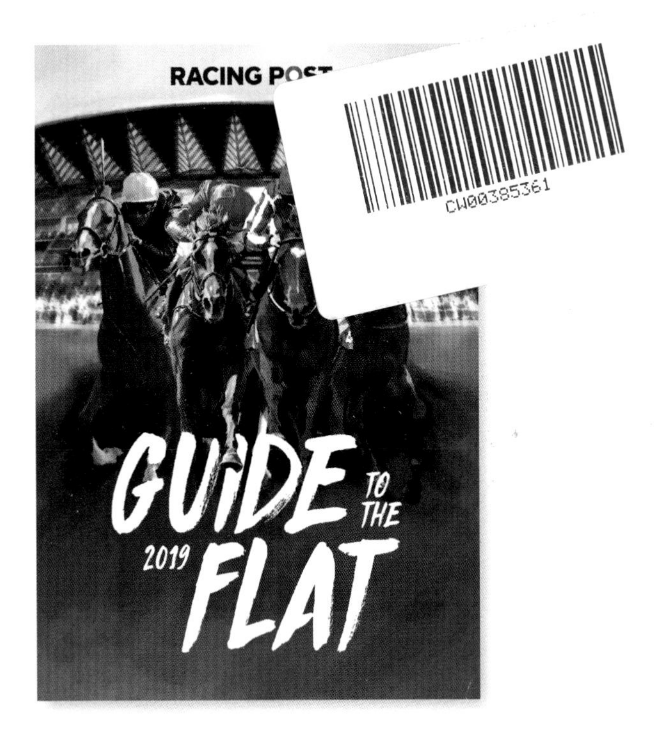

Edited and designed by David Dew

Contributors

Richard Birch
Scott Burton
Tom Collins
Andrew Dietz
Nicholas Godfrey
David Jennings
Paul Kealy
Pietro Innocenzi
David Milnes
Ollie O'Donoghue
Justin O'Hanlon
Dave Orton
Maddy Playle
Graeme Rodway
Peter Scargill
Tom Segal
Brian Sheerin
James Stevens
Alan Sweetman
Kitty Trice
Tom Ward
Nick Watts
Robbie Wilders
Andrew Wilsher
Ron Wood

Cover artwork by Samantha Creedon

Published in 2019 by Racing Post Books, Raceform, 27 Kingfisher Court, Hambridge Road, Newbury, RG14 5SJ

ISBN: 978-1839500015

Printed by Buxton Press Limited

THE TRAINERS

THE LOWDOWN JOHN GOSDEN

Plethora of stars can help master secure his fourth trainers' title

THE LOWDOWN JOSEPH O'BRIEN

Young gun eyes more glory with smart team

THE EXPERTS

THE KEY HORSES

DAVID O'MEARA

THE LOWDOWN MARK JOHNSTON

Bidding to build on record-breaking 'incredible' season

The course specialists primed to do it again

I ADVISED six Brighton specialists to follow in this book last year, and was rewarded with multiple wins from the likes of Roy Rocket and Pour La Victoire. In fact, the returns I accumulated from Brighton bets ultimately proved the difference between a winning and losing 2018.

Course form is something many punters fail to pay sufficient attention to when making their selections. There are many horses who at certain tracks consistently run 5lb or more above the level they produce round other venues. And with that in mind, fill your boots by following these ten course specialists in 2019 . . . .

THE STATS

THE LOWDOWN RALPH BECKETT

De Vegas hold the key to successful campaign

WINNERS IN LAST FOUR YEARS 88, 66, 101, 80

IF last year was a good one for trainer Ralph Beckett then there is every reason to believe this season could be an even better one – mainly because of two words: De Vega.

The single-minded pursuit of offspring of the stallion Lope De Vega by the Classic-winning trainer and London-based owners Waverley Racing unearthed four fillies who look to possess above-average levels of ability and look well placed to make an impact in big races this season.

"It was a good year and it looks like we have a nice bunch of three-year-olds going into this season," Beckett offers. "They were everything we hoped of them in the end and there's plenty to play for this year.

"It all rather fell into place for us with the Lope De Vegas. I'd be fortunate in that I'd trained a few of the same make and shape by that sire, horses like She Is No Lady and Isabel De Urbina, whose sister is Manuela De Vega; I was forewarned and forearmed in terms of what might be coming if we played our cards right."

Manuela De Vega won on her debut before following up in the Listed Silver Tankard Stakes at Pontefract. Feliciana De Vega and Antonia De Vega were also debut winners before landing black-type races, while Dancing Vega put up an eyecatching performance to win her only start.

"**Manuela De Vega** was a bit more forward than her sister at the same stage and I felt once she'd won her maiden then Pontefract

DID YOU KNOW?

Before going into training, Ralph Beckett got experience from all over the world when working with David Loder in England, Arthur Moore in Ireland, Tommy Skiffington in the US and Colin Hayes in Australia.

Ralph Beckett oversees his string on the gallops

was always going to be my first choice for her," Beckett says. "I thought the stiff mile would really suit her as would the turning nature of the course. It was a good effort to beat the colts and she ran through the line really well.

"She's wintered well and I hope we can get her to the place we want her to be. She'll have to start in the Classic trials straight away and that's the right thing to do anyway. I'm more inclined to look at Oaks trials rather than in the Guineas as I'm not convinced she has that speed."

Antonia back on track

The 1,000 Guineas route is more likely for Group 3 Prestige Stakes winner Antonia De Vega, while Feliciana De Vega, who romped to a Listed success in France, could head back to the continent for her early Classic engagements.

"**Antonia De Vega** came back with a split pastern after her run in the Fillies' Mile at Newmarket, but she's training well now. We'd be looking more towards Guineas trials for her straight off – she's unlikely to go further than that at this stage," Beckett says.

"**Feliciana De Vega** would be a bigger, rawer unit than the other two. It's difficult to say exactly what will be the route for her but I'd say we're most likely to end up factoring ground into what she does, at least in the short term. The way she's made and the way she moves indicates she wants a bit of juice so that's the way we'll lean for now.

"She might end up being one to go back to France with if we have a dry spring and she'll start in a trial too. She'll have a Guineas entry for Newmarket, but the ground will dictate her programme to begin with."

If three Classic contenders for one set of owners was not enough, Waverley Racing also have the totally unexposed **Dancing Vega**, who scooted to success at Doncaster in October, in the process defeating a subsequent Listed winner.

Beckett says: "Dancing Vega is the one most difficult to get a handle on as she rather trained off after her debut win. Initially I'd wanted to run her again but we had to put her away so that didn't come to pass.

"I thought her win was as impressive as any performance we had from one of our runners in a maiden last year. I would think, again, she's going to have to run in a Classic trial and is another who would want a bit of juice in the ground initially."

Beckett could well be saddling runners in the more familiar colours of owner Khalid Abdullah in Classics this season too with Chaleur and Sand Share putting up bold performances in stakes races last season.

More to come from Chaleur

Chaleur was third to Pretty Pollyanna in the Duchess of Cambridge Stakes before dismissing her rivals in the Jersey Lily Nursery, while Sand Share finished third in the May Hill Stakes before getting run down in the closing stages of the Prix Reservoirs.

"Chaleur's a lovely filly and could start off in the Fred Darling at Newbury," Beckett says. "She should progress and I think she's definitely worth having a crack at one of the trials with as I think she'll get a mile well. Whether she gets further, I don't know.

"**Sand Share** will be another for a Classic trial. It didn't work in France as I think the jockey got rather sucked into playing her too soon and got swamped late. I wouldn't blame him for that as it happens from time to time.

"She's definitely better than that run and I'm hopeful for the season ahead with her. She's a big filly and I don't think anyone would have ever described her as being particularly forward, so you'd think with only three runs under her belt she'd be able to progress again this year."

All three of Beckett's Classic victories have been with fillies (Look Here, 2008 Oaks; Talent, 2013 Oaks; Simple Verse, 2015 St Leger) and, as has been outlined so far, it is

SUPER STATS

Beckett's best tracks for punters are York (+£31.08), Ayr (+£17.35) and Pontefract (+£14.31). The venues to avoid are at Ascot (-£38.25), Salisbury (-£26.29) and Sandown (-£25.55)

Take note when he runs his horses at Yorkshire tracks – Beckett was three from five at Pontefract last year and had one winner from two runners at Ripon

Beckett tends to do best with horses running over 1m6f and 1m7f and has a 20 per cent strike-rate with a profit of £47.28

His best months are typically early in the season. In March 2017 Beckett had a 33 per cent strike-rate, while in the same month last year he was on the mark with 44 per cent of his runners

Statistics cover the last five years unless stated

the girls who are once again leading the way at Kimpton Down Stables. But that is not to say the boys are incapable. They certainly are capable, and middle-distance handicaps and stakes races could feature some formidable contenders from the Beckett yard.

'Something to look forward to'

Topping that list is surely **Stormwave**, a once-raced maiden scorer and brother to Beckett's All-Weather Marathon and Listed-winner Moonrise Landing.

"Stormwave showed a lot at two, especially for a son of Dalakhani," Beckett muses. "His mother [Celtic Slipper] was a pretty good two-year-old but you don't get many Dalakhani's showing up as well as he did at two. I think he's a really nice horse.

"He had a blip after his only run and we had to do a minor procedure on him which is why he didn't run again. He's quite laid-back, which will definitely help him as his sister wasn't like that at all. But if he's anything like her he should progress as he

gets older and that's something to really look forward to."

The same sentiments apply to Nivaldo, Skymax, Fearless Warrior and Brasca, who all showed plenty of promise as juveniles but are bred, and look like, horses to do better as they get older.

"**Nivaldo** showed plenty from the outset even with as backward a pedigree as he has. He's done well over the winter and is quite exuberant. I can see him running in the Dee Stakes at Chester," Beckett says.

"**Skymax** is a long-distance handicapper in the making, or potentially better, and will get better as we go further. He could be a horse for the King George V at Royal Ascot and then maybe on to races like the Melrose after that.

"**Fearless Warrior** could be another for the King George V, although I wouldn't know if he'd get further. He's certainly a 1m4f horse to go to war with in those better handicaps for the rest of the year."

Beckett adds: "**Brasca** might be a slower burner who may come online later in the year – it will depend on how it goes for him in the next couple of months. His sister Highgarden got better as she got older and I can see him being the same."

Eagle ready to fly high

Beckett has a template for the likes of Brasca in **Rock Eagle**. Bred by owner Jeff Smith,

Stormwave made a good impression when winning at Salisbury on his sole start last season as a two-year-old

the four-year-old was unraced this time last year but progressed to win the Old Rowley Cup on his final start. Like his paternal half-brother, Melbourne Cup winner Cross Counter, it looks like a case of the further the better for Rock Eagle.

"Rock Eagle was one we had to be patient with last year and he was an immature individual," Beckett says. "I'm hoping we'll be able to campaign him a bit more aggressively this year. He enjoys fast ground and I think a step up in trip at some point would be an obvious way to go with him. He's on the cusp of being a stakes horse now and hopefully that all comes together for him."

If Rock Eagle could be progressing out of handicaps, he leaves a suitable space for the likeable **Here And Now** to step into.

Beckett says: "I'd love to run him in the Ebor because he loves York. Equally we might try the Chester Cup with him first as he's fully effective around there and beat a certain Stradivarius there, albeit a long time ago."

Ascot targets for course specialist

While York is the course of choice for Here And Now, **Di Fede** is never better than when running at Ascot. The four-year-old ended last season with an impressive Listed win at the course, and has recorded her three highest Racing Post Ratings at the track.

Beckett says: "Di Fede thrives at Ascot and runs better there than anywhere else and I think she should pay her way. She's a tough girl and will get an entry in the Duke of Cambridge Stakes at Royal Ascot as she runs so well there. She could also start in the Victoria Cup, or alternatively go for the Chartwell Stakes at Lingfield on the same day."

Beckett is highly likely to be thumbing his way through the continental programme book this year too having claimed numerous prizes abroad last season, headed by the two Group victories of the evergreen **Air Pilot** in the Prix Exbury and Prix d'Harcourt.

"He'll go the same route again this year and is the most extraordinary horse," Beckett says, exuding pride at the ten-year-old's enthusiasm and vigour. "He's a real stable favourite and he's been great fun to have here and he still enjoys it. If we place him right he'll win more races.

"It's a great shame for me that he's never really done it in England, it's always been Ireland and France. I'd love him to win something at the level he's achieved on the continent back here."

Bright outlook for Vista

Air Pilot could be joined in his continental missions by **Dolphin Vista**, with the six-year-old having a distinct preference for soft ground.

Beckett took charge of the 2017 Cambridgeshire winner midway through last year and saddled him to win a Listed race at Ayr on the second of his two starts for the trainer.

"In a way they're likely to have similar campaigns and could end up taking each other on," Beckett says. "Ground is important to him and he could start in something like the Prix Exbury which is run at Saint-Cloud at the end of March. Races like the Earl of Sefton at Newmarket and such are the way he'll likely go.

"He's a talented horse when conditions are on his side and there's plenty of mileage left in him yet in my view."

Beckett adds: "**Mitchum Swagger** also has a good bit left to work with. He's a lovely horse and should pick up something nice along the way. He might start in the Doncaster Mile at the Lincoln meeting."

There will be few yards approaching the season with the optimism and excitement of Beckett's and if only a handful of the horses mentioned reach their potential then the stable is in for a good time of things in 2019. If they all reach the level they have promised, it could well be a truly memorable year. Viva De Vega.

Interview by Peter Scargill

RALPH BECKETT

KIMPTON, HAMPSHIRE

	Number of horses	Races run	1st	2nd	3rd	Unpl	Per cent	£1 level stake
2yo	55	161	27	26	18	90	16.8	-35.31
3yo	52	258	46	47	34	131	17.8	-23.82
4yo+	23	103	15	16	10	62	14.6	-19.38
Totals	**130**	**522**	**88**	**89**	**62**	**283**	**16.9**	**-78.51**
2017	136	464	66	59	69	269	14.2	-103.21
2016	133	506	101	70	55	279	20.0	+7.55

BY MONTH

2yo	W-R	Per cent	£1 level stake	3yo	W-R	Per cent	£1 level stake
Jan	0-0	0.0	0.00	Jan	1-10	10.0	-2.00
Feb	0-0	0.0	0.00	Feb	1-2	50.0	+0.50
Mar	0-0	0.0	0.00	Mar	0-7	0.0	-7.00
Apr	1-3	33.3	+3.00	Apr	6-29	20.7	+33.00
May	0-7	0.0	-7.00	May	7-41	17.1	-0.08
June	1-7	14.3	-5.67	June	5-44	11.4	-26.32
July	2-18	11.1	0.00	July	7-35	20.0	-12.32
Aug	3-30	10.0	-18.00	Aug	7-35	20.0	-13.84
Sep	9-37	24.3	+18.63	Sep	5-27	18.5	-1.00
Oct	7-29	24.1	-5.42	Oct	5-20	25.0	+8.50
Nov	3-22	13.6	-15.09	Nov	2-7	28.6	-2.27
Dec	1-8	12.5	-5.75	Dec	0-1	0.0	-1.00

4yo+	W-R	Per cent	£1 level stake	Totals	W-R	Per cent	£1 level stake
Jan	1-10	10.0	-7.50	Jan	2-20	10.0	-9.50
Feb	0-1	0.0	-1.00	Feb	1-3	33.3	-0.50
Mar	0-4	0.0	-4.00	Mar	0-11	0.0	-11.00
Apr	2-8	25.0	-2.75	Apr	9-40	22.5	+33.25
May	3-15	20.0	+5.75	May	10-63	15.9	-1.33
June	2-18	11.1	-7.00	June	8-69	11.6	-38.99
July	2-11	18.2	-3.50	July	11-64	17.2	-15.82
Aug	2-11	18.2	+4.63	Aug	12-76	15.8	-27.21
Sep	1-11	9.1	+4.00	Sep	15-75	20.0	+21.63
Oct	0-7	0.0	-7.00	Oct	12-56	21.4	-3.92
Nov	2-6	33.3	0.00	Nov	7-35	20.0	-2.27
Dec	0-1	0.0	-1.00	Dec	1-10	10.0	-2.00

DISTANCE

2yo	W-R	Per cent	£1 Level Stake	3yo	W-R	Per cent	£1 level stake
5f-6f	7-56	12.5	-19.92	5f-6f	6-38	15.8	-0.40
7f-8f	17-98	17.3	-19.52	7f-8f	15-84	17.9	-1.33
9f-13f	3-7	42.9	+4.13	9f-13f	23-120	19.2	-13.00
14f+	0-0	0.0	0.00	14f+	2-16	12.5	-9.09

4yo+	W-R	Per cent	£1 level stake	Totals	W-R	Per cent	£1 level stake
5f-6f	0-4	0.0	-4.00	5f-6f	13-98	13.3	-24.32
7f-8f	5-31	16.1	-7.13	7f-8f	37-213	17.4	-27.98
9f-13f	8-49	16.3	-4.63	9f-13f	34-176	19.3	-13.50
14f+	2-19	10.5	-3.63	14f+	4-35	11.4	-12.72

TYPE OF RACE

NON-HANDICAPS				HANDICAPS			
	W-R	Per cent	£1 level stake		W-R	Per cent	£1 level stake
2yo	24-135	17.8	-21.31	2yo	3-26	11.5	-14.00
3yo	12-96	12.5	-22.99	3yo	34-162	21.0	-0.83
4yo+	6-30	20.0	+5.00	4yo+	9-73	12.3	-24.38

Statistics relate to all runners in Britain from January 1, 2018 to December 31, 2018

Here And Now (far side) beats Stradivarius at Chester – he could be heading back to the course this season

THE LOWDOWN RICHARD FAHEY

Vibes are good as Mali spearheads smart team

WINNERS IN LAST FOUR YEARS 190, 200, 198, 235

SINCE starting out on a small farm near Malton in North Yorkshire in 1993, Richard Fahey has grown to be one of Britain's most prominent Flat trainers.

While not at the height of Aidan O'Brien or John Gosden, Fahey continues to boast a stable filled with talented horses who can pull off big wins at big odds.

In 2018 he posted a total of 190 winners in Britain and another in Ireland, returning a profit for punters at 11 tracks. That includes Ascot where, despite having just one winner from the 27 horses he sent there, 28-1 shot **Sands Of Mali** scored in the Champion Sprint as the curtain came down to give Fahey his sole Group 1 winner of the season.

The star sprinter was the stable's standout performer last year, also scooping a Group 3 at Chantilly and the Group 2 Sandy Lane Stakes at Haydock as well as finishing second in the Commonwealth Cup at Royal Ascot.

Fahey is hopeful Sands Of Mali can push on from that big victory on Champions Day last year, starting with a tilt in Dubai.

The trainer says: "He's looking as good as ever. It's easy planning for him, and I think he'll run a maximum of six times this year. He's heading to Meydan to run on World Cup Night, and all being well from that he'll be going to Royal Ascot again and all of the top sprints. The July Cup is certainly an option."

SUPER STATS

Follow Fahey for a profit at Nottingham (+£50.51), Musselburgh (+£27.33) and Newbury (+£27.13). Tread carefully at York (-£159.25), Haydock (-£138.89) and Wolverhampton (-£130.94)

Keep an eye out for Fahey's juvenile runners at Newbury where he has a profit of £36.63

Fahey has a good record with his three-year-old runners at Musselburgh with a 22 per cent strike-rate and a profit of £32.20

Watch out for older horses in claimers – Fahey has a 26 per cent strike-rate (+£35.78)

Oisin Murphy is three from three when riding for the stable and boasts a profit of £12 with those wins

Statistics cover the last five years unless stated

A trip to the Middle East may not be the only travelling Sands Of Mali does this year, as Fahey also pinpoints a potential conquest in Australia, saying: "There's been some talk of sending him for the VRC Sprint Classic on Emirates Stakes Day at Flemington, but that's a long way off. We'll start in Dubai and take it from there."

Another renowned flagbearer for Fahey's yard who is showing no signs of stopping is ten-year-old **Gabrial**. He ran 15 times last year and remains a feature at all the big

meetings, finishing second in the Diomed Stakes at Epsom and appearing in the Royal Hunt Cup and Queen Elizabeth II Stakes at Ascot.

Fahey is absolutely delighted with him, and says: "He's an unbelievable horse and an absolute legend. We're looking at starting him off in the Lincoln, but I'll need to speak to Marwan [Koukash, owner] about it. He'll be running off a mark of 107 though which isn't easy. Still, he's in great form and we'll also look at some races at York and Chester."

'He's done very well over winter'

It was Chester's Huxley Stakes in which five-year-old **Forest Ranger** earned his biggest win last season, which followed up success in the Earl of Sefton at Newmarket. While the remainder of his season wasn't quite so successful, the son of Lawman was beaten only a neck in the Darley Stakes back at Newmarket on his final run and has impressed over the break.

"He's done very well over the winter and is still such a big horse. We'll likely take the same route as last year seeing as that worked out well, but we'll get through the first two and take it from there."

Last year's two-year-old class included plenty of black-type earners, so it is no wonder Fahey is excited for the upcoming campaign to see how they progress at three.

One who broke on to the scene in a big way was **Red Balloons**, who defied odds of 33-1 to scoop the Premier Yearling Stakes at the Ebor Festival.

That victory was secured by an impressive three lengths, but Fahey is not getting carried away and suggests he will take a bit more time in deciding which route to take with the daughter of Kyllachy.

Forest Ranger (left) powers home to land Chester's Huxley Stakes

RICHARD FAHEY

MUSLEY BANK, NORTH YORKSHIRE

	Number of horses	Races run	1st	2nd	3rd	Unpl	Per cent	£1 level stake
2yo	108	493	54	65	62	312	11.0	-160.93
3yo	82	571	79	79	67	345	13.8	+4.24
4yo+	66	535	57	55	62	360	10.7	-92.36
Totals	**256**	**1599**	**190**	**199**	**191**	**1017**	**11.9**	**-249.05**
2017	298	1749	200	220	218	1109	11.4	-505.32
2016	294	1739	198	194	223	1121	11.4	-396.09

BY MONTH

2yo	W-R	Per cent	£1 level stake	3yo	W-R	Per cent	£1 level stake
Jan	0-0	0.0	0.00	Jan	1-17	5.9	-12.50
Feb	0-0	0.0	0.00	Feb	2-16	12.5	+3.00
Mar	0-2	0.0	-2.00	Mar	3-24	12.5	+1.00
Apr	2-14	14.3	-0.50	Apr	7-40	17.5	-1.50
May	9-44	20.5	+8.88	May	11-75	14.7	-18.37
June	8-60	13.3	-9.34	June	14-85	16.5	+49.50
July	12-82	14.6	-17.58	July	15-83	18.1	-2.80
Aug	12-101	11.9	-24.51	Aug	10-80	12.5	-27.09
Sep	2-82	2.4	-56.00	Sep	6-66	9.1	-5.50
Oct	6-60	10.0	-32.38	Oct	5-51	9.8	+20.00
Nov	1-31	3.2	-26.50	Nov	2-22	9.1	-6.00
Dec	2-17	11.8	-1.00	Dec	3-12	25.0	+4.50

4yo+	W-R	Per cent	£1 level stake	Totals	W-R	Per cent	£1 level stake
Jan	1-23	4.3	-19.25	Jan	2-40	5.0	-31.75
Feb	1-22	4.5	-13.00	Feb	3-38	7.9	-10.00
Mar	5-30	16.7	+8.00	Mar	8-56	14.3	+7.00
Apr	8-44	18.2	+15.75	Apr	17-98	17.3	+13.75
May	8-79	10.1	-30.21	May	28-198	14.1	-39.70
June	12-88	13.6	+0.13	June	34-233	14.6	+40.29
July	9-68	13.2	-5.75	July	36-233	15.5	-26.13
Aug	6-59	10.2	+5.23	Aug	28-240	11.7	-46.37
Sep	3-62	4.8	-29.25	Sep	11-210	5.2	-90.75
Oct	3-44	6.8	-19.00	Oct	14-155	9.0	-31.38
Nov	1-14	7.1	-3.00	Nov	4-67	6.0	-9.00
Dec	0-2	0.0	-2.00	Dec	5-31	16.1	+2.50

DISTANCE

2yo	W-R	Per cent	£1 Level Stake	3yo	W-R	Per cent	£1 level stake
5f-6f	42-338	12.4	-84.05	5f-6f	32-193	16.6	+9.01
7f-8f	12-148	8.1	-69.88	7f-8f	31-255	12.2	-8.27
9f-13f	0-7	0.0	-7.00	9f-13f	16-120	13.3	+6.50
14f+	0-0	0.0	0.00	14f+	0-3	0.0	-3.00

4yo+	W-R	Per cent	£1 level stake	Totals	W-R	Per cent	£1 level stake
5f-6f	15-155	9.7	-15.25	5f-6f	89-686	13.0	-90.29
7f-8f	26-223	11.7	-15.02	7f-8f	69-626	11.0	-93.17
9f-13f	12-125	9.6	-42.25	9f-13f	28-252	11.1	-42.75
14f+	4-32	12.5	-19.83	14f+	4-35	11.4	-22.83

TYPE OF RACE

NON-HANDICAPS				HANDICAPS			
	W-R	Per cent	£1 level stake		W-R	Per cent	£1 level stake
2yo	43-351	12.3	-86.80	2yo	11-142	7.7	-74.13
3yo	14-98	14.3	+2.29	3yo	65-473	13.7	+1.95
4yo+	13-64	20.3	+10.35	4yo+	44-471	9.3	-102.71

Statistics relate to all runners in Britain from January 1, 2018 to December 31, 2018

Charming Kid in the winner's enclosure after scoring at Dundalk over the winter

He says: "I haven't got any real plans yet for Red Balloons, but we'll look at getting her some black type as the first priority. She's a really tough filly in general, and I'm sure there'll be races for her. We'll start at 6f but that could change."

Patient approach can pay off

Fahey is not one to rush into things and enjoys taking each race as it comes, so plans for the likes of Wasntexpectingthat – third in the £300,000 2-Y-O Stakes at Doncaster – and Sabre – second in a pair of Listed races last term – are fluid.

The trainer says: "**Sabre** had a little setback at the end of last season, so we've been dealing with that. He's back in training now and we're happy with him, but we'll take it easy with him for now and see how he progresses.

"**Wasntexpectingthat** was gelded over the winter and has since started showing some of his best form. It's still too early to tell where we'll go with him, but he's very well handicapped and we'll look for decent ground."

Other three-year-olds flagged up as ones to follow this campaign are Charming Kid, Cosmic Law and Space Traveller.

Charming Kid tasted success on the all-weather over winter which has earned him a place on finals day at Lingfield in April, while **Cosmic Law** showed steady progression as a two-year-old, finishing ninth in the Coventry before improving that to sixth in the Vintage Stakes and third in the Rockingham.

Fahey says: "Cosmic Law did well over the winter and I'm very happy with him. The plan is to start him off handicapping and take it from there. One at Newmarket or York would be right up his street, but he doesn't want the ground too quick."

DID YOU KNOW?

Richard Fahey developed an interest in training when buying and selling horses during his riding career. The first Royal Ascot winner he saddled was Superior Premium in 2002. He cost just 2,800gns.

Trip mission for Traveller

In France **Space Traveller** was narrowly beaten into second in a Group 3 at Maisons-Laffitte but then disappointed at Newmarket

George Bowen scores at York last season and will be heading back there this year

and York. Fahey says: "We'll go with a three-year-old handicap to start and see how he gets on. I'm still not sure whether he's a sprinter or would prefer further, but he's a good-minded horse and we'll use that handicap to find out a bit more."

The Fahey stable has consistently thrived in big handicaps over the years, and the trainer has another stout line-up of runners to go to war with this term.

Seven-year-old **Growl** has been a regular on the scene but was unable to win last year, although he was placed four times. Fahey says: "It was a frustrating year for him. He wants soft ground ideally but after the summer we had it just didn't work out. He's still well handicapped and in good form."

George Bowen is another seven-year-old handicapper in Fahey's ranks, but he says this could be a tricky year for him: "He won a couple last year and was sixth in the Wokingham, but he isn't getting any younger and 103 is a tough mark to start off at. We'll aim him at York and hopefully get a couple more wins."

Instead the trainer has another one to follow in handicaps this year – a winner at Doncaster in 2018 and purchased from

Richard Fahey cools down one of his string after morning exercise

Godolphin by Marwan Koukash over the winter.

"**Brian The Snail** ran in nine handicaps last year and there'll be more of the same," says Fahey. "I think he could do with a step up in trip and Marwan is keen to run him in the Lincoln, so we could go there and see how he handles a mile."

Plenty of new recruits

As is typical in the Flat scene, a number of those within the Fahey battalion who scored last season will not be returning this year.

Listed winners Kimberella and Dance Diva have been retired, as has Listed runner-up Clubbable, while Vange and Ninetythreetwenty, who finished fourth and sixth in last year's Coventry Stakes at Royal Ascot, have been sold to race in Hong Kong. French Group 3 runner-up Kodyanna has also been sold.

Fahey, however, remains upbeat about the new campaign and fresh crop of talent that will be coming through the ranks.

"Unfortunately we sold six of our best, but that's the nature of our business," he says. "We're offered money we can't refuse and we have to take it – it's a natural consequence if you keep turning out winners.

"Still, we have a good bunch in this year and a broad spectrum of runners. There are some really nice two-year-olds who could do something, and the three-year-olds we have left are still very decent."

Fahey is tight-lipped about any particular juveniles who could spring a surprise, but he does reveal they are a good bunch and that he is very happy with their progress.

Considering he was represented by three runners in last season's Coventry Stakes – finishing fourth (25-1), sixth (33-1) and ninth (11-1) – and had a number of other youngsters place in Group and Listed company, it is safe to assume he will get this year's crop in shape for further success.

Interview by Andrew Wilsher

"Alexa, what's my Flash Briefing?"

THE LOWDOWN JOHN GOSDEN

Plethora of stars can help master secure his fourth trainers' title

JOHN GOSDEN won his third British trainers' title last year in a very familiar pattern – it was three years after the previous one.

Having broken his duck soon after returning to Newmarket in 2012, Gosden doubled his tally in 2015 thanks to the likes of Golden Horn before bagging the trio last December when the likes of Enable, Roaring Lion and Cracksman weighed in.

In each of those instances, it was common practice that the intervening times were seen as rebuilding years in which old stars had

Enable (left) charges towards a second victory in the Arc and will bid for the hat-trick this season

WINNERS IN LAST FOUR YEARS 178, 138, 142, 133

moved on to stud. Although a repeat of that trend would indicate Gosden may have to wait until 2021 for his next crown, don't be surprised if he wins it again this year, especially with the decision to keep dual Arc winner **Enable** in training.

Although Khalid Abdullah's star generated most of her prize-money overseas in bagging her second Arc and first win at the Breeders' Cup in 2018, she could contribute more this year with Royal Ascot pencilled in as a summer target followed by another crack at the King George VI & Queen Elizabeth Stakes she first won in 2017.

Although Roaring Lion and Cracksman may have gone, Gosden's senior team also includes staying phenomenon Stradivarius, Group 1 St James's Palace Stakes winner Without Parole, top staying prospect Lah Ti Dar not to mention prolific all-weather winner Wissahickon.

On top of that, Gosden has the highest-rated juvenile since Frankel in 2011 in his armoury in the shape of Too Darn Hot who is already favourite for the Qipco 2,000 Guineas and Investec Derby without a ball even being kicked on the turf.

The son of Dubawi is already assured a place at Dalham Hall Stud when his racing days are over with his breeder Andrew Lloyd Webber selling a half share in the colt to Sheikh Mohammed before his devastating display in the Group 1 Dewhurst Stakes at Newmarket last October.

That defeat of Advertise topped an unbeaten four-race campaign as a juvenile which encompassed back-to-back wins at Sandown, including the Group 3 Solario Stakes, before another commanding display in the Group 2 Champagne Stakes at Doncaster.

If that was not enough ammunition for the top table, Gosden has Calyx waiting in the wings to bolster the Group 1 cavalry after his easy win in the Group 2 Coventry Stakes at Royal Ascot in June.

All roads lead back to Paris

Gosden says: "Every year is a rebuilding year as you start again on zero. We'll miss Roaring Lion and Cracksman just as we missed Golden Horn and Taghrooda when they retired. You've got to look forward though and we've got some young and some proven horses to look forward to for 2019."

Queen of the proven stock is **Enable** for whom all roads lead to a bid to surpass the mighty Treve and win the Arc for a record third time in October.

Her trainer says: "It's been well publicised that Enable had an injury last spring that was operated on and she did brilliantly to come back from it. She had a hiccup between her comeback race at Kempton and the Arc which wasn't ideal but she showed a lot of courage to win in Paris and then overcame quite a lot to win at the Breeders' Cup."

Before her injury, Enable was last year pencilled in to make her reappearance in the Group 1 Coronation Cup at Epsom and that 1m4f contest is also on her radar this time.

Gosden adds: "Enable has had a good winter – she's had an easy time and she'll be heading into June before she's seen in action with races like the Coronation Cup and the Prince of Wales's Stakes at Royal Ascot on her agenda. Beyond that, it's all about where we have her on the first Sunday in October."

In his latest title-winning year, Gosden reached a highest ever tally of 178 winners and over £8.5 million in prize-money to boot.

Stradivarius supplemented his earnings last season with a £1m bonus for winning the Weatherbys Hamilton Stayers' Million and was unbeaten in his five starts.

The five-year-old is likely to have the same targets as last year in a bid to scoop the cash for a second year although the series has been expanded.

Gosden says: "Stradivarius is in good order and we look forward to the challenge again. I see there are now qualifying races in France, Ireland, Germany and Dubai added to the four races here which makes it more interesting.

"Stradivarius started off last year in the Yorkshire Cup in May and the plan is to go there again before Royal Ascot, Goodwood and back to York for the Lonsdale Cup."

Group 1s for Winter Derby ace

Before the domestic action gets going at Newbury and at the Craven Meeting at Newmarket in April, Gosden plans to be busy on World Cup night in Dubai on March 30 when he could have three runners headlined by prolific all-weather performer **Wissahickon**.

The four-year-old mopped up three races on the Polytrack at Lingfield through the winter, culminating in an easy defeat of stablemate Court House in the Group 3 Winter Derby and is set for a move up to Group 1 level.

Gosden says: "Wissahickon is improving and could go to Dubai for the Sheema Classic. He's also in the Easter Classic at

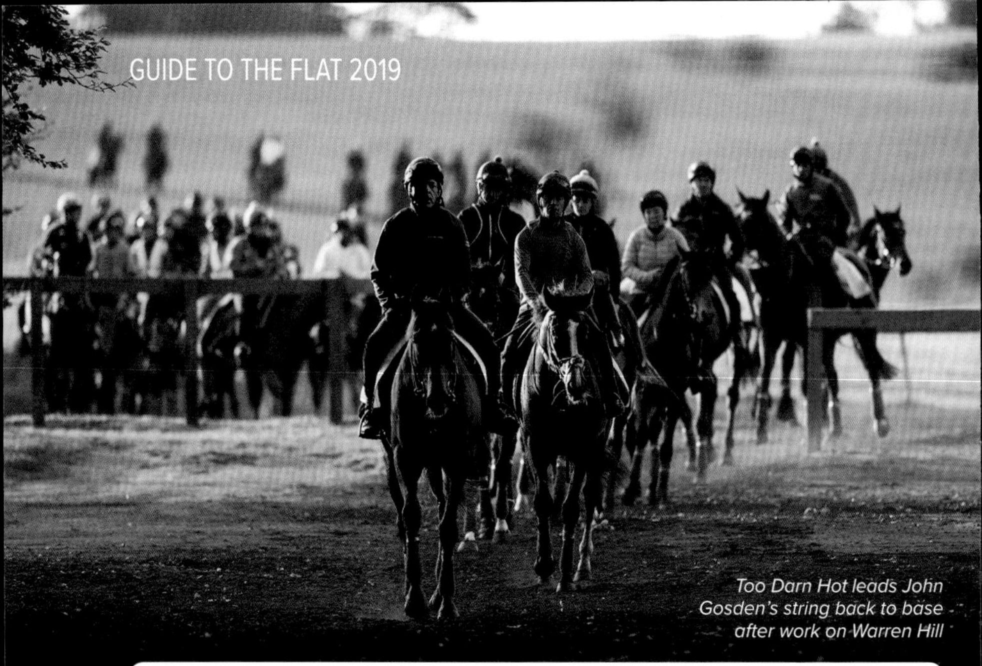

Too Darn Hot leads John Gosden's string back to base after work on Warren Hill

JOHN GOSDEN

NEWMARKET, SUFFOLK

	Number of horses	Races run	1st	2nd	3rd	Unpl	Per cent	£1 level stake
2yo	89	228	53	49	24	102	22.8	-28.48
3yo	105	394	104	72	56	162	26.4	-27.86
4yo+	25	83	21	10	10	42	25.3	-2.37
Totals	**219**	**705**	**178**	**131**	**90**	**306**	**25.1**	**-58.71**
2017	225	690	138	91	102	358	20.0	-81.86
2016	211	613	142	106	78	287	23.2	+7.64

BY MONTH

2yo	W-R	Per cent	£1 level stake	3yo	W-R	Per cent	£1 level stake
Jan	0-0	0.0	0.00	Jan	6-24	25.0	-3.78
Feb	0-0	0.0	0.00	Feb	4-11	36.4	+7.03
Mar	0-0	0.0	0.00	Mar	3-17	17.6	-10.57
Apr	0-0	0.0	0.00	Apr	17-50	34.0	+18.40
May	1-4	25.0	-1.00	May	20-72	27.8	+1.80
June	4-10	40.0	+1.23	June	11-57	19.3	-24.73
July	7-22	31.8	-2.02	July	9-39	23.1	-16.68
Aug	5-22	22.7	-6.59	Aug	11-39	28.2	-6.80
Sep	9-45	20.0	-1.52	Sep	9-34	26.5	+7.10
Oct	9-55	16.4	-22.39	Oct	7-28	25.0	+2.85
Nov	9-42	21.4	-1.73	Nov	3-16	18.8	-5.27
Dec	8-28	28.6	+5.55	Dec	4-7	57.1	+2.80

4yo+	W-R	Per cent	£1 level stake	Totals	W-R	Per cent	£1 level stake
Jan	0-1	0.0	-1.00	Jan	6-25	24.0	-4.78
Feb	1-2	50.0	+4.00	Feb	5-13	38.5	+11.03
Mar	0-5	0.0	-5.00	Mar	3-22	13.6	-15.57
Apr	3-5	60.0	+7.20	Apr	20-55	36.4	+25.60
May	7-20	35.0	-1.13	May	28-96	29.2	-0.33
June	3-18	16.7	-4.96	June	18-85	21.2	-28.46
July	1-7	14.3	-5.20	July	17-68	25.0	-23.90
Aug	2-6	33.3	+7.36	Aug	18-67	26.9	-6.03
Sep	1-7	14.3	-5.47	Sep	19-86	22.1	+0.11
Oct	2-9	22.2	-5.17	Oct	18-92	19.6	-24.71
Nov	1-3	33.3	+7.00	Nov	13-61	21.3	+1.73
Dec	0-0	0.0	0.00	Dec	12-35	34.3	+2.80

DISTANCE

2yo	W-R	Per cent	£1 Level Stake	3yo	W-R	Per cent	£1 level stake
5f-6f	13-36	36.1	+9.39	5f-6f	3-18	16.7	-9.15
7f-8f	37-176	21.0	-31.86	7f-8f	43-165	26.1	-39.54
9f-13f	2-16	12.5	-6.00	9f-13f	56-194	28.9	+33.38
14f+	0-0	0.0	0.00	14f+	2-17	11.8	-12.55

4yo+	W-R	Per cent	£1 level stake	Totals	W-R	Per cent	£1 level stake
5f-6f	1-5	20.0	-3.09	5f-6f	17-59	28.8	-2.85
7f-8f	2-20	10.0	-11.00	7f-8f	82-361	22.7	-82.40
9f-13f	13-48	27.1	+12.14	9f-13f	71-258	27.5	+39.52
14f+	5-10	50.0	-0.42	14f+	7-27	25.9	-12.97

TYPE OF RACE

NON-HANDICAPS				HANDICAPS			
	W-R	Per cent	£1 level stake		W-R	Per cent	£1 level stake
2yo	48-209	23.0	-27.06	2yo	4-19	21.1	-1.42
3yo	77-265	29.1	+5.62	3yo	27-129	20.9	-33.49
4yo+	14-46	30.4	-7.15	4yo+	7-37	18.9	+4.78

Statistics relate to all runners in Britain from January 1, 2018 to December 31, 2018

Lingfield but we'll take it a step at a time and he'll need to freshen up at some point. We had a plan since the Cambridgeshire and he's performed very well."

Also on the plane to Dubai could be last year's Group 1 St James's Palace Stakes winner **Without Parole**.

Gosden reveals: "He's had a good winter and we could be looking at starting off in the Group 1 Dubai Turf at Meydan. After that he'll operate back here over a mile or 1m2f. He was slightly late maturing but he's bigger and stronger now at four."

Making up the UAE trio is likely to be improving stayer **Weekender**, who has long been invited for the Group 2 Dubai Gold Cup.

Mares ready to sparkle

Of the older females still around at Clarehaven, **Lah Ti Dar** had an interrupted season which meant missing the Epsom Oaks, but she could be in for a decent year.

Gosden says: "She's wintered nicely and we'll be looking at the fillies' races over 1m2f-1m4f. She ran a great race to finish second in the St Leger where she was a little green through the middle of the race but finished very strongly.

"There's a good middle-distance programme for fillies these days and she could have races like the Lancashire Oaks and Yorkshire Oaks on her radar."

Staying in training at five is **Coronet**, who finished in front of Lah Ti Dar when last seen in a Group 1 at Ascot last October.

Gosden is pleased with her progress and says: "Coronet has had a great winter and ran some fabulous races last year including when winning a Group 2 and beaten a nose in a Group 1 in France. The owner is very game in keeping her in training to try to win that elusive Group 1 and she'll have similar targets this year."

Top of the tree among the Classic generation is **Too Darn Hot** who is to go the Frankel route and have a prep for the 2,000 Guineas in the Group 3 Greenham Stakes at Newbury in April.

DID YOU KNOW?

In a Racing Post interview with Ronnie Wood, the Rolling Stones legend revealed John Gosden is a huge fan of his band saying, "He knows everything about the Stones." Wood also described Gosden as a Dylanologist – a fan of Bob Dylan.

Since being crowned champion juvenile, Too Darn Hot has looked a little like Frankel in the mornings as he now has his own lead horse in the shape of **Whitlock** for whom Andrew Lloyd Webber shelled out 200,000 guineas last October.

Gosden says: "We're very pleased with him. He's grown a bit and is stronger and is now a powerful colt who has a lot of speed."

On the decision to get the son of Dubawi a lead horse, Gosden adds: "He likes to settle in behind another horse and he knows Whitlock well as he's in the box next door. Later on it could be that Whitlock could lead him if he races against older horses especially if there's a small field."

Not a million miles behind Too Darn Hot in the Guineas betting is **Calyx**, who has not been sighted in public since his devastating Royal Ascot win, but he could yet go down the sprinting route.

The champion trainer adds: "Calyx is cantering away nicely and his programme could be between 7f and a mile but he'll be given an entry in the Group 1 Commonwealth Cup.

"He comes out of the gate quickly and travels strongly. He's a big, powerful, fast horse for whom we're keeping our options open."

Azano and Warrior on the up

Among the other colts, **Azano** was second in the Group 3 Horris Hill Stakes at Newbury last backend and could be out early. His

trainer says: "Azano ran well to be second at Newbury and is unusual in that he's by Oasis Dream and likes it soft."

Many commentators were impressed by the debut win of **Dubai Warrior** at Chelmsford in November and he could have some fancy entries this spring. Of the son of the now-retired Dansili, the trainer says: "Dubai Warrior will probably come back for a novice at the Craven Meeting over 1m2f. He's in good form and will appreciate middle distances this year. He won very nicely considering we don't drill them at home before their debuts."

Others in the potential Derby hopes bracket also include **Humanitarian**, who broke his maiden at the second time of asking when scoring by five lengths at Lingfield in November.

The trainer says: "Humanitarian won well last time and I think we'll go 1m2f with him in something like the Group 3 Sandown Trial or the Listed Newmarket Stakes."

In a similar mould is **Turgenev**, who was last seen in the Vertem Futurity Trophy and could also be stepped up in trip this year.

On the son of Dubawi, Gosden says: "It might have happened a bit quickly in a race of that level for Turgenev at Doncaster but he's a nice type who's another in the 1m2f department this year."

At lesser distances, **Beatboxer** won his first two starts as a juvenile in impressive fashion but disappointed when favourite for the Group 2 Royal Lodge Stakes at Newmarket in October – but there was a reason for that.

Gosden reveals: "We had Beatboxer's wind checked after Newmarket and it wasn't satisfactory so he's since had a soft palate operation. He's wintered well and will start back at a mile."

Three set to improve

Of the less exposed types, Gosden picks out three to watch. He says: "We have **Almashriq**, who won his only start – on the all-weather at Newcastle. He's a nice type and looks a miler. We also have **Battle For Glory**, who won at Newmarket and is another War Front and should improve on what he did last year.

Stradivarius streaks to victory in the Lonsdale Cup

I also like **Daarik** who got injured on his first start at Nottingham and returned to win at Newcastle. He's been given an entry in the French 2,000 Guineas."

Of the fillies, the 105-rated **Angel's Hideaway** was last seen finishing second in the Group 3 Oh So Sharp Stakes, her first foray beyond 6f.

Gosden adds: "She's done very well over the winter and I think we'll start her off in the Group 3 Nell Gwyn Stakes at the Craven Meeting. I think she was crying out for 7f last year and we'll see if she gets the mile. She's in the French 1,000 Guineas and that would be one option for her."

Stablemate **Shambolic** signed off with a fourth in the Group 1 Fillies' Mile at Newmarket and could be working to a middle-distance ticket.

Gosden says: "She won her first two races and could go straight to 1m2f, while we also have **Sparkle Roll**, who has improved a lot in her racing and I can see her going to a novice and then hopefully an Oaks trial."

Interview by David Milnes

SUPER STATS

Gosden has a fine level-stake record at Salisbury (+£36.36), Kempton (+£34.95) and Yarmouth (+£25.52), but is best avoided at Chelmsford (-£46.07), Goodwood (-£37.64) and Doncaster (-£33.70)

Gosden's best record with juveniles is at Ascot where he has a 30 per cent strike-rate with a profit of £24.25

Keep an eye out for Gosden's three-year-olds at Wetherby (three from four) and Chepstow (four from seven)

Oisin Murphy does well when teaming up with Gosden. They have a 44 per cent strike-rate and a profit of £13.72

Kieran O'Neill has a good record when riding Gosden's juveniles with a 21 per cent strike rate and a profit of £18

Statistics cover the last five years unless stated

THE LOWDOWN MARK JOHNSTON

Bidding to build on record-breaking 'incredible' season

THE year 2018 was certainly one to remember for Mark Johnston.

When Poet's Society won a mile handicap at York in August, the North Yorkshire-based trainer recorded the 4,194th winner of his career and became the most prolific trainer in the history of British racing, supplanting Richard Hannon Snr at the top table and entering rarefied air.

"It was incredible," Johnston says. "I suppose I knew quite some time ago that I was likely to break the record last year but I

WINNERS LAST FOUR YEARS 226, 215, 195, 204

honestly didn't expect there to be the reaction there was. I'm not joking when I say I wasn't sure anyone would notice.

"I was astounded at the public and media reaction as it's not often racing gets on News at Ten. That was far and away the highlight of the season."

A highlight indeed – a crown jewel in a year in which the trainer went on to record 226 winners and register more than £3 million in prize-money for the first time.

However, these statistics leave Johnston only partially satisfied – 2018 did not yield a winner at Group 1 level and that is something of a thorn in the side for the trainer after what was otherwise a triumphant season.

"It was a great year for us. I'd say you always feel a little disappointed if you don't get a Group 1 win – that was the only downside to the season really.

"We went into it with so many horses we thought could get us that top-level victory, but as the season progressed some of them fell by the wayside."

'Exciting Cup horse'

After a marvellous runner-up performance in the Derby, **Dee Ex Bee** looked capable of planting the Johnston flag in any number of middle-distance and staying Group 1s.

"He started last season in a handicap and nobody expected him to be one of the star horses of the season for us, but by the time we got to the end we were a little disappointed," Johnston says.

"At the beginning of the year if you'd asked me whether I'd settle for Dee Ex Bee being second in the Derby the answer would have been absolutely yes. Yet by the end of the

DID YOU KNOW?

When Mark Johnston became Britain's winningmost trainer in August he had actually equalled the record five days earlier and endured a rotten bit of luck before finally ending the drought with a 20-1 winner.

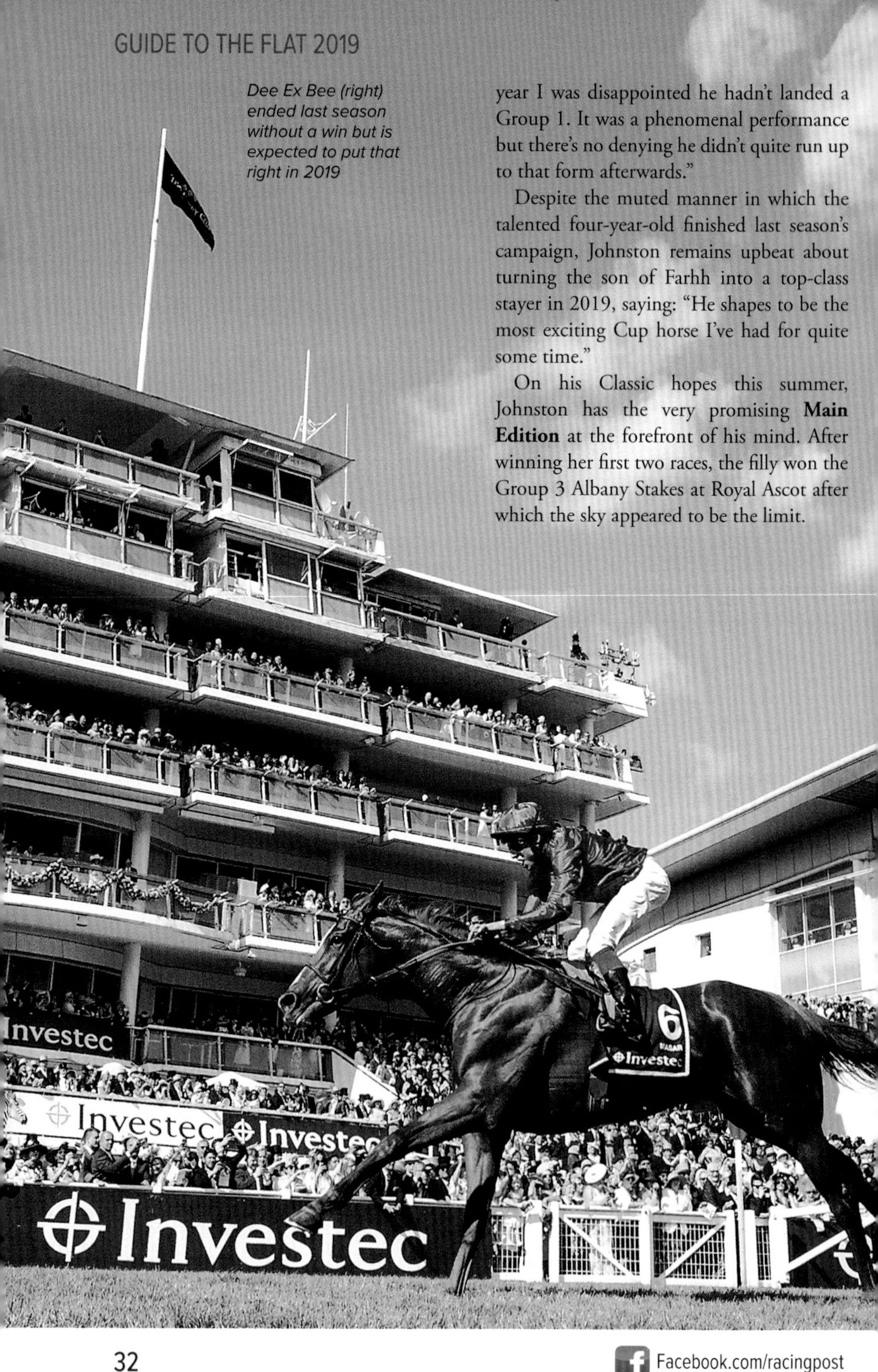

Dee Ex Bee (right) ended last season without a win but is expected to put that right in 2019

year I was disappointed he hadn't landed a Group 1. It was a phenomenal performance but there's no denying he didn't quite run up to that form afterwards."

Despite the muted manner in which the talented four-year-old finished last season's campaign, Johnston remains upbeat about turning the son of Farhh into a top-class stayer in 2019, saying: "He shapes to be the most exciting Cup horse I've had for quite some time."

On his Classic hopes this summer, Johnston has the very promising **Main Edition** at the forefront of his mind. After winning her first two races, the filly won the Group 3 Albany Stakes at Royal Ascot after which the sky appeared to be the limit.

"Around Royal Ascot we were thinking she was a contender to win a Group 1 before the year was out, so it was a little sad not to have finished on a high note.

"Providing we can get the best out of her, the dreams are all there. We'll stick to a mile initially, we're certainly not ruling out the Guineas – that's got to be the first target."

More joy expected from Natalie's

Equally exciting is the lightly raced **Natalie's Joy** who, after her debut success, was sent off the 5-4 favourite for the Chesham Stakes at Royal Ascot and finished fifth before winning a Listed contest at Newbury the next month.

"She's had time off since July and has developed calluses on her tibia," Johnston confirms. "It's very common when horses start cantering on return from a break.

"It's a bit of a race to get her to the Guineas but we think she's top-class and we're confident she should be back at the highest level."

Promise from **I'll Have Another** did not go unnoticed and, after Pattern success in

SUPER STATS

Johnston does well with older runners in apprentice races, showing a profit of £5.75 in the last five years and a profit of £18.25 last season alone

Punters can profit most from Johnston runners at Yarmouth (+£43.45), Goodwood (+£42.83) and Ripon (+£26.62). He is best avoided at Wolverhampton (-£114.20), Kempton (-£83.90) and Ascot (-£78.88)

Johnston has a good record with his three-year-old runners at Musselburgh where last season he enjoyed a strike-rate of 29 per cent and a profit of £32

Keep an eye out for Johnston's juvenile runners in October. He registered a profit of £28.91 in 2018 and £28.83 in 2017

Statistics cover the last five years unless stated

Germany last summer, Johnston is hopeful of more to come: "I think she probably surpassed everybody's expectations last year and the next stepping stone will be trying to win a Pattern race in Britain."

Hoping Vision can return to best

The world looked to be at the feet of the Godolphin-owned **Dark Vision** after he ran out a dominant winner of the Group 2 Vintage Stakes at Glorious Goodwood, but an injury suffered at Doncaster last September has Johnston worried.

"We've still got concerns as he hasn't yet returned to those pre-Doncaster days," the trainer says. "I'd desperately like to get him back to the top – the Guineas has still got to be the plan."

Marie's Diamond, who finished last season down the field in the Breeders' Cup Juvenile Turf, is "not bred to be a sprinter and he doesn't look like a sprinter, so initially we'll be thinking about the climb to a mile," his trainer says.

Arctic Sound closed his season by winning the Group 3 Tattersalls Stakes at Newmarket and Johnston says: "The trip is still up for debate. We've got him entered in the Irish Derby and we're dreaming about 1m4f races but his best form is at 7f."

Mildenberger shapes to be the most promising of the four-year-old generation at Kingsley Park stables.

After a two-year-old season that saw the son of Teofilo finish third behind Roaring Lion in the Royal Lodge Stakes at Newmarket, 2018 began with victory in the Feilden Stakes followed by a runner-up performance in the Dante – from there everything looked set for a Classic season centred around Epsom.

"The Derby was originally the plan for him but he then had a problem mid-season," his trainer says. "We're hoping he can pick up where he left off and that he's a Group 1 winner in the making.

"We'll be dreaming of Coronation Cups and the like with him but we haven't yet decided where he starts as yet."

Sky still the limit for Elarqam

Another colt about whom much was made last year was the regally bred **Elarqam**, whose fourth place in the 2,000 Guineas on his return to action put him firmly in the mix with the likes of Saxon Warrior, Masar and Roaring Lion. That promise was not built on, but Johnston has by no means given up on the son of Frankel.

"This time last year he would've been our number one hope but after the Guineas the rest of the season was not quite what we were hoping for.

"He has the very best of pedigrees and we've got to be aiming to get him back on track – we want him to be a Group 1 winner."

Talented four-year-old fillies **Nyaleti** and **Threading** spent much of last season contesting races in Pattern company, yet inconsistency seemed to hold them back

from making a real splash in Group 1 company.

"She's been a brilliant horse," Johnston says of Nyaleti, whose Group 2 success in the German 1,000 Guineas was the start of a sequence that saw her take in four Group 1 races and a Group 2.

"I think she stays 1m2f well and we'll be looking for that elusive Group 1 with her and I see no reason why she can't get it," the trainer says.

On the prospects of Threading, Johnston adds: "The form is not consistent and that's been disappointing. On her day she's very good, it's a just a matter of getting her absolutely right."

Cardsharp could be a player

Of a similar profile is **Cardsharp**, whose talent appears to be hindered somewhat by his roguish tendencies, but Johnston hopes a recent gelding operation may go some way to addressing that.

"He's his own worst enemy but he's got loads of ability. Hopefully that operation should calm him down – if it does the trick he's capable."

Similarly owned by Sheikh Hamdan Bin Mohammed Al Maktoum, **Communique** began last season running in handicaps before graduating to Pattern class and winning the Listed Godolphin Stakes at Newmarket.

"He's now clearly into Pattern class and he should be in the mix in a fair few of them," Johnston says.

Beyond the firepower he possesses for Group and Listed contests, Johnston, as ever, will have an enviable roster of top-class handicap performers at his disposal.

Nyaleti speeds to success in the Group 3 Princess Margaret Stakes at Ascot

Cesarewitch also-ran **Making Miracles** will be "sticking to distance handicaps for the moment", with the likes of the Ebor being possibilities, while **Elegiac**, a three-time winner last season, could also be aimed at York's showpiece handicap.

Johnston sees **Austrian School** as very much in the same category as those consistent handicappers and suggests the Northumberland Plate could be on the agenda for a horse who finished outside the top three only twice from 11 starts in 2018.

Talented as those three may be in handicap class, Johnston has no problem admitting he could easily see all three "eventually making that transition to Pattern class if progress continues".

"A nice one for handicaps" will be **Lake Volta**, who despite winning the Listed Surrey Stakes at Epsom last season looks set to make the most of "a very realistic mark we know he can win good races from".

Masham ready to go again

Masham Star, a five-year-old from the same ownership as Nyaleti, ran 25 times last season and exceeded all expectations when winning the Group 3 Premio Ribot Memorial Loreto Luciani at Capannelle in November. He clearly holds a special place in Johnston's heart.

"He's a fantastic advert for running a horse regularly as the last outing of his very busy season was his best – he owes us nothing.

"He's entered in the Lincoln and it will be more of the same really – running plenty and possibly back to Italy in November."

Johnston's affections also stretch to the eight-year-old **Fire Fighting**, whose two-win seven-year-old season is a testament to the abilities of the trainer and the importance he places on running racehorses with regularity.

On the 81-race veteran, Johnston adds: "He's another we like to keep as active as possible. We're hoping for more of the same from him, he owes us and his owners absolutely nothing.

Stars of the future

On his two-year-old crop for this year Johnston says: "We have a fantastic team of two-year-olds this year, possibly our biggest ever. However, there's not a great deal to say about the ability of any of them just yet."

That said, there are some notable pedigrees that catch the trainer's eye, most notably **Motion**, an Invincible Spirit filly out of Attraction, who "looks very like her mother but looks sharper than much of her progeny. We're very excited about her."

Others to note include the New Approach colt **Flashing Approach**, a brother to 2012 Chesham winner Tha'ir as well as four of Frankel's offspring who although "on the lower end of Frankel's price range, all look very promising and are exciting to have at the yard."

Interview by Tom Ward

MARK JOHNSTON

MIDDLEHAM MOOR, NORTH YORKSHIRE

	Number of horses	Races run	1st	2nd	3rd	Unpl	Per cent	£1 level stake
2yo	103	461	84	56	61	258	18.2	-134.04
3yo	95	676	102	97	109	368	15.1	-139.23
4yo+	29	303	40	38	33	191	13.2	-65.90
Totals	**227**	**1440**	**226**	**191**	**203**	**817**	**15.7**	**-339.17**
2017	217	1379	215	187	164	807	15.6	-223.79
2016	237	1413	195	206	175	836	13.8	-317.31

BY MONTH

2yo	W-R	Per cent	£1 level stake	3yo	W-R	Per cent	£1 level stake
Jan	0-0	0.0	0.00	Jan	3-20	15.0	-10.90
Feb	0-0	0.0	0.00	Feb	1-18	5.6	-14.75
Mar	0-3	0.0	-3.00	Mar	9-47	19.1	-3.63
Apr	3-13	23.1	-3.00	Apr	4-40	10.0	-16.15
May	13-41	31.7	+5.95	May	17-104	16.3	-13.47
June	18-63	28.6	-5.53	June	19-116	16.4	-24.77
July	16-61	26.2	-1.51	July	22-116	19.0	-14.05
Aug	12-68	17.6	-17.65	Aug	8-79	10.1	-41.50
Sep	12-86	14.0	-34.11	Sep	7-63	11.1	-15.13
Oct	5-79	6.3	-55.44	Oct	7-44	15.9	+24.80
Nov	2-34	5.9	-17.25	Nov	2-17	11.8	-5.00
Dec	3-13	23.1	-2.50	Dec	3-12	25.0	-4.68

4yo+	W-R	Per cent	£1 level stake	Totals	W-R	Per cent	£1 level stake
Jan	3-9	33.3	+5.25	Jan	6-29	20.7	-5.65
Feb	6-14	42.9	+19.63	Feb	7-32	21.9	+4.88
Mar	2-30	6.7	-20.50	Mar	11-80	13.8	-27.13
Apr	3-20	15.0	0.00	Apr	10-73	13.7	-19.15
May	8-55	14.5	-11.25	May	38-200	19.0	-18.77
June	7-53	13.2	-23.27	June	44-232	19.0	-53.57
July	4-30	13.3	-1.25	July	42-207	20.3	-16.81
Aug	4-38	10.5	+5.00	Aug	24-185	13.0	-54.15
Sep	1-25	4.0	-21.25	Sep	20-174	11.5	-70.49
Oct	0-16	0.0	-16.00	Oct	12-139	8.6	-46.64
Nov	2-7	28.6	+3.75	Nov	6-58	10.3	-1.25
Dec	0-6	0.0	-6.00	Dec	6-31	19.4	-10.68

DISTANCE

2yo	W-R	Per cent	£1 Level Stake	3yo	W-R	Per cent	£1 level stake
5f-6f	36-184	19.6	-45.61	5f-6f	6-65	9.2	-38.17
7f-8f	45-250	18.0	-73.91	7f-8f	38-260	14.6	-82.39
9f-13f	3-27	11.1	-14.52	9f-13f	52-310	16.8	-11.74
14f+	0-0	0.0	0.00	14f+	6-41	14.6	-6.93

4yo+	W-R	Per cent	£1 level stake	Totals	W-R	Per cent	£1 level stake
5f-6f	0-8	0.0	-8.00	5f-6f	42-257	16.3	-91.78
7f-8f	14-90	15.6	-6.27	7f-8f	97-600	16.2	-162.57
9f-13f	14-124	11.3	-21.50	9f-13f	69-461	15.0	-47.76
14f+	12-81	14.8	-30.13	14f+	18-122	14.8	-37.06

TYPE OF RACE

NON-HANDICAPS				HANDICAPS			
	W-R	Per cent	£1 level stake		W-R	Per cent	£1 level stake
2yo	72-352	20.5	-78.76	2yo	12-109	11.0	-55.28
3yo	24-158	15.2	-51.07	3yo	78-518	15.1	-88.16
4yo+	3-29	10.3	-18.88	4yo+	37-274	13.5	-47.02

Statistics relate to all runners in Britain from January 1, 2018 to December 31, 2018

Communique (fourth right) makes his way to victory at Newbury last season

THE LOWDOWN JOSEPH O'BRIEN

Young gun eyes more glory with smart team

IT IS a little under a decade ago that Joseph O'Brien announced himself to the racing world when riding his first winner aboard Johann Zoffany at Leopardstown.

The spotlight hasn't been too far away since that day and in recent years, through a number of big-race successes across both codes, racing's fresh-faced genius has proved himself an exceptional custodian of the historic Owning Hill Stables in his role as trainer.

There have been many milestones in an exceptionally short space of time. Too many to list, but right up there with the Melbourne Cup success achieved with Rekindling in November 2017 would have been the breakthrough Classic victory he earned alongside brother Donnacha with Latrobe in

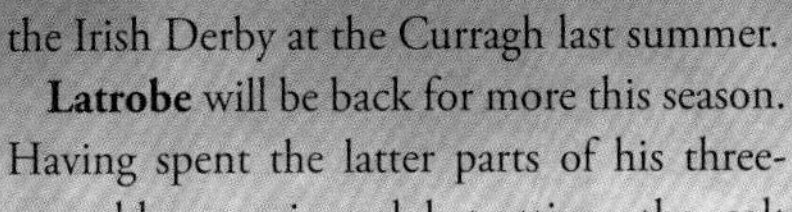

the Irish Derby at the Curragh last summer.

Latrobe will be back for more this season. Having spent the latter parts of his three-year-old campaign globetrotting, the colt earned a well-earned break, and while Camelot's best son is back in light work, a target has yet to be decided upon for his seasonal return.

On his stable star, O'Brien says: "He had a great season last year, winning the Irish Derby before he acquitted himself well on the international stage.

"He's had a good break after running in the Hong Kong Vase and he's back in light work. We're looking forward to this season with him. He has options from 1m2f-plus

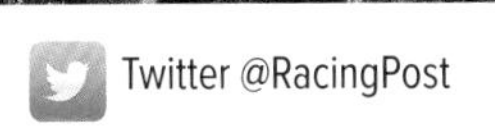

and, while it's a bit early to outline any definitive targets, we have big hopes for him."

This will be the first year O'Brien has any real older prospects, given he has only been officially training since 2016. **Speak In Colours** is one of those prospects.

A Group 3 winner over 6f at the Curragh last term, Speak In Colours finished down the field in his three attempts at Group 1 level, but O'Brien has not given up on the idea of the four-year-old being a force at the highest level this year.

He says: "He won a Group 3 at the Curragh for us last season and the plan would be to start off in Group races this season. The big aim for him would be to try and win a Group 1 sprint and I think he's capable of that. He has to step up to do that but we're hoping he can."

Smart stayer a new recruit

Cimeara is an interesting recruit to the team. A four-time winner for Jim Bolger, she holds a rating of 102, and is one O'Brien hopes can be a force at staying trips.

Celebrations after Latrobe's victory in the Irish Derby

IN THE
PADDOCK
ROYAL
ASCOT

DID YOU KNOW?

Joseph O'Brien enjoyed a fantastic career in the saddle and made history when becoming the youngest winning rider in the Breeders' Cup by landing the Turf aboard St Nicholas Abbey in 2012 at the age of 18. He also enjoyed wins in the 2,000 Guineas, St Leger and two successes in the Derby.

"She's a nice addition. She won a Group 3 and a Listed race last season and looks a nice staying type," he says.

Classic hopes with Iridessa

If O'Brien can record his second Classic victory, **Iridessa** looks the most likely type to deliver. An impressive winner of the Group 1 Fillies' Mile at Newmarket on her final start as a two-year-old *(above)*, she is said to have done well during the winter and will be ready to start back in the spring.

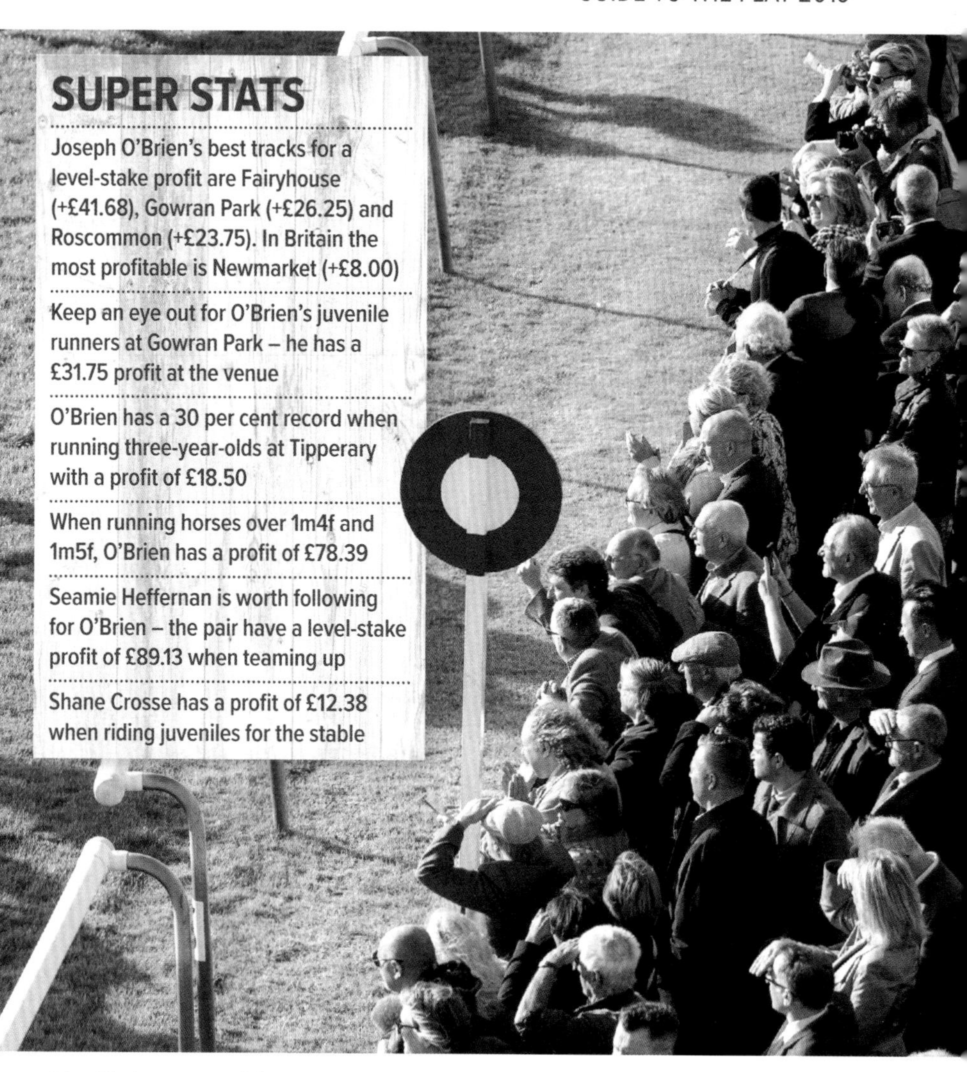

SUPER STATS

Joseph O'Brien's best tracks for a level-stake profit are Fairyhouse (+£41.68), Gowran Park (+£26.25) and Roscommon (+£23.75). In Britain the most profitable is Newmarket (+£8.00)

Keep an eye out for O'Brien's juvenile runners at Gowran Park – he has a £31.75 profit at the venue

O'Brien has a 30 per cent record when running three-year-olds at Tipperary with a profit of £18.50

When running horses over 1m4f and 1m5f, O'Brien has a profit of £78.39

Seamie Heffernan is worth following for O'Brien – the pair have a level-stake profit of £89.13 when teaming up

Shane Crosse has a profit of £12.38 when riding juveniles for the stable

The filly has occupied favouritism for the Oaks at a general 16-1 after that Newmarket win, and O'Brien says: "She was a brilliant performer for us last year, winning the Group 1 Fillies' Mile at Newmarket on her final start. We're all excited about her.

"She'll start off in a Guineas trial and that will determine where we go. At the moment, she's a contender for the 1,000 Guineas.

"I know she's by Ruler Of The World, and her pedigree would suggest she'll get further than a mile, but we'll cross that bridge when we come to it. We're looking forward to starting back and seeing where she takes us."

Another promising middle-distance filly for O'Brien to look forward to this term, judging by a taking debut victory at Dundalk in January, is **Altair**.

"We really like her," he says. "She was impressive on her debut at Dundalk and she's having a nice break after that.

"She's one we'll be aiming at a Guineas or an Oaks trial and I guess she's more of a middle-distance type filly in time.

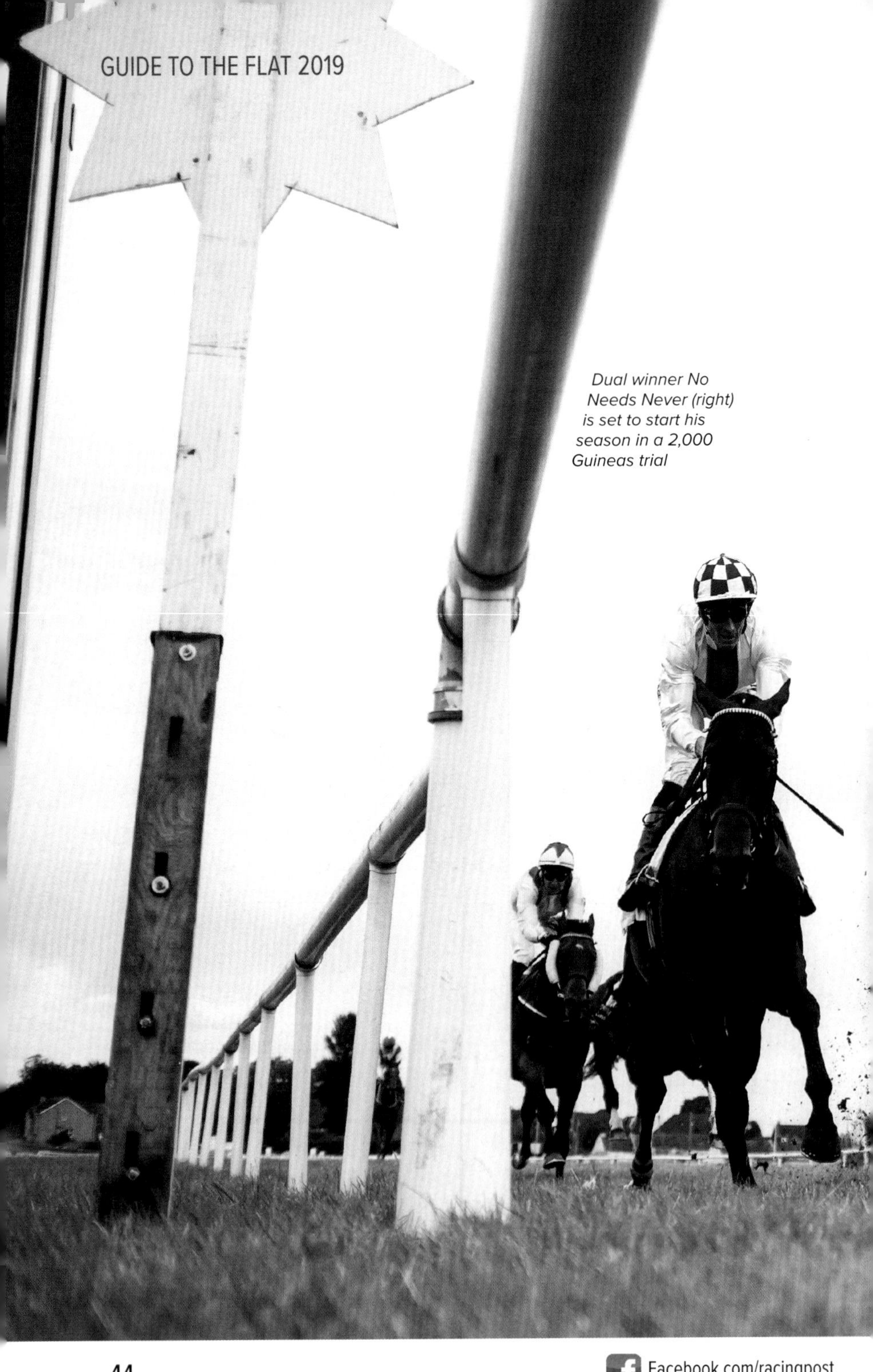

Dual winner No Needs Never (right) is set to start his season in a 2,000 Guineas trial

"She's got that type of build and was a little bit weak at two, which is why she only started this year. She's got a big engine and we're looking forward to her."

No Needs Never is an exciting colt for the young maestro. A son of sire of the moment No Nay Never, he landed a Listed contest over 7f at Dundalk in October and will be aimed at a 2,000 Guineas trial.

"Good ground is what he needs. He's a stakes-winning two-year-old over 7f.

"Whether he'll get much further than a mile is questionable but we'll probably start off in a trial and see where the season takes us," he says.

Cosmic Horizon, owned by the Ireland rugby boss Joe Schmidt, Grandmaster Flash, Pasley, Crockford, Millswyn and Cerberus are other potentially nice colts, according to the trainer.

He says: "**Cosmic Horizon** was a good winner at Roscommon last season but he disappointed in a Group race and was possibly unlucky in a handicap after that. He'll start off in a premier three-year-old handicap.

'He's a very nice colt'

"**Grandmaster Flash** is a very nice colt. He's run well in a couple of maidens and has had a nice break. He'll be back for a maiden in the spring and could be one for a Derby trial. He's nice."

O'Brien adds: "**Crockford** has run well in a couple of nice maidens and is another we like. He'll have no trouble winning his maiden and then hopefully he can step into stakes company.

"**Millswyn** won his maiden well and we think he wants soft ground. He's a nice hardy type of horse.

"**Pasley** is also a nice colt. He finished

Statistics for O'Brien cover the last three years

mid-division on his only run but we think he's a bit better than that and we're looking forward to seeing how he progresses. **Cerberus** is well up to winning his maiden as well and he's got plenty of ability."

'She's exciting, for sure'

There are plenty more exciting three-year-old fillies, including **Cava**, winner of her maiden over 6f at Fairyhouse before finishing less than a length behind So Perfect and Skitter Scatter when third in the Group 3 Grangecon Stud Stakes at the Curragh.

She hasn't raced since because of a minor problem but O'Brien reports the daughter of Acclamation to have done well over the winter.

He says: "Her form has worked out very well. She had a little setback after her second run. She's Group-placed already and whether she starts off in a Guineas trial or a sprint, we haven't quite decided yet. She's exciting, for sure."

Dramatise, Lovee Dovee, Cnoc An Oir, Crotchet and Rainbow Moonstone are also capable of mixing it at a higher level.

The trainer says: "**Dramatise** won her maiden well but was a bit disappointing at Dundalk. She's done well over the winter and will be trained for some nice handicaps and maybe some black type during the summer.

"**Lovee Dovee** has a couple of nice runs under her belt. We think she's up to winning her maiden and she'll go on the hunt for black type after that.

"**Cnoc An Oir** won her only start, and a Guineas trial in the spring could be an option for her, while **Crotchet** is a nice filly who came from Richard Fahey.

"She had a few good runs in Britain and we'd be hoping she's up to getting black type. **Rainbow Moonstone** will probably go on the hunt for some black type as well."

Top handicaps the plan for Field

O'Brien did particularly well with his handicappers last season and has a nice bunch to look forward to again this term, including the 105-rated **King's Field**.

"He went to Dubai and ran very well on his first run but he picked up an injury so he's had a little break after that and will be back for some premier handicaps in the summer," the trainer says.

Downdraft and Ming are others capable of snaring a big prize, with O'Brien adding: "**Downdraft** finished off his season well, winning a good handicap at Naas. He's done well since and he should have a nice season.

"**Ming** disappointed us at Dundalk during the winter and we gave him a break. We'll have him back for some nice handicaps."

Interview by Brian Sheerin

Dramatise (right) has done well during the winter and will be sent in pursuit of black type this season

THE LOWDOWN DAVID O'MEARA

Hot on the big-race trail with team full of quality

IT SEEMS like only yesterday that a fresh-faced David O'Meara burst on to the training scene but this year marks the 42-year-old's tenth season since starting out in 2010, a period in which he has mastered his craft and built up one of the biggest teams in Britain.

The Irishman approaches the landmark campaign in high spirits after collecting just shy of £2 million in domestic prize-money – his most profitable term – and surpassing a century of winners for the sixth consecutive year.

Although success at the highest level eluded the stable, flagbearer Lord Glitters led the gold rush with placed efforts in the Queen Anne and Sussex Stakes.

O'Meara, a former jump jockey, has established a reputation for working miracles with other people's cast-offs, and some interesting new recruits feature in a 135-strong team bristling with quality at his purpose-built Willow Farm near York.

"It was a good year for us as we achieved the most prize-money we've won and

DID YOU KNOW?

David O'Meara has enjoyed rapid growth over the past few years. In his first year of training he had 25 victories and just three years later he sent out 136 winners. O'Meara has hit the century every season since.

WINNERS IN LAST FOUR YEARS 113, 109, 103, 122

operated well at the highest level through the likes of Lord Glitters and Suedois," O'Meara says.

"We were a bit frustrated at times and we'll be hoping to turn those seconds and thirds in the big races into winners. We're very happy with how the horses are running and we've got our strongest ever squad of horses to go to war with."

The undoubted stable star is **Lord Glitters**, who was unlucky not to have more than a Group 3 win at York to show for his consistency in the big mile races.

After his success in the Strensall Stakes, the grey was sent out to Canada for the Woodbine Mile – a race O'Meara won in 2015 with Mondialiste – but his travel plans were heavily disrupted and he could manage only sixth place come the day.

"He was brilliant for the majority of the season and then we took him to Woodbine and things didn't work out as he was stuck en route in Amsterdam for a few days," says O'Meara.

"We're targeting the Dubai Turf over 1m1f and then he'll possibly take a similar route to last season with the Queen Anne, in which he was narrowly beaten, the big aim. We'll see how he does over a mile and there might be a stage where we look at going over 1m2f."

Another classy performer likely to be seen on the international stage is 2017 Shadwell Turf Mile winner **Suedois**, whose best performance last year came when beaten a short head in the Group 2 Lennox Stakes.

"His best form has come over a mile round a bend and hopefully he'll rediscover the good form he showed in the middle of last year," the trainer says. "We'll be looking at the mile Listed race at Doncaster as a starting point and if that comes too soon he could go to Sandown."

Intisaab, winner of a big handicap pot at the Curragh last July, has been in action in Dubai over the winter and will be given a break before the summer.

"We'll get him back and freshen him up for the quicker-ground summer handicaps and possibly Listed and Group 3 races," says O'Meara. "He's at his best with a strong gallop so some of these better handicaps suit him – it just depends what mark he gets."

Tumbling down the handicap

So Beloved, who has racked up £350,000 in earnings, has never been short of talent but the nine-year-old will be looking to snap a winless run stretching back to May 2016.

"He probably has as much ability as we've had over the years but he doesn't get his head in front all that often," says the trainer. "He might be getting older but he's coming down the weights, so hopefully we can target a big handicap over 7f round a bend."

Another with stacks of ability is **Escobar**, who finished a first season for the stable with a massive run when second in the Balmoral Handicap on British Champions Day.

"We weren't sure the straight mile on soft ground at Ascot would be to his liking but he ran his best race for us," O'Meara says. "As he likes to get cover, a race like the Royal Hunt

Waarif (right): improved his official handicap mark by 22lb last season

Cup would be an obvious target for him and he's definitely capable of winning a good handicap."

Still more to come from Waarif

Winning proved no problem at all for **Waarif**, whose official rating soared 22lb in 2018, and there is a feeling the handicapper might not have his measure yet.

"He was a fantastic horse for us last year, winning four races," the trainer says. "He ran a great race at York at the end of the season off his current mark, so it doesn't look like the handicapper is on top of him just yet. We'll start off in the Lincoln and the fact he handles cut in the ground gives us some encouragement."

The Lincoln, a race O'Meara won in 2017 with Bravery and finished second in last year with Lord Glitters, is also under consideration for new arrivals Humbert and Remarkable.

"We're happy with what we've seen from **Humbert** so far and, as he's shown form in good handicaps on slower ground, he'll be

SUPER STATS

David O'Meara's most profitable tracks are Wetherby (+£45.75) and Ripon (+£13.38). Caution is advised at York (-£125.00), Wolverhampton (-£116.27) and Newcastle (-£91.40)

O'Meara has a 33 per cent strike-rate (+£12.13) with juveniles at Doncaster

He has sent just three juvenile runners to Newmarket with two of them winning and one finishing third (+£13)

Last July O'Meara clocked a 20 per cent strike-rate

Silvestre de Sousa should be backed when riding juveniles for the yard – he is two from four with a profit of £5.50

James Doyle does well when teaming up with O'Meara and the pair have notched a profit of £21.50

Statistics cover the last five years unless stated

DAVID O'MEARA

UPPER HELMSLEY, NORTH YORKSHIRE

	Number of horses	Races run	1st	2nd	3rd	Unpl	Per cent	£1 level stake
2yo	32	141	17	18	11	94	12.1	-28.72
3yo	38	251	32	35	22	161	12.7	-21.17
4yo+	78	683	64	97	75	446	9.4	-249.90
Totals	**148**	**1075**	**113**	**150**	**108**	**701**	**10.5**	**-299.79**
2017	174	1078	109	125	131	710	10.1	-247.14
2016	164	975	103	124	115	633	10.6	-336.62

BY MONTH

2yo	W-R	Per cent	£1 level stake	3yo	W-R	Per cent	£1 level stake
Jan	0-0	0.0	0.00	Jan	0-1	0.0	-1.00
Feb	0-0	0.0	0.00	Feb	0-2	0.0	-2.00
Mar	1-2	50.0	+2.00	Mar	0-7	0.0	-7.00
Apr	0-5	0.0	-5.00	Apr	3-17	17.6	+1.25
May	1-10	10.0	-2.00	May	3-36	8.3	-22.00
June	1-12	8.3	+5.00	June	4-39	10.3	-16.13
July	4-18	22.2	+10.88	July	6-38	15.8	-11.42
Aug	4-26	15.4	-10.75	Aug	5-37	13.5	+1.38
Sep	2-18	11.1	-13.38	Sep	6-35	17.1	+5.25
Oct	2-20	10.0	0.00	Oct	4-25	16.0	+29.50
Nov	2-18	11.1	-3.47	Nov	0-8	0.0	-8.00
Dec	0-12	0.0	-12.00	Dec	1-6	16.7	+9.00

4yo+	W-R	Per cent	£1 level stake	Totals	W-R	Per cent	£1 level stake
Jan	0-33	0.0	-33.00	Jan	0-34	0.0	-34.00
Feb	0-21	0.0	-21.00	Feb	0-23	0.0	-23.00
Mar	0-22	0.0	-22.00	Mar	1-31	3.2	-27.00
Apr	6-35	17.1	+10.03	Apr	9-57	15.8	+6.28
May	10-86	11.6	-30.42	May	14-132	10.6	-54.42
June	11-107	10.3	-46.67	June	16-158	10.1	-57.80
July	19-91	20.9	+14.67	July	29-147	19.7	+14.13
Aug	8-79	10.1	-34.96	Aug	17-142	12.0	-44.33
Sep	6-73	8.2	+5.00	Sep	14-126	11.1	-3.13
Oct	1-58	1.7	-47.00	Oct	7-103	6.8	-17.50
Nov	3-45	6.7	-11.56	Nov	5-71	7.0	-19.56
Dec	0-33	0.0	-33.00	Dec	1-51	2.0	-24.00

DISTANCE

2yo	W-R	Per cent	£1 Level Stake	3yo	W-R	Per cent	£1 level stake
5f-6f	14-97	14.4	-18.47	5f-6f	16-127	12.6	-2.42
7f-8f	3-44	6.8	-10.25	7f-8f	15-103	14.6	-4.75
9f-13f	0-0	0.0	0.00	9f-13f	1-21	4.8	-14.00
14f+	0-0	0.0	0.00	14f+	0-0	0.0	0.00

4yo+	W-R	Per cent	£1 level stake	Totals	W-R	Per cent	£1 level stake
5f-6f	22-190	11.6	-62.59	5f-6f	52-414	12.6	-83.48
7f-8f	30-321	9.3	-94.39	7f-8f	48-468	10.3	-109.39
9f-13f	9-158	5.7	-86.71	9f-13f	10-179	5.6	-100.71
14f+	3-14	21.4	-6.21	14f+	3-14	21.4	-6.21

TYPE OF RACE

NON-HANDICAPS				HANDICAPS			
	W-R	Per cent	£1 level stake		W-R	Per cent	£1 level stake
2yo	14-104	13.5	-18.47	2yo	3-37	8.1	-10.25
3yo	8-55	14.5	-14.63	3yo	24-196	12.2	-6.54
4yo+	12-98	12.2	-47.11	4yo+	52-585	8.9	-202.79

Statistics relate to all runners in Britain from January 1, 2018 to December 31, 2018

aimed at the Lincoln," adds O'Meara.

"**Remarkable** is a brother to Watchable, so he's from a family we know well. He missed a year but has loads of ability and, while we'll aim him at the Lincoln, it might be a big ask after such a long time off."

Other recent acquisitions include Arecibo and Time's Arrow, who have been bought from France to race for the same connections as Suedois.

"**Arecibo** is a high-class sprinter who has size and scope and hopefully he can improve from three to four," O'Meara says. "**Time's Arrow** was originally with Sir Michael Stoute and has been running in Group and Listed races. He's the type we've done well with."

Ex-Godolphin five-year-old **Tamleek**, who has been off the track since August 2017, might be another to benefit for a switch to O'Meara, having shown promise before his long absence.

"He's a lovely horse with plenty of size and a high level of ability and we're hoping he can recover his good form after time off," the trainer says.

Frankuus, a two-time Group 3-winning son of Frankel, has already been in action on the all-weather after joining the stable at the end of last year.

O'Meara says: "We'll target one of the big

On the gallops at David O'Meara's Yorkshire stables and (above left) Frankuus

handicaps at the Dante meeting and we think going left-handed round a bend on softer ground is key to him."

High hopes for Gardenia

With 17 juvenile winners, the trainer had a prolific year with his two-year-olds and there are high hopes for the three-year-old crop. **Blue Gardenia**, owned and bred by Sir Robert Ogden, takes high rank among them, having signed off the campaign with a Listed victory at Newmarket.

"We were delighted with her last season as she got better with each run and we may target the Musidora as Sir Robert loves a runner at York," says O'Meara. "She's strengthened up over the winter and we're hopeful she'll see out 1m2f."

Fastman won two of his first three starts before finishing fourth in the Rockingham Stakes on his final start and his attitude is expected to stand him in good stead.

"He's a very genuine horse, who improved with each run last year," says the trainer. "He's done well over the winter and can hopefully take a step forward in the three-year-old 6f handicaps and progress from there."

Dream has plenty of promise

Leodis Dream did not make his debut until October but made up for lost time with two wins and a second in the space of a month.

"He did well last year and has loads of speed, and we'll look to run him in the 5f three-year-old handicap at the Dante meeting," the trainer adds.

Lovin was a big eyecatcher in a fillies' maiden at Glorious Goodwood and, after winning at Chelmsford, ran in a Listed race at Chantilly, where she finished tenth of 11.

O'Meara says: "She showed loads of ability and speed early on and ran very well in a hot maiden at Goodwood. She's very fast and 5f is her trip."

At the opposite end of the experience scale, the ever-dependable **Firmament** will be back for a crack at the 7f and mile handicaps after competing in 17 races during 2018.

"He's performed solidly in all the high-class handicaps and returning on a slightly lower mark, hopefully he can be competitive again," the trainer says.

The colours of Gallop Racing are also likely to be carried in some of the big sprint handicaps by **Muscika**, who notched two wins during a generally progressive season.

"He's a big, raw horse who matured through last season and there should be more to come," says O'Meara. "He has plenty of ability and is one for the Saturday 6f handicaps and possibly the Wokingham."

Top handicaps on the agenda

The Royal Ascot sprint handicap features on **Summerghand**'s agenda too following a highly productive campaign featuring five victories in 14 starts.

The trainer adds: "He has loads of size and scope. We always thought he'd improve and we got to see his true potential. He'll be running in all the top 6f handicaps, starting at the Dante meeting and with the Wokingham later on."

Hajjam is another handicapper capable of improvement, although he will be seen to better effect away from summer ground.

"He's tough and genuine, just like his half-brother Salateen, and is at his best on soft ground over 7f," O'Meara says.

Likewise **Cold Stare** wants give underfoot and could feature at the Lincoln meeting at the end of March.

"He's a very good horse who loves soft ground and a strong gallop," the trainer adds. "Hopefully he can start the season with a win or two and we'll target him at the 6f handicap on the Sunday at Doncaster."

Every victory counts as O'Meara sets off on his annual pursuit of 100 winners and although reaching a century has become the norm, it is no mean feat. However, you get the sense from the ambitious trainer that returning to the Group 1 fold would transform a good season into a great one.

Interview by Andrew Dietz

ROYAL WINDSOR
RACECOURSE
DASH
TO THE
FINALE
29TH JULY 2019
sky bet
Summer
SPRINT SERIES

Looking to future with new system set to reap dividends

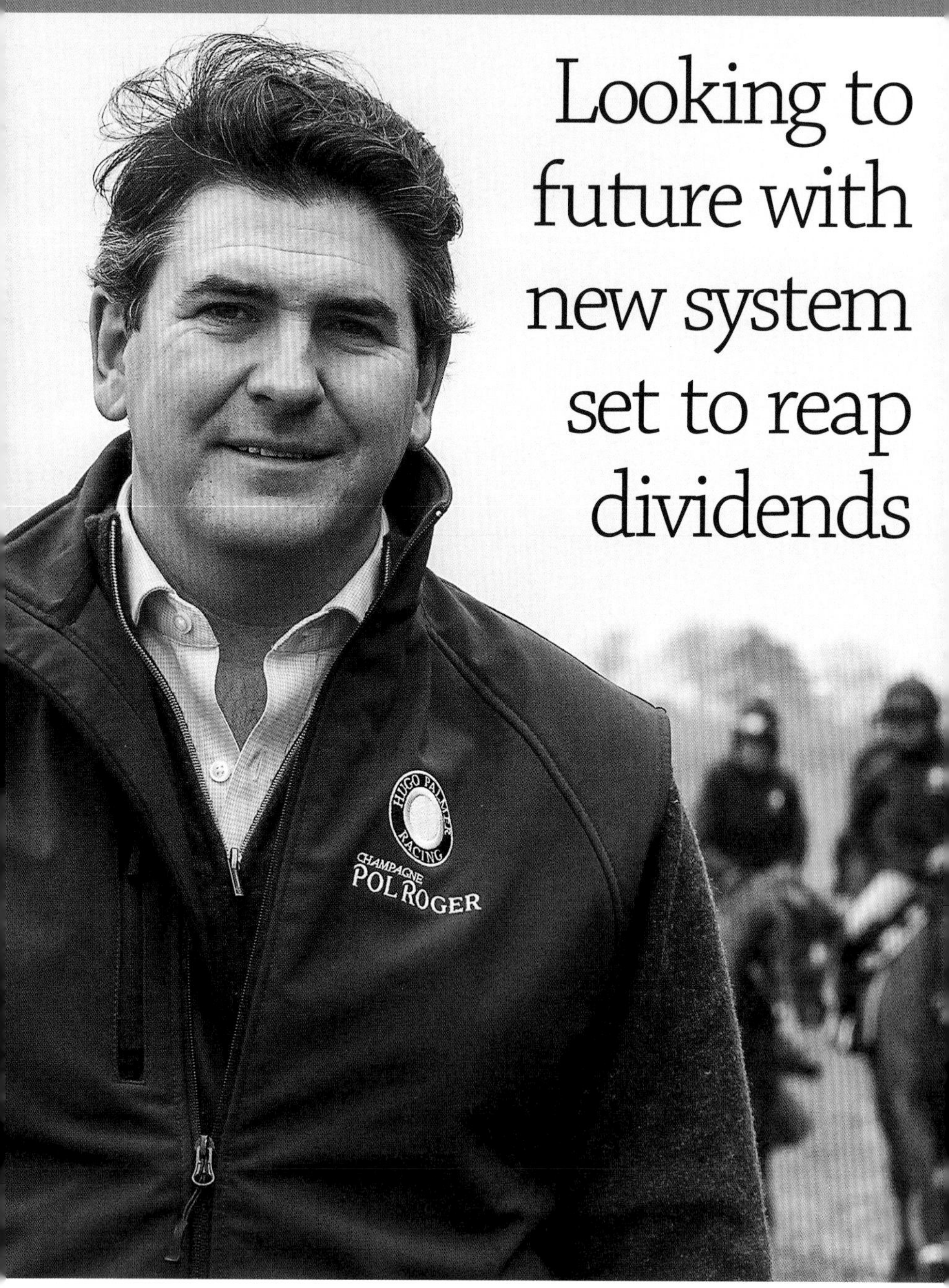

WINNERS IN LAST FOUR YEARS 87, 77, 71, 34

HUGO PALMER has centralised his Newmarket operation for 2019 after relinquishing his second yard on the Hamilton Road and is hoping the new regime can match last year's top tally of 87 winners with a nice spread of established and promising types.

The master of Kremlin Cottage, who tasted 2,000 Guineas success with Galileo Gold in 2016, now has 96 boxes at his premises on the Snailwell Road and rents a further 12 from William Jarvis nearby, a system that is already working out for the better.

He says: "We rented Yellowstone Park across town last year but we had pushing 180 horses then and we're much more manageable having them all on one site. Last year was our

fourth consecutive year topping £1 million in win and place prize-money and we managed a very respectable 17th in the trainers' title."

The biggest contributor to Palmer's prize-money haul over the years has been smart speedster **Gifted Master**, who is shortly to embark on his career as a six-year-old with just shy of £750,000 next to his name.

Last year's Stewards' Cup winner did not cover himself with glory when last seen in a Listed contest at Lingfield in November but is to start his season in Dubai in March.

Palmer says: "Gifted Master is a yard favourite and the plan is to take him out to Dubai for the Group 3 Nad Al Sheba Trophy on Super Saturday. If he were to win or run well there we'd look at World Cup night."

Dukhan ready to step up

Apart from that stalwart, Palmer's senior team consists of a clutch of promising four-year-olds, many of them 'Saturday horses' who could figure in some of the more valuable televised handicaps this summer.

Among them is **Dukhan**, who was a weak-looking son of Teofilo last year, but has strengthened up over winter.

Palmer says: "We had high hopes for Dukhan this time last year but he lost his

Gifted Master (leading) sprints to success over 6f at Newmarket last May

way on quick ground in the summer. He did come back to win on soft ground at Newbury at the backend and could be a horse for something like the John Smith's Cup at York."

In the same 1m2f to 1m4f handicap bracket is **Collide**, a striking son of Frankel who won three of his six races last year but disappointed when last stepped up to Listed company at Newmarket in November.

The trainer says: "Collide was progressive last year apart from his last start but he scoped dirty after that. He hasn't many miles on the clock and could be a player this year when he could get 1m4f."

Also owned by Khalid Abdullah is

SUPER STATS

The most profitable tracks at which to back Palmer's runners are Haydock (+£83.20), Bath (+£26.79) and Chepstow (+£22.00). A watching brief is advised at Newmarket (July) (-£53.70), Sandown (-£25.50) and Windsor (-£25.34)

Backing Palmer's three-year-olds shows a profit of £39.39

Wolverhampton is a track at which Palmer does well with his juveniles – he has a 32 per cent strike-rate and a £21.35 profit

It is worth noting Palmer has a good record when sending his three-year-old runners north. Last year he had five winners from six runners at Carlisle and three winners from four runners at Hamilton

Palmer has a 23 per cent strike-rate when running horses between 1m6f and 1m7f with a profit of £26.75.

Palmer's three-year-old runners show a profit of £63.60 when running over 1m4f and 1m5f

Statistics cover the last five years unless stated

DID YOU KNOW?

Hugo Palmer got into racing when he was 16 and first went into a bookies with a friend. He claims the pair went in with £3 and walked out with £60 each having backed eight or nine winners. He was completely hooked after Benny The Dip won the Derby in 1997.

progressive sprinter **Encrypted**, who won the Listed Golden Rose Stakes at Lingfield in November. Not surprisingly, the son of Showcasing is on his way back there.

Palmer says: "Encrypted has been the surprise package for me and he's done so well from three to four that he's now built like a tank. The plan is to go back to Lingfield for Good Friday and beyond that there is a wonderful programme of 6f sprints."

As well as Gifted Master, Palmer is taking the classy **Mootasadir** out to Dubai and he could yet figure on World Cup night if all goes well in his prep.

The trainer reveals: "Mootasadir is being targeted at the Group 3 Nad Al Sheba Trophy on Super Saturday and if he wins or runs well there he could go for the Group 3 Dubai Gold Cup as I expect him to get 2m. In time he could well turn out to be a Melbourne Cup horse as he has the class."

Classic entries for smart Set Piece

The oldest part of Kremlin Cottage is the yard in which Derby winners Kahyasi and High-Rise stood when Luca Cumani trained there – and it is now where Palmer has some of his most promising Classic generation stock.

Among the colts housed there is **Set Piece**, who is unbeaten in two starts on the all-weather this winter.

Palmer says: "He had to make up a lot of ground when winning first time at Kempton and looked workmanlike when following up at Newcastle, although he was giving 7lb to a subsequent winner that day. He's entered in the 2,000 Guineas here and in France and in the French Derby. It could be that we take him to the Craven Stakes or the Feilden. Other than that, there's the Listed Burradon Stakes at Newcastle."

Two out of two and more to give

Also unbeaten in two runs on the all-weather is **Dahawi**, most recently over 6f at Kempton in February – and Palmer is not afraid to step up the son of Heeraat in trip. He says: "Luke Morris is adamant he'll be even better over 7f and he could be even better on turf. If he's in the 85-100 bracket he could prosper like Encrypted did last year."

Others of note include **Almufti**, about whom Palmer says: "We've always liked him. He won his novice well at Kempton last September and then found the ground too soft in the Horris Hill at Newbury. We think he'll get a mile and he could run on Good Friday Finals day at Lingfield."

HUGO PALMER

Newmarket, Suffolk

	Number of horses	Races run	1st	2nd	3rd	Unpl	Per cent	£1 level stake
2yo	34	114	18	18	10	68	15.8	-43.81
3yo	67	329	59	35	35	198	17.9	+54.63
4yo+	15	65	10	8	8	39	15.4	+7.75
Totals	**116**	**508**	**87**	**61**	**53**	**305**	**17.1**	**+18.57**
2017	134	493	77	69	51	295	15.6	-126.71
2016	102	344	71	54	49	169	20.6	+13.28

BY MONTH

2yo	W-R	Per cent	£1 level stake	3yo	W-R	Per cent	£1 level stake
Jan	0-0	0.0	0.00	Jan	0-15	0.0	-15.00
Feb	0-0	0.0	0.00	Feb	1-9	11.1	-7.27
Mar	0-0	0.0	0.00	Mar	1-11	9.1	-8.00
Apr	0-1	0.0	-1.00	Apr	4-23	17.4	-7.95
May	0-5	0.0	-5.00	May	10-45	22.2	+14.35
June	2-16	12.5	-13.31	June	6-42	14.3	+85.22
July	3-20	15.0	-9.75	July	5-51	9.8	-33.51
Aug	2-16	12.5	-11.85	Aug	7-39	17.9	-7.72
Sep	2-20	10.0	-10.00	Sep	12-47	25.5	+5.87
Oct	4-18	22.2	-2.75	Oct	8-31	25.8	+25.00
Nov	0-6	0.0	-6.00	Nov	5-12	41.7	+7.63
Dec	5-12	41.7	+15.85	Dec	0-4	0.0	-4.00

4yo+	W-R	Per cent	£1 level stake	Totals	W-R	Per cent	£1 level stake
Jan	2-4	50.0	-0.18	Jan	2-19	10.5	-15.18
Feb	2-4	50.0	+0.55	Feb	3-13	23.1	-6.72
Mar	0-7	0.0	-7.00	Mar	1-18	5.6	-15.00
Apr	1-6	16.7	+7.00	Apr	5-30	16.7	-1.95
May	1-6	16.7	+3.00	May	11-56	19.6	+12.35
June	2-7	28.6	-0.63	June	10-65	15.4	+71.28
July	0-6	0.0	-6.00	July	8-77	10.4	-49.26
Aug	2-10	20.0	+26.00	Aug	11-65	16.9	+6.43
Sep	0-6	0.0	-6.00	Sep	14-73	19.2	-10.13
Oct	0-4	0.0	-4.00	Oct	12-53	22.6	+18.25
Nov	0-4	0.0	-4.00	Nov	5-22	22.7	+3.63
Dec	0-1	0.0	-1.00	Dec	5-17	29.4	-5.00

DISTANCE

2yo	W-R	Per cent	£1 Level Stake	3yo	W-R	Per cent	£1 level stake
5f-6f	5-33	15.2	-19.06	5f-6f	10-44	22.7	+38.13
7f-8f	13-78	16.7	-21.75	7f-8f	19-127	15.0	-50.61
9f-13f	0-3	0.0	-3.00	9f-13f	29-153	19.0	+68.85
14f+	0-0	0.0	0.00	14f+	1-5	20.0	-1.75

4yo+	W-R	Per cent	£1 level stake	Totals	W-R	Per cent	£1 level stake
5f-6f	2-24	8.3	+6.00	5f-6f	17-101	16.8	+25.07
7f-8f	5-28	17.9	+7.80	7f-8f	37-233	15.9	-64.56
9f-13f	3-13	23.1	-6.05	9f-13f	32-169	18.9	+59.80
14f+	0-0	0.0	0.00	14f+	1-5	20.0	-1.75

TYPE OF RACE

NON-HANDICAPS				HANDICAPS			
	W-R	Per cent	£1 level stake		W-R	Per cent	£1 level stake
2yo	14-92	15.2	-46.81	2yo	4-22	18.2	+3.00
3yo	26-140	18.6	+42.78	3yo	33-189	17.5	+11.85
4yo+	3-26	11.5	+3.58	4yo+	7-39	17.9	+4.17

Statistics relate to all runners in Britain from January 1, 2018 to December 31, 2018

Gearing up for the new season

Of the fillies, **Zofelle** was spoken of as a 1,000 Guineas possible when winning on her debut at Doncaster in the summer but things did not pan out after that.

Palmer explains: "She came back very shin sore and had to be given plenty of time. By the time we got her back the ground had gone when she disappointed on soft at Newbury. She's had a very good winter and the plan is to take her to a novice on the all-weather before looking at a Classic trial."

Unraced **Iron Clad** has not been in the yard long and has Palmer dreaming of big things: "He came in late last year and is a nice type who has done some good bridle work of late. He's one to dream about all right and the plan is to get him out in March. He should be effective at 1m2f in time but we'll start him off at a mile."

Names to note early on

The Kremlin Cottage outfit usually has one or two forward types to go to war with at either the Newmarket Craven Meeting or the Qipco Guineas Festival and this year could be no exception.

Palmer says: "We have some nice two-year-olds and we've been sent one by Sheikh Fahad for the first time.

Among the more forward brigade is a half-brother to former stable star Aktabantay. Palmer says: "He's by Dubawi and we picked him up at Tattersalls for only 105,000gns which we are hoping is a sound investment."

The trainer picks out two fillies who could be early, saying: "We have one by first-season sire Gutaifan out of Payphone called **Vintage Polly** we like and also an Oasis Dream filly of Juddmonte's called **Oasis Joy**."

Interview by David Milnes

Flying up the Warren Hill gallops in Newmarket

EQUESTRIAN
SURFACES LTD

GALLOP
WITH CONFIDENCE

THE LOWDOWN KEVIN RYAN

Yorkshire's got talent!

THERE is excitement and anticipation for Kevin Ryan and his team as several of last year's exciting two-year-olds look set to make a mark in their Classic campaigns.

And the older brigade, spearheaded by the admirably consistent stalwart Brando, will also attempt to build on an excellent 2018 season giving plenty of reason for optimism for this year.

Having saddled 76 winners and over

WINNERS IN LAST FOUR YEARS 76, 76, 94, 73

KEVIN RYAN

Hambleton, North Yorkshire

	Number of horses	Races run	1st	2nd	3rd	Unpl	Per cent	£1 level stake
2yo	48	172	25	22	20	105	14.5	-29.26
3yo	43	205	31	30	29	115	15.1	-24.92
4yo+	35	243	20	29	30	163	8.2	-43.00
Totals	**126**	**620**	**76**	**81**	**79**	**383**	**12.3**	**-97.18**
2017	124	661	76	94	73	418	11.5	-216.46
2016	127	733	94	91	93	455	12.8	-102.24

BY MONTH

2yo	W-R	Per cent	£1 level stake	3yo	W-R	Per cent	£1 level stake
Jan	0-0	0.0	0.00	Jan	2-6	33.3	+3.00
Feb	0-0	0.0	0.00	Feb	2-13	15.4	-7.50
Mar	0-0	0.0	0.00	Mar	3-13	23.1	-1.63
Apr	1-6	16.7	+7.00	Apr	8-33	24.2	+13.50
May	5-22	22.7	+0.13	May	4-27	14.8	-3.54
June	1-22	4.5	-19.80	June	1-27	3.7	-16.00
July	3-30	10.0	-22.58	July	2-21	9.5	-14.25
Aug	6-37	16.2	-11.25	Aug	3-21	14.3	-2.50
Sep	9-38	23.7	+34.25	Sep	2-24	8.3	-12.50
Oct	0-10	0.0	-10.00	Oct	2-8	25.0	+1.50
Nov	0-6	0.0	-6.00	Nov	1-9	11.1	+8.00
Dec	0-1	0.0	-1.00	Dec	1-3	33.3	+7.00

4yo+	W-R	Per cent	£1 level stake	Totals	W-R	Per cent	£1 level stake
Jan	1-13	7.7	-11.00	Jan	3-19	15.8	-8.00
Feb	3-16	18.8	+61.50	Feb	5-29	17.2	+54.00
Mar	4-19	21.1	+15.50	Mar	7-32	21.9	+13.87
Apr	2-21	9.5	-11.00	Apr	11-60	18.3	+9.50
May	2-29	6.9	-19.00	May	11-78	14.1	-22.41
June	1-27	3.7	-19.00	June	3-76	3.9	-54.80
July	0-30	0.0	-30.00	July	5-81	6.2	-66.83
Aug	1-27	3.7	-20.00	Aug	10-85	11.8	-33.75
Sep	1-26	3.8	-22.50	Sep	12-88	13.6	-0.75
Oct	2-17	11.8	+0.50	Oct	4-35	11.4	-8.00
Nov	3-14	21.4	+16.00	Nov	4-29	13.8	+24.00
Dec	0-4	0.0	-4.00	Dec	1-8	12.5	+3.00

DISTANCE

2yo	W-R	Per cent	£1 Level Stake	3yo	W-R	Per cent	£1 level stake
5f-6f	25-140	17.9	+2.74	5f-6f	11-72	15.3	-18.38
7f-8f	0-32	0.0	-32.00	7f-8f	18-98	18.4	+18.13
9f-13f	0-0	0.0	0.00	9f-13f	2-34	5.9	-23.67
14f+	0-0	0.0	0.00	14f+	0-1	0.0	-1.00

4yo+	W-R	Per cent	£1 level stake	Totals	W-R	Per cent	£1 level stake
5f-6f	5-100	5.0	-60.50	5f-6f	41-312	13.1	-76.14
7f-8f	9-69	13.0	+47.50	7f-8f	27-199	13.6	+33.63
9f-13f	6-73	8.2	-29.00	9f-13f	8-107	7.5	-52.67
14f+	0-1	0.0	-1.00	14f+	0-2	0.0	-2.00

TYPE OF RACE

NON-HANDICAPS				HANDICAPS			
	W-R	Per cent	£1 level stake		W-R	Per cent	£1 level stake
2yo	19-146	13.0	-35.26	2yo	6-26	23.1	+6.00
3yo	13-82	15.9	-13.92	3yo	18-123	14.6	-11.00
4yo+	6-23	26.1	+24.00	4yo+	14-220	6.4	-67.00

Statistics relate to all runners in Britain from January 1, 2018 to December 31, 2018

£1.6 million in prize-money last year, hopes are high once again with leading owners Jaber Abdullah and TA Rahman represented by some well-bred recruits.

"We've got good horses and they've got good races to go for, so if we pick up one or two along the way then we'll be very happy," Ryan says.

Leading the way is **Brando**, winner of the Group 1 Prix Maurice de Gheest in 2017. He enjoyed another fruitful campaign in 2018, which included a second win in the Group 3 Abernant Stakes at Newmarket and two runner-up spots at Group 1 level in the July Cup and Sprint Cup.

A similar campaign awaits the seven-year-old son of Pivotal and Ryan says: "He's come back in great form and his route is mapped out. He'll start at the Craven Meeting and then go on to York followed by the July Cup – a similar route to last year."

The gelding, who has earned £860,000 in prize-money, finished his season with a respectable fourth behind Sands Of Mali in the Champion Sprint at Ascot on Champions Day and it would be no surprise to see him reach similar heights at the very top level this term.

More to come from Jonesy

Also among the older brigade at Hambleton Lodge is **Hey Jonesy**, who underwent a gelding operation after finishing second in a Listed contest at Doncaster in November. He has his trainer hopeful of a good campaign who says: "He'll possibly start at Doncaster and has come back bigger and stronger this time around. He finished last year with a great run and hopefully he can build on that this year. He has grown up."

Major Jumbo, who was bought for 17,000gns as a foal at Tattersalls, is another

Brando (yellow and purple) is set to start his season at Newmarket's Craven Meeting

stalwart who enjoyed a consistent time last season with two wins and six places from nine starts. He landed the valuable Coral Sprint Trophy Handicap on his final start of the campaign at York in October and Ryan believes the son of Zebedee can make an impact at a higher level.

The trainer says: "He'll be ready to go early on and hopefully can step up into Group company this year."

East going in right direction

Ryan's sole Classic victory came with The Grey Gatsby in the 2014 French Derby but he is hopeful of more success and has an enviable team of Classic possibles.

The Yorkshire-based trainer is particularly excited by the prospects of **East**, a talented daughter of Frankel who won the Group 3 Prix Thomas Bryon at Saint-Cloud and followed up with an excellent second in the Breeders' Cup Juvenile Fillies' Turf after a difficult draw.

The three-year-old, who was sold for €315,000 at the Goresbridge Breeze-Up Sales last May has quotes of 14-1 for 1,000 Guineas glory despite having beaten ante-post favourite Just Wonderful at Churchill Downs, and looks another bright prospect for the stable's team.

Ryan says: "She's entered in the English and French Guineas and will go to either one of them without a prep run. She's a very exciting filly for this year."

On East's brother, the two-year-old **Zabeel King**, Ryan adds: "It's early days as he's only just started cantering."

DID YOU KNOW?

Ryan's best horse The Grey Gatsby – winner of the French Derby and Irish Champion Stakes – was actually bought by a different owner who decided he did not want him as a yearling. Ryan was unsure whether to buy the horse for an owner but on the morning of the sale decided to buy the horse. He describes it as the luckiest phone call of his career.

Newspaperofrecord strolls home to win the Breeders' Cup Juvenile Fillies' Turf in which the Kevin Ryan-trained East (right) was runner-up

Gimcrack winner in good shape

Emaraaty Ana is another Classic hopeful who could fly the flag for Ryan. He finished his juvenile campaign with a respectable fifth behind Ten Sovereigns in the Middle Park Stakes having earlier won the Group 2 Gimcrack Stakes.

The Sheikh Mohammed Obaid Al Maktoum-owned colt will head straight to Newmarket for the 2,000 Guineas and could also step up in trip for a crack at the Prix du Jockey Club at Chantilly.

Ryan says: "He's done well over the winter and will go straight to the Guineas – he also has an entry in the French Derby. If he runs well in the Guineas then we'd probably step him up in trip. His pedigree suggests he should be able to get a trip like that."

Hello Youmzain was another to enjoy Group success as a juvenile, landing the Group 2 Criterium de Maisons-Laffitte in October. The form is solid as back in second was Ayr Group 3 scorer Queen Of Bermuda and Gimcrack runner-up Legends Of War.

Given the son of Kodiac is a half-brother to Royal Youmzain, a Group winner over 1m2f, stamina for the mile trip of the 2,000 Guineas does not look an issue but Ryan adds a Guineas trial could also be on the cards.

He says: "He finished off by winning a Group 2 in France, which he did very well, and he'll probably start off in a Guineas trial. It's debatable whether he'll stay the mile of the Guineas but he could start off at Newbury. We'll find out whether he stays but if he doesn't he'll go back sprinting."

Interview by Kitty Trice

SUPER STATS

In terms of profit, Ryan's runners perform best at Wolverhampton (+£38.93), Hamilton (+£33.46) and Musselburgh (+£25.13), while there are significant losses at York (-£80.25), Ayr (-£53.13) and Haydock (-£51.75)

Ryan's juveniles have a good record at Wolverhampton – 20 per cent strike-rate and a profit of £73.25 last season

Ryan does well with three-year-olds at Beverley with a profit of £37.25

Ryan is especially good with older horses running over 1m and 1m1f and shows a profit of £62.25

Andrew Mullen enjoyed a good partnership when riding for Ryan last year (+£22.50)

Ryan had a profit of £11 when running his horses in claiming and Listed company last season

Keep an eye out for Ryan's two-year-old runners over 7f – he had a level-stake profit of £10.34 last year

Statistics cover the last five years unless stated

Gimcrack winner Emaraaty Ana leads Kevin Ryan's string

THE LOWDOWN ROGER VARIAN

Going for glory with fine mix spanning the ages

WINNERS IN LAST FOUR YEARS 106, 109, 97, 100

IT HAS not taken long for Roger Varian to establish himself as one of the top trainers in the business with his eight-year career characterised by an arc of steady progression.

Few trainers can boast a Group 1 win in their first year of holding a licence – and 13 further top-level victories have followed Nahrain's success in the 2011 Prix de l'Opera.

Although last year saw Varian draw a rare blank at the highest level in Britain, he did land an international Grade 1 in Canada with the now-retired filly Sheikha Reika in the E.P. Taylor Stakes at Woodbine.

SUPER STATS

The most profitable tracks at which to follow Varian have been Doncaster (+£40.48), Wolverhampton (+£22.84) and Lingfield (+£17.77). He has been best avoided at Ascot (-£51.27), York (-£48.88) and Newmarket (July) (-£37.34)

Varian has a 67 per cent record with juvenile runners at Beverley (+£9.08)

He has a 22 per cent strike-rate with runners in novice company (+£30.37)

Epsom has proved a happy hunting ground for Varian's three-year-olds. He had a 45 per cent strike-rate at the venue last year (+£14.15)

Joe Fanning has a 45 per cent record when riding for Varian with a profit of £19.71

Statistics cover the last five years unless stated

"Last season was pretty solid, we performed to a high level domestically and I thought the numbers looked good at the end of the year," reflects the Classic-winning trainer. "You go through peaks and troughs in any season and it's important the graph is pointing in the right direction at the end, which I think it was. A Group 1 win on home soil would have been nice and we'll aim to rectify that this year.

"We had a whole stack of two-year-old winners with some promising types among them and that should set us up for a better season."

For someone who has grown so accustomed to saddling Pattern-race winners it is somewhat surprising Varian has not tasted Royal Ascot success since Cursory Glance won the Albany Stakes in 2014 – and the trainer mentions a first Royal winner in five years as another intended target for the upcoming season.

"It's been a few years since we scored at Royal Ascot so striking there would be high up on the priority list," he adds. "I feel we have a really strong team throughout in all departments, though. We have some nice older horses combined with some unexposed but promising three-year-olds.

"It's crucial we try to better last season and it'd be nice to chalk up a few more winners."

Powerful owner Sheikh Mohammed Obaid has been a loyal patron for the yard in recent years and continues to supply Varian with substantial ammunition.

He has shown a particular fondness for older horses and his team is headed by **Defoe**, who ran in last season's Prix de l'Arc de Triomphe.

"Defoe has been gelded for the core reason that he didn't look to have the profile of a commercial stallion," says Varian.

"We hope we can elongate his career and he should have a lot more to offer as a

DID YOU KNOW?

Roger Varian was initially a jumps rider who worked with Josh Gifford – he rode seven winners in Britain. He has found far greater success as a trainer and since taking over from Michael Jarvis in 2011 has developed his team into one of the biggest and most successful in Newmarket.

Defoe (2): set to start his campaign in the John Porter at Newbury again

gelding. He's very solid at 1m4f and is pretty versatile groundwise, but I still don't believe he wants fast ground.

"It's not beyond the realms of possibility we'll try him over staying trips at some point. We'll probably look to start him back at Newbury in the John Porter again.

"**Sharja Bridge** is a good horse. I'd expect him to go on to better things this year. We probably spent most of last year avoiding soft ground but he seemed to relish the testing surface when winning the Balmoral Handicap at Ascot on Champions Day.

"I think he might have confused us as a young horse appearing not to handle soft ground, but maybe he was just a bit weak. He could well start in the Doncaster Mile at the Lincoln meeting. I'd expect him to improve into a Pattern performer at a mile.

Old favourite back for more

"**Barsanti** is a real favourite at the yard and is back for another year, but whether he's going to improve as a seven-year-old we'll have to see. He's never won a Group race but he's a genuine Listed performer and is a fun horse to have around. He could start back in something like the Buckhounds Stakes at Ascot – a race he won last year.

"**Laugh A Minute** is a solid horse. He has some good sprint form and it could be his year as a four-year-old. He's a bit stronger and could hopefully hold his own in some of the better sprint races throughout the year.

"**Cape Byron** was a bit unlucky not to win last year and I really think he's capable of landing a Victoria Cup or a Hunt Cup – one of those big summer handicap highlights. He might still go on to be a stakes performer, I think he's good enough – he needs everything to click, and I'm sure he's handicapped to win a big pot.

"**Fujaira Prince** has been delicate throughout his career but if he can stay in one piece he is capable of progressing to the higher ranks with time."

An older horse with the potential to dine at the top table is **Pilaster**, who progressed well to win the Group 2 Lillie Langtry Stakes at Glorious Goodwood last season. Pitching her into the Champion Fillies & Mares Stakes at Ascot in the autumn was a big statement from Varian and she bids to add more black type to her burgeoning CV this season, although her best trip remains up for debate.

"Pilaster is a nice filly who has done well through the winter," says the trainer. "She looks stronger this year and we think she's improved. There are a lot of good 1m4f fillies' options throughout the summer and she could start in the Further Flight Stakes at Nottingham.

"We'll also look at races like the Lancashire Oaks and she'll tell us whether she is going to excel over middle distances or whether she'll stay over further – there's a pretty good programme for her."

Kingston Hill was a genuinely top-class three-year-old and ensured Varian added his name to the roster of Classic-winning trainers in 2014, backing up a second to Australia in the Epsom Derby by going one place better in the St Leger at Doncaster.

A second Classic victory has so far eluded Varian but he appears to have a handful of runners who will be campaigned with such targets in mind this year.

All roads lead to 1,000 Guineas

"I think **Mot Juste** is a very nice filly," he says. "I don't think there was any fluke about her victory in the Oh So Sharp Stakes. I watched it back a few times and she was very professional. She's wintered very well and she could have her prep run in the Nell Gwyn en route to contesting the 1,000 Guineas.

"**San Donato** is a smart horse who has loads of gears. We're going to ask him the question of staying a mile and we've put him in the French 2,000 Guineas. He could reappear in the Greenham en route to the Classic. Hopefully he'll get the mile but we always have the option of going back to sprint distances.

ROGER VARIAN

Newmarket, Suffolk

	Number of horses	Races run	1st	2nd	3rd	Unpl	Per cent	£1 level stake
2yo	66	161	29	21	26	84	18.6	-4.98
3yo	78	313	56	61	45	150	17.9	-45.29
4yo+	31	129	21	25	11	71	16.3	-60.18
Totals	**175**	**603**	**106**	**107**	**82**	**305**	**17.7**	**-110.45**
2017	162	558	109	113	91	244	19.5	-117.57
2016	167	554	97	72	65	317	17.5	-141.34

BY MONTH

2yo	W-R	Per cent	£1 level stake	3yo	W-R	Per cent	£1 level stake
Jan	0-0	0.0	0.00	Jan	0-3	0.0	-3.00
Feb	0-0	0.0	0.00	Feb	0-1	0.0	-1.00
Mar	0-0	0.0	0.00	Mar	0-3	0.0	-3.00
Apr	0-0	0.0	0.00	Apr	2-49	4.1	-44.25
May	0-1	0.0	-1.00	May	7-57	12.3	-4.38
June	1-7	14.3	-1.50	June	11-50	22.0	+10.56
July	2-8	25.0	-3.42	July	9-38	23.7	-5.87
Aug	2-18	11.1	-11.64	Aug	8-36	22.2	-14.43
Sep	8-35	22.9	+10.94	Sep	9-35	25.7	+9.07
Oct	9-43	20.9	+20.40	Oct	5-28	17.9	-7.75
Nov	6-34	17.6	-10.34	Nov	4-9	44.4	+18.25
Dec	2-15	13.3	-8.43	Dec	1-4	25.0	+0.50

4yo+	W-R	Per cent	£1 level stake	Totals	W-R	Per cent	£1 level stake
Jan	0-2	0.0	-2.00	Jan	0-5	0.0	-5.00
Feb	0-3	0.0	-3.00	Feb	0-4	0.0	-4.00
Mar	1-5	20.0	-3.09	Mar	1-8	12.5	-6.09
Apr	4-13	30.8	-0.50	Apr	6-62	9.7	-44.75
May	8-26	30.8	+2.08	May	15-84	17.9	-3.30
June	4-16	25.0	-8.17	June	16-73	21.9	+0.89
July	0-15	0.0	-15.00	July	11-61	18.0	-24.29
Aug	2-18	11.1	-12.00	Aug	12-72	16.7	-38.07
Sep	1-18	5.6	-14.50	Sep	18-88	20.5	+5.51
Oct	1-10	10.0	-1.00	Oct	15-81	18.5	+11.65
Nov	0-3	0.0	-3.00	Nov	10-46	21.7	+15.25
Dec	0-0	0.0	0.00	Dec	3-19	15.8	+0.50

DISTANCE

2yo	W-R	Per cent	£1 Level Stake	3yo	W-R	Per cent	£1 level stake
5f-6f	8-36	22.2	-5.97	5f-6f	6-29	20.7	-8.69
7f-8f	20-121	16.5	-2.51	7f-8f	32-179	17.9	-12.34
9f-13f	2-4	50.0	+3.50	9f-13f	16-96	16.7	-23.01
14f+	0-0	0.0	0.00	14f+	2-9	22.2	-1.25

4yo+	W-R	Per cent	£1 level stake	Totals	W-R	Per cent	£1 level stake
5f-6f	0-29	0.0	-29.00	5f-6f	14-94	14.9	-43.66
7f-8f	11-58	19.0	-12.84	7f-8f	63-358	17.6	-27.69
9f-13f	9-40	22.5	-20.09	9f-13f	27-140	19.3	-39.60
14f+	1-2	50.0	+1.75	14f+	3-11	27.3	+0.50

TYPE OF RACE

NON-HANDICAPS				HANDICAPS			
	W-R	Per cent	£1 level stake		W-R	Per cent	£1 level stake
2yo	28-154	18.2	-6.98	2yo	2-7	28.6	+2.00
3yo	36-186	19.4	-1.12	3yo	20-127	15.7	-44.17
4yo+	8-35	22.9	-15.93	4yo+	13-94	13.8	-44.25

Statistics relate to all runners in Britain from January 1, 2018 to December 31, 2018

Varian can see Pilaster (left) mixing it in top company in the months ahead

"**Yourtimeisnow** was a smart two-year-old. I'm not sure if she'll get a mile, though. We've entered her in the French 1,000 Guineas and it's possible she could reappear in the Fred Darling at Newbury. I think she's quite talented and if she doesn't stay a mile, like San Donato, we can always drop back to sprinting trips.

"**Nabeyla** is a promising filly who impressed me at Wolverhampton and will hopefully go on to better things. She could well take in a novice under a penalty in a few weeks' time.

"**Prince Eiji** is also promising. We probably threw him in a bit at the deep end last year after he won his novice but I retain faith in him. I'd hope he'd be good enough to contest some of the better three-year-old races throughout the year.

"**Nearooz** is quite nice we think – she's been entered up well. I'm still not completely sure of her optimum trip but we're likely to start at a mile and see where we go.

Pattern aspirations for Comets

"I like **Three Comets**. I thought he might have achieved more last year but he's by Sea The Moon, whose progeny always tend to improve with age. I'd hope he can progress into a Pattern performer over middle distances.

"**Surfman** looked quite smart when winning his maiden at Nottingham in the autumn. He's a half-brother to the Group 1 winner Kitesurf and looks a pretty promising ten-furlong horse.

"**Nausha** is another filly we hold in quite high regard. She won on her only start at Newbury and should have more to offer as she grows this year.

"**UAE Jewel** is a horse we've always liked but he was just a bit too immature to see the track in the autumn last year. I think he's full of potential and will hopefully

be winning some nice races later in his career.

"**Apparate** was second at Newbury on his sole start at two which I thought was a good debut. He struck me likely to excel over middle distances. He was under pressure from halfway but all he did was keep staying on until the line. We'll likely start him in a 1m2f novice in the spring before stepping up in trip."

It is important to possess quality in all departments and Varian's team of older horses is bolstered by a promising squad of juveniles.

"We had a lot of two-year-old winners last season and I really like what I've seen of this year's crop at this stage," says the trainer.

"We definitely like **Desert Emperor**. He's a good-moving Camelot colt showing all the right signs at home and has a Derby entry.

Smart prospects

"**Postileo** is also entered in the Derby and is showing all the right signs at home on the gallops.

"**Retrospect** is another who has the Derby entry. He's a nice mover with a good temperament but we'll need to learn more about him to find out just how good he can be. He's another entered in the Derby.

"**Solar Screen** is a half-brother to Sheikha Reika but is going to take time to develop. I'd be looking at races in the second half of the season for him.

"**Good Humour** is another well-bred type as a brother to Mot Juste. He goes nicely at this stage."

Exiting the Carlburg Stables conveyor belt are a cluster of familiar names, including Emmaus, who has departed to race elsewhere. Grade 1 winner Sheikha Reika is embarking on a second career in the paddocks, along with Group 3 winner Tomyris, 2017 Cheveley Park third Madeline and the unbeaten Newmarket maiden winner Turaya.

Interview by Robbie Wilders

Yourtimeisnow (yellow colours) will be tested over a mile and has an entry in the French 1,000 Guineas

Three talented trainers and their smart recruits

JAMES TATE

THERE has been plenty of movement within James Tate's yard since the end of last season, but **Invincible Army** remains the stable star at Jamesfield Place and will look to rectify what was a disappointing end to a fine campaign.

Now a four-year-old, the colt won the Group 3 Pavilion Stakes at Ascot last May and finished second to Sands Of Mali by a whisker in the Group 2 Sandy Lane Stakes at Haydock before failing to deliver in the Commonwealth Cup and Hackwood Stakes.

He has not been seen since but after a lengthy absence Tate is optimistic Invincible Army can return to his best, with the Dante meeting at York earmarked.

The trainer says: "He lost his way in the summer on the fast ground so we made the decision to give him a break. He's been absolutely flying at home which is fantastic and his rider can barely hold him at times!

"The primary aim for us is the Group 2 Duke of York in May, but we might give him a prep race in Listed company just to make sure."

Scurry Stakes winner Haddaf and the impressive Iconic Sunset have left Tate, but he has another ace up his sleeve in the form of top miler **Hey Gaman**.

The four-year-old finished in the first three in a trio of Group races last season, including the French 2,000 Guineas at Longchamp where he was edged out by only a neck.

Tate believes he can build on that form, and says: "He's a massive horse and one you'd expect to improve from three to four. That said, he only needs to improve slightly and I'll be happy.

"He's at his best on right-handed turning tracks with easy ground, so the French courses like Longchamp suit him. He hasn't had a black-type win yet so we might start in a Listed or Group 3 and then work our way up."

After making only two appearances last season, **Kyllang Rock** is a sprinter who won't be appearing on too many radars. However, one of those runs produced a Class 2 victory at Musselburgh that saw the now five-year-old defeat subsequent Group 1 Nunthorpe winner Alpha Delphini by half a length.

He picked up an injury in the Listed Sole Power Sprint Stakes at the Curragh and finished sixth, but Tate says: "He's one I've got a lot of faith in. He looked like a sprinter going places before his injury, but he's healthy now and will return for the top sprints this year where he'll hopefully take off."

Tate believes he has plenty of potential in his stable and says this looks to be the most promising group he's ever had.

The trainer says: "**Astonished** is a huge Sea The Stars filly who won her sole start last year when scoring at Kempton. She could return in a novice or go straight for a Listed race, but she's one we think a lot of. **New Graduate** finished second to a horse who was third at Royal Ascot on his debut and should be a black-type horse."

Tate also flags up a couple of three-year-olds, saying: "**Name The Wind** has run once and won, beating 2-9 shot Buffalo River at Kempton. He will hopefully be in a Guineas trial this year.

"**Sameem** is rated 81 but is a lot better than that and broke his maiden by six lengths at Beverley in September. He should progress and on the optimistic end of the scale I'll look at a Derby trial for him."

Asked whether there are any two-year-olds who have caught his eye, Tate mentions one in particular who he is already extremely fond of.

James Tate has some decent firepower at his disposal, including Hey Gaman (centre, facing page)

"**Lyrical Beauty** is a No Nay Never filly out of Virginia Celeste. She was bought at the end of last November and I absolutely love her action. She's cantered great on the all-weather and grass, and has all the makings of a quality filly. I'd make her the one to follow."

CHARLIE FELLOWES

THE Flat season tends to wind up towards the end of October with Champions Day at Ascot, but for Charlie Fellowes the excitement was only just beginning.

His globe-trotting superstar **Prince Of Arran** headed to Australia having already won in Dubai and placed in the US with the Melbourne Cup in mind.

He defied all expectations and came third in the famous Group 1 contest. Now Fellowes is eyeing domestic success for the son of Shirocco.

He says: "After he returns to Britain from Dubai we'll look at the Hardwicke at Royal Ascot. He likes Ascot and it suits him well."

Asked if a trip back to Flemington is on the cards, Fellowes makes no attempt to hide his intentions.

"Absolutely. We'll stick to 1m4f or so over the summer but we've certainly got another go at the Melbourne Cup in mind."

Another six-year-old who could turn into a hot commodity for Fellowes is **Chiefofchiefs**, who followed up victory at Kempton in January by finishing behind Wissahickon in the Lingfield Winter Derby Trial and the Winter Derby itself. Now a tilt at the Lincoln could be on the cards.

The Lincoln opens the Flat season at the end of March, and Fellowes does not hold back on Chiefofchiefs' chances of kicking the season off with a winner.

"It's perfect for him. He's well handicapped and is at his best on a straight, flat track with soft ground. A mile's right up his street and it's something to aim at. He's very much the Lincoln horse for us."

One young gun who could break on to the scene this year is three-year-old **King Ottokar**, who made a winning debut in September. That was a Class 4 victory at

Newbury, and the son of Motivator went on to run in the Group 1 Futurity Stakes at Doncaster a month later, finishing eight lengths behind winner Magna Grecia.

Fellowes says: "Our plan is to start low and look at novice company to get his head back in front and we'll take it from there. His owners have lofty targets and dreams, and he holds an entry for the Irish Derby.

"I think he's a very good colt and is one of the best-looking horses I've trained. He's a real favourite of mine and we'll likely start over a mile this term and end up at 1m4f."

With black type-winning mares Carolinae and Crimson Rosette retired, it is up to these younger horses to step up and Fellowes believes his string of three-year-olds can do just that.

"We've got a really nice bunch of three-year-olds. **Maid For Life** finished second first time out at Chelmsford and should progress, and we've got a few unraced horses to go to war with.

"There's no Snazzy among the two-year-olds this year, but **Obligada** is nice and one of my more forward types. **Lady Bamford** has looked good as well."

Charlie Fellowes' string stretch their legs on Warren Hill in Newmarket

JOHN BERRY

IT WOULD be impossible to look at the stable of John Berry without first considering **Roy Rocket**, the nine-year-old Beverley House flagbearer who has developed a cult-like following on the Sussex coast.

The horse who loves to be beside the seaside ran eight times at Brighton last year, winning three and finishing in the first three on four other occasions.

Victory on an absymal August afternoon cemented his status as a course legend when he became the joint-winningmost horse at the track with nine wins – and Berry is not secretive about plans for the new campaign.

"The plan is to keep going back to Brighton!" he says.

"Picking races for Roy is easy because I just mark up the Brighton meetings that have a middle-distance race for his rating and only look elsewhere if there's a gap in the schedule."

Another pair of contenders from the Berry camp are Hope Is High and Sussex Girl, who enjoyed winning campaigns in 2017 but struggled to build on that last year.

"It was a frustrating year. **Hope Is High** won four handicaps in 2017 so started off at her maximum feasible rating, and kept running well without winning so her mark

never decreased by much. She'll likely make her return in early June.

"**Sussex Girl** won her last two starts of 2017 as a three-year-old and I thought she would progress from three to four but it just hasn't really happened."

Kryptos had a tremendous campaign two years ago, winning three of his five runs, but missed all of last year through injury. Berry reports he is now having a long rest and likely won't appear until the autumn.

Konigin arrived at Beverley House in November following the retirement of Luca Cumani but, having earned two places from three runs, the four-year-old filly has already shown plenty of promise.

Berry says: "She's a very big horse and I think she's the type to improve markedly from three to four because of her size. Her dam's a sister to St Leger winner Milan so she's bred to improve for time and distance."

Loving Pearl has arrived from Ralph Beckett's stable. A daughter of Dunaden, she finished second twice over the summer and Berry is optimistic she can build on those runs.

He says: "She showed decent form as a two-year-old and you'd hope she would improve significantly as she gets older. I'm hoping she can progress from what she's done so far."

Also among his ranks is Nathaniel filly **Sacred Sprite**, who was not broken in until she was a three-year-old and had her first run last December.

"She's a well-bred filly and if she progresses I'd hope she has the makings of a nice stayer."

Interviews by Andrew Willsher

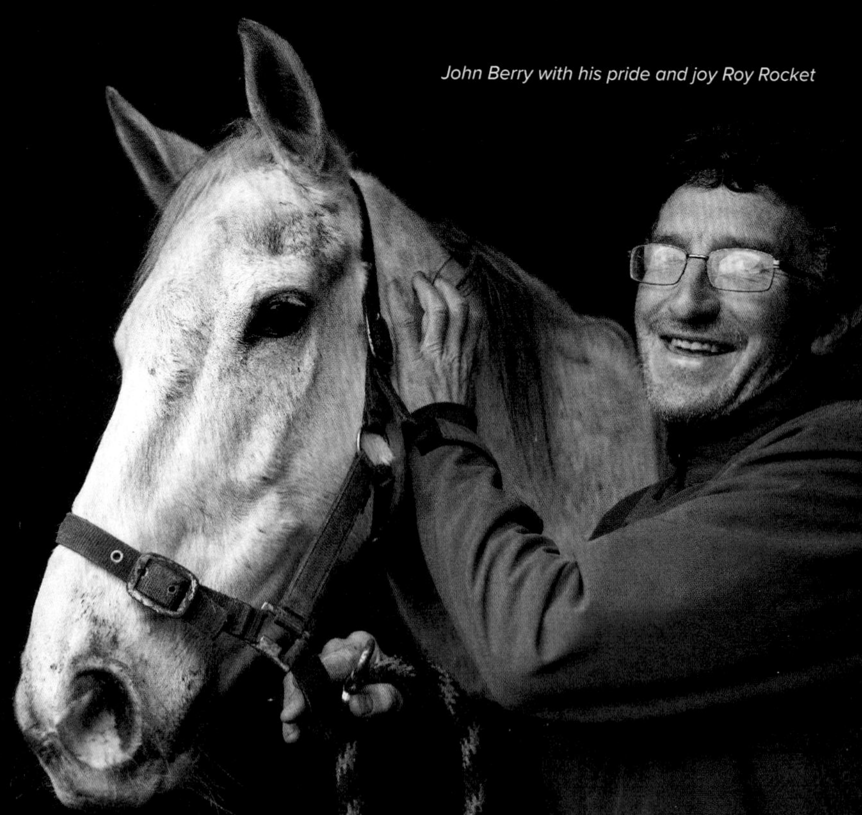

John Berry with his pride and joy Roy Rocket

THE EXPERTS

VIEW FROM IRELAND ALAN SWEETMAN

Hoping smaller trainers can continue to prosper

LOOKING BACK

Novelty and variety were a feature during the Flat season in Ireland in 2018 when the usual theme of Aidan O'Brien dominance was not as pervasive as usual.

The possibility of a fresh perspective is fascinating after a year in which Ireland's star performer was a filly, Alpha Centauri, trained by one of the country's top jumps trainers Jessica Harrington, one of three new Classic-winning trainers, along with Ken Condon, who won the Irish 2,000 Guineas with Romanised, and Joseph O'Brien who saddled Latrobe to deprive his father of a 13th Irish Derby win.

Ballydoyle's flying start to the British Classic campaign with Saxon Warrior was not maintained. The fall from grace of the 2,000 Guineas winner was a blow to the Coolmore team whose three-year-old cohort was short on the crucial middle-distance talent it aims to cultivate. Some late compensation was afforded by big wins over staying trips for Kew Gardens in the St Leger and Flag Of Honour in the Irish St Leger.

O'Brien's two-year-old team contributed several major wins, despite a rare failure to land any of the three domestic Group 1s. The Phoenix Stakes and the National Stakes went for export courtesy of the Martyn Meade-trained Advertise and Godolphin's Quorto respectively, while Skitter Scatter won the Moyglare Stud Stakes for Patrick Prendergast, whose decision not to renew his licence was a major shock when revealed early in the year.

LOOKING FORWARD

Ten Sovereigns, third in the European Classification on 121, completed an unbeaten three-race sequence with a smart performance to beat **Jash** in the Middle Park. He gives the impression of being a potential sprint champion, but there is just about enough stamina in the family to suggest he may be afforded a shot at the Guineas.

The 118-rated **Anthony Van Dyck** beat stablemates **Christmas** and **Mohawk** in the Group 2 Futurity Stakes at the Curragh and upheld form with the pair when second to Quorto in the National Stakes. His third place behind Too Darn Hot and Advertise in the Dewhurst should probably be seen as a more accurate guide to his potential at three than a rather lifeless effort in the Breeders' Cup Juvenile Turf.

Magna Grecia arrived relatively late on the scene to stake a claim as one of the stable's most promising colts with a late September maiden win at Naas. Beaten a neck by the French-trained Persian King in the Group 3 Autumn Stakes at Newmarket, he gave O'Brien a ninth win in the Vertem Futurity Trophy (formerly Racing Post Trophy) at Doncaster, with stablemates **Western Australia** and **Circus Maximus** third and fourth. Magna Grecia, by Invincible Spirit out of a Galileo mare, does not hold a Derby entry but could be a force at 1m2f after a possible Irish 2,000 Guineas bid.

Other O'Brien-trained colts likely to feature in middle-distance Pattern races include **Japan** and **Mount Everest**, who finished in reverse order in terms of market expectations when winner and second in the Beresford Stakes. There is also Zetland winner **Norway**, who possibly has the makings of a St Leger type. At the other end of the distance spectrum, Cornwallis winner **Sergei Prokofiev** should make his presence felt in the sprint division.

Outside of Ballydoyle, the most interesting Group 1 prospect among the colts is **Madhmoon**, trained by Kevin Prendergast for Hamdan Al Maktoum. Unbeaten in two starts, the Dawn Approach colt defeated O'Brien's subsequent Royal Lodge and Criterium de Saint-Cloud runner-up **Sydney Opera House** in a maiden at Leopardstown in August and was an emphatic winner of the mile Group 2 event on the same venue's Irish Champions card.

The O'Brien-trained second **Broome** did his bit for the form when losing out by only a neck to Royal Marine in the Prix Jean-Luc Lagardere.

One of the most interesting once-raced maiden winners from the latter stages of the season was the Dermot Weld-trained **Tankerville**. From the same stable, **Masaff** – twice Group-placed after a debut win – is a useful middle-distance prospect in the Aga Khan colours.

The progress made by **Skitter Scatter** – from a third placing in a 5f Dundalk maiden in March to Classic contender – provided a heart-warming narrative in 2018, involving a popular and hard-working trainer reaping well-deserved reward against the odds.

Prendergast's decision to join John Oxx as assistant trainer means the filly is now in a stable which has won only two Group races since 2012 and endured a miserable 2018 campaign, failing to reach double figures.

Oxx, who has suffered a significant loss of profile in the ten years since Sea The Stars carried all before him, retains the affection of the Irish racing public who will hope to see the filly spearhead a revival.

One of three Irish-trained fillies to win a Group 1 in 2018, she looks a more obvious Guineas type than Joseph O'Brien's **Iridessa**, whose manner of victory in the Fillies' Mile at Newmarket and status as a daughter of Ruler Of The World marks her down as more of an Oaks prospect.

Skitter Scatter came into her own from late July on when stepped up to 7f for her final three runs. She emerged best in two clashes with Ballydoyle's Fillies' Mile runner-up **Hermosa**, who ended the season with a creditable second against the colts in the Criterium International at Chantilly.

The Guineas trip should prove ideal for Skitter Scatter. The same could not be said with certainty of Ballydoyle's best juvenile filly **Fairyland**, a daughter of Kodiac campaigned exclusively at 6f in five runs at two. Beaten only once, when third in the Albany Stakes, she was a narrow winner from

Kew Gardens (left) could do well in Cup races this season

The Mackem Bullet in the Lowther and the Cheveley Park. There is a lot of speed in the pedigree, although her half-sister Now Or Later won a mile Group 3 at three.

O'Brien's Cheveley Park third **So Perfect**, who beat Skitter Scatter in a 6f Group 3 race at the Curragh at the beginning of July, is another with a sprint-oriented pedigree. Best of three runners for the stable when runner-up in the Phoenix Stakes, she ended the season with a creditable third in the Breeders' Cup Juvenile Turf Sprint.

Just Wonderful also ended the season brightly enough at Churchill Downs, finishing fourth to Newspaperofrecord in the Breeders' Cup Juvenile Turf, after showing uneven form in Britain and Ireland. She failed to deliver in the Albany Stakes and in the Moyglare before redeeming herself with a Rockfel Stakes victory which put her in the Guineas picture.

Goddess, a superbly bred daughter of Camelot, impressed with a ten-length maiden win at Leopardstown in July but flopped in a Group 3 a fortnight later and was not seen again. She remains of significant interest.

A Listed race at Leopardstown on Irish Champion Stakes day in which Iridessa finished third may continue to be informative. The Harrington-trained pair **Sparkle'n'joy** and **Trethias**, winner and fourth respectively, look capable of Pattern success, as well as runner-up **Foxtrot Liv**, who did Pat Twomey's small County Tipperary yard proud when second to Hermosa in a Group 3 event at Naas in October.

Lady Kaya is another high-class prospect for a small stable. Sheila Lavery's filly was runner-up in the Moyglare and not beaten far in sixth in the Cheveley Park.

Ballydoyle houses several lightly raced fillies with potential to make the grade in Pattern company. **Chablis**, winner of a 7f maiden at Gowran Park in October, could be the pick of them.

Having finished last season by chasing home Enable in the Breeders' Cup Turf, **Magical** stays in training at five in a bid to supplement the 1m4f Group 1 honours gained at Ascot last October. **I Can Fly**, a 33-1 chance when going close against Roaring Lion in the Queen Elizabeth II Stakes, is also afforded another season.

Although beaten only four lengths when seventh behind Enable in the Arc, **Kew Gardens** has work to do in order to establish himself as a top-flight 1m4f performer at four, and may be more profitably employed as a Cup horse, since **Flag Of Honour** did not show quite enough on his final two starts of the campaign to suggest he can step into the shoes vacated by Order Of St George.

Joseph O'Brien's Irish Derby winner **Latrobe**, second to Flag Of Honour in the Irish Leger, later went very close over 1m2f in the Mackinnon Stakes at Flemington, an effort that augurs well for an international middle-distance campaign at four.

Too Darn Hot looks every inch the real deal

2,000 GUINEAS / DERBY

There is only one place to start and that is with John Gosden's **Too Darn Hot**, who was an exceptional two-year-old.

He won all his four starts, going up the ladder from maiden to Group 3, to Group 2, and finally to Group 1 success in the Dewhurst.

All of his wins were characterised by one thing – they were easy. His narrowest winning margin was a length and three-quarters, achieved in the Champagne Stakes at the expense of Phoenix Of Spain who was arguably unlucky not to win the Futurity on his next start.

His most impressive display, however, was saved for the Dewhurst. He was racing on the fastest ground he had encountered, he was on and off the bridle and looked to be struggling around halfway. However, when Frankie Dettori pulled him out the response was electric and he went on to thrash the Group 1-winning Advertise with Anthony Van Dyck in third.

There seems no good reason why he shouldn't train on, his breeding suggests he ought to get a Derby trip and his family aren't fragile – his dam Dar Re Mi raced for four seasons, his sister Lah Ti Dar ran five times last season including in a St Leger and on Champions Day, while Too Darn Hot managed four races in little over two months last year between August and October.

If he lands the 2,000 Guineas – a race Gosden has yet to win – then I think connections will find it hard to pass up the opportunity of a run at Epsom.

If you wanted more of a Derby-St Leger type then the Aidan O'Brien-trained **Norway** might interest you more.

He has a real middle-distance pedigree being a brother to Ruler Of The World and a half-brother to King George winner Duke Of Marmalade.

Last season he might have won only two of his five starts, but they did include a comfortable win in the Zetland Stakes at Newmarket, a race that has increased in importance for the Ballydoyle team in recent seasons.

Norway will most likely appear in a Derby trial somewhere and don't be surprised if he has a similar campaign to Kew Gardens, who went Queen's Vase, Grand Prix de Paris and Voltigeur on his way to Classic success at Doncaster.

1,000 GUINEAS

The fillies' department is much more open and it's 10-1 the field for the 1,000 Guineas.

Unsurprisingly Aidan O'Brien supplies the current favourite in Just Wonderful, but he also has **So Perfect** a bit lower down the betting.

She ran seven times as a two-year-old, arguably putting in her best performance when beating Moyglare winner Skitter Scatter by half a length in a Group 3 at the Curragh.

She took on the boys in the Phoenix Stakes

and again acquitted herself well to finish within half a length of Advertise, who showed the form in a positive light with an excellent run in the Dewhurst.

The hard thing to ascertain is what her best trip will be – she stayed on dourly to beat Skitter Scatter over 6f, suggesting further should be within her remit, but as yet she hasn't run beyond that trip.

Maybe she will get the chance to run in a trial to test her stamina, but if that fails there are always races like the Commonwealth Cup she can go for. She did go to Royal Ascot last season and excelled herself to finish a close-up fourth in the 5f Queen Mary.

OAKS

The Oaks is even more open with bookies going 16-1 the field so there is some value and British stables can come to the fore.

Ralph Beckett has proved time and again how adept he is with fillies and he has an interesting contender in **Manuela De Vega** – two from two as a juvenile.

She won at Salisbury on her debut in September and then went north to Pontefract for an easy Listed win over a mile. Beckett is already thinking of an Oaks trial for her and it wouldn't be a surprise to see her head to Lingfield, a race the trainer has won three times, while his 2008 Oaks winner Look Here was second in the race.

William Haggas also has a lively one in **Rainbow Heart**, currently 33-1 for Epsom success. She ran in two Newmarket maidens late last season, showing promise in the first before winning the second by eight lengths.

Both of those races were over 7f but she should stay the mile, being by Sea The Stars' brother Born To Sea and related to a German 1m3f Listed winner on the dam's side.

Too Darn Hot could prove a major force in the Classics

GETTING AN EDGE RICHARD BIRCH

The course specialists primed to do it again

I ADVISED six Brighton specialists to follow in this book last year, and was rewarded with multiple wins from the likes of Roy Rocket and Pour La Victoire. In fact, the returns I accumulated from Brighton bets ultimately proved the difference between a winning and losing 2018.

Course form is something many punters fail to pay sufficient attention to when making their selections. There are many horses who at certain tracks consistently run 5lb or more above the level they produce round other venues. And with that in mind, fill your boots by following these ten course specialists in 2019 . . .

CHRISTMAS NIGHT Beverley

Enterprising tactics often pay maximum dividends at Beverley and my idea of the perfect horse for the track is a prominent racer or front-runner who can hug the inside rail and kick for home on the run into the straight. Christmas Night did just that under Ben Robinson (who rides Beverley well) to land a 7½f handicap by two lengths last May off a mark of 60. He finished a close third on his only subsequent visit the following month, and is currently rated 63. There will be plenty of opportunities for him during the summer and I'd expect him to take one or two at least.

DE VEGAS KID Brighton

His course form figures at the seaside venue read 41122, and this five-year-old is still going the right way. Trained by Tony Carroll, a dab hand at finding the right opportunities for his handicappers at Brighton, De Vegas Kid won Class 5 handicaps on consecutive days last September off 66 in tremendous style. He acquitted himself with real credit in a higher grade at Epsom and Lingfield, and the return to Brighton in 2019 will see him back in the winner's enclosure. The best is yet to come and I fancy him to win the valuable Brighton Mile in August.

A summer scene at Brighton, where De Vegas Kid can enhance his smart course form figures

LUXFORD Brighton

This diminutive mare did well for John Best, but could take another step forward now she has joined Gary Moore. She boasts a 50 per cent strike-rate at Brighton – two wins from four starts – and is particularly well suited by a mile. Invariably fast out of the stalls which enables her to take up a good early position, Luxford has won off a mark of 56 at Chelmsford yet starts the new turf campaign rated just 50. I will be surprised if she isn't placed to win two or three handicaps this season at Brighton. She acts on any ground and confirmed she retains all her ability when going close at Chelmsford over 1m2f in December.

POUR LA VICTOIRE Brighton

The archetypal Brighton specialist. You only had to watch the way he handled the tricky gradients during his first win there in August 2013 to realise he would prove a regular money-spinner on his trips to the south coast. Nearly six years later he has now won nine times at Brighton, including three during a golden three-week spell last summer. Effective at trips from 6f to a mile, Pour La Victoire is a standing dish at the Brighton festival and comfortably landed the Brighton Bullet for a second time last August by three-quarters of a length from Big Lachie. A lofty handicap mark may make things more difficult in the short term, but I would bet serious money Carroll will be campaigning him for another strike in August.

REDARNA Ayr

This chestnut comes alive when racing at his beloved Ayr over 7f with some cut in the ground. Unbeaten in four visits to the Scottish track, the Dianne Sayer-trained five-year-old has that priceless knack of not winning by very far which means not too much damage can be done to his handicap rating. Successful from marks of 55, 59, 60 and 66, Redarna remains lightly raced and there ought to be a bit more improvement to come. He does particularly well in the autumn when there is plenty of juice underfoot, and could be one to watch for at the Ayr Gold Cup fixture.

REGAL MIRAGE Hamilton

Tim Easterby enjoyed his best Flat season last year, and Regal Mirage was one of those who contributed to the record tally with victories at Hamilton and Beverley. It is at the Scottish track where Regal Mirage performs best. Unbeaten there in three starts in Class 5 and 6 company, the son of Aqlaam looks capable of holding his own in a higher grade at the track, and it would be no surprise if he manages to land a decent prize over 1m3f or 1m5f at some stage this summer. He doesn't possess high mileage for a five-year-old and, with further improvement, should be capable of winning off marks in the high 70s and low 80s.

ROY ROCKET Brighton

A grey legend who needs no introduction to Brighton regulars, Roy Rocket's success story soared last year as another series of wonderful performances on Race Hill made headline news. John Berry's stable star has now won nine times at Brighton over 1m2f or 1m4f, and seems particularly effective on baking hot days when the ground is firmer than it would be at other tracks. He has yet to score outside of Class 6 and 5 company. John Egan has a strong rapport with the nine-year-old, but two of his three wins in 2018 came under Ross Birkett and Rob Hornby. Clearly well handicapped when taking an amateur riders' handicap by four lengths from Pour L'Amour off 55 last June, he starts the new turf season rated 14lb higher. His mark may have to come down a few pounds before he can get competitive again, but when it does just listen to the reception he'll receive from the Brighton crowd for win number ten.

AL SHAQAB LOCKINGE DAY

SATURDAY 18 MAY

The Al Shaqab Lockinge Stakes has been run at Newbury Racecourse since its inauguration in 1958. Named after a parish north of the racecourse, the first winner of the race Pall Mall, was owned by Her Majesty Queen Elizabeth II, and was coming from a win in the 2,000 Guineas at Newmarket. Having been promoted to Group 1 status in 1995, the race was closed to three-year olds – making it the first mile race for older horses in the flat season calendar.

In recent years, the race has been won by some of the leading names in the industry including the legendary Frankel, Canford Cliffs and more recently by Ribchester.

This year Ladies Day will form part of the celebrations as we welcome the summer season in spectacular style. Following on from the success of Rhododendron's win in 2018 and the first filly to succeed in the Group 1 showpiece, since Red Evie in 2007, Saturday 18 May seems a fitting new home for the occasion.

AL SHAQAB

Racecourse Rd, Newbury RG14 7NZ

Tel: 01635 40015 | info@newburyracecourse.co.uk | www.newburyracecourse.co.uk

SHARP OPERATOR Brighton

I hailed Sharp Operator the 'new Pour La Victoire' after watching him win a Class 6 handicap over a mile at Brighton last May. The manner in which he handled the unique ups and downs of the track suggested he would develop into a proper course specialist. Problems with the starting stalls halted his progress, but he did return to land another Class 6 in July, once again showing a smart turn of foot to seal matters before idling late on. Although possessing plenty of quirks, Sharp Operator's style of running – travels strongly and can produce one telling burst – is perfect for this track, and he is high on my list of potential money-spinners for the summer. A mile is definitely his best trip, and I am far from convinced 1m2f – over which he was been campaigned on the all-weather during the winter – plays to his strengths.

SHOW OF FORCE Chepstow

If I was in the market for buying a horse I would have bid for Show Of Force when she was sent by trainer Jonny Portman to the Tattersalls Ireland Ascot Sale last November.

Summer action at Chepstow where Show Of Force should be in winning form later this year

Picked up by Nick Mitchell for just £4,800, that could prove a bargain when he campaigns her at Chepstow – where his form figures read 121 – this summer. Sent for home a long way out when beating Branscombe by two and a half lengths at the Welsh track last July, Show Of Force will start the new turf campaign only 1lb higher after a string of subsequent defeats at other tracks. Chepstow doesn't suit every horse, but this four-year-old filly loves it there, and looks the type to pop up at a decent price.

SUPER FLORENCE Catterick

A sprinter with exceptional trapping ability and early pace, which she utilised to maximum effect when running riot off 57 over 6f at Catterick last July. A winner by seven lengths that day, the Iain Jardine-trained speedster is tailor-made for sprints at that track since front-runners and prominent racers usually hold a significant advantage – it is devilishly difficult to come from well off the pace round there. Super Florence returned to Catterick for a competitive Class 5 handicap over 6f in August and made another bold attempt to make all, just caught in the final strides by Extrasolar. Later campaigned at 7f, I feel she would be better suited by a drop to the minimum trip, and there will be abundant opportunities for her to excel over 5f and 6f at the Yorkshire track this summer. She starts off on 69 and has the definite makings of a 75-plus filly when conditions are in her favour.

NAMES TO MAKE IT PAY PAUL KEALY

From Hilalee to Rascal: back these 12 horses to help lock in a profit

AL HILALEE

This Charlie Appleby-trained three-year-old broke his duck with an impressive victory on the July course at the height of summer. A Racing Post Rating of 93 for that debut was pretty high and Al Hilalee duly stepped up on the performance when just holding on in a three-way photo from fellow British raiders Duke Of Hazzard and Great Scot in a Deauville Listed contest in August. The trainer had been thinking in terms of the Vertem Futurity at Doncaster before that, so there may have been a problem or he might just have decided he wasn't quite up to it at that stage of his career. He hasn't been seen on a racecourse since but, given his pedigree (by Dubawi out of a Group 1-winning dam), he ought to progress with a further step up in trip this term.

Dom Carlos got off the mark on his third start, improving significantly to score in fine style

DESERT FRIEND

I like the profile of this colt. He is by Mark Johnston's teak-tough Universal and, while that hardly makes him a horse with a fashionable pedigree, the fact he managed to win two of his three starts as a juvenile, all from September onwards, is surely a good sign. Universal didn't hit his peak until he was four, so you would hope there is more improvement to come and Desert Friend starts life looking very temptingly handicapped off a mark of 83 following his debut success at Leicester and second victory at Kempton in October. Given his pedigree, he certainly ought to be improving for a step up to 1m2f and 1m4f this season and I'll be disappointed if he isn't at least a stone better than his mark by the end of the campaign.

DOM CARLOS

This colt was called a slow learner by Joseph O'Brien last season and that certainly looked to be the case as it took him three runs to get off the mark. He did show huge improvement to score, though, slamming his rivals by four lengths and more at the Curragh. That probably wasn't much of a race, but just a couple of weeks later Dom Carlos was sent out to contest the Windsor Castle at Royal Ascot, a race which turned out to be surprisingly good. He was a massive eyecatcher as he was miles behind at halfway and must have had the best part of 20 horses to pass during the final furlong. He got past most of them, though, finishing third to Soldier's Call. He didn't race again last season, but hopefully there is nothing wrong as he looks the type to improve again and I'd be interested to see him back at Royal Ascot in the Commonwealth Cup or the Jersey Stakes, a race won by his sire Gale Force Ten.

DUBAI WARRIOR

The horse everyone wants to see from the John Gosden yard in 2019 is undoubtedly Too Darn Hot – but there will surely be more than one three-year-old star in the powerful Newmarket stable this season. Dubai Warrior might well be one of them as he looked a bit special when scorching clear to win on his debut by four and a half lengths at Chelmsford in November. That was only a lowly novice contest, but Dubai Warrior won with any amount in hand and the five-length third is now rated 77 and the eight-length fourth will probably be rated higher after winning his maiden by eight lengths next time – he earned a Racing Post Rating of 86. Gosden has introduced some top-class performers in all-weather maidens in the last two months of the year – the likes of Enable, Jack Hobbs and Without Parole spring to mind – and Dubai Warrior has the potential to develop into a serious Derby contender. He has a long way to go before he can seriously be considered for that and early quotes of 16-1 are hardly giving anything away, but he is by Dansili out of a mare who won at Grade 1 level in South Africa and Grade 2 in Dubai, latterly when trained by William Haggas. Dubai Warrior's brother Mootasadir is an all-weather specialist, who has won all four starts on artificial surfaces (including a Group 3) but hasn't run well in two on turf, so he'll have that to prove.

FRANKELLINA

This William Haggas-trained daughter of Frankel is one from one having won her maiden at Yarmouth in October. She opened up at odds-on that day (drifted to 5-4) so was clearly expected to win, but ran a bit green and keen and just got up to win only in the last strides. Given Frankel's progeny all seem to stay well and she is by a filly who won the 1m4f Galtres Stakes on only her fourth start (three wins), there is every chance Frankellina is going to need all of 1m4f in time. She has an Irish Oaks entry, and although it's a long way from running an RPR of 77 on her debut and becoming a Group 1 performer, there is every reason to hope this filly will prove well above average this season.

HARRY'S BAR

James Fanshawe does really well with sprinters and this one is from a family he knows well as he is a brother to Mazzini (who has finally developed into a classy sprinter over the last few months) and out of Firenze, whom Fanshawe trained to win at Listed level in 2006-07. There isn't too much

Quorto is unbeaten in three starts – including the Group 1 National Stakes – and looks an ideal candidate for Classic honours

to say about him at this point as he has raced only once and finished only fifth of seven at Yarmouth, recording a Racing Post Rating of 68. However, he was clearly very green and did stay on nicely at the end to be beaten about five lengths by Emblazoned, who two starts later finished a close third in the Commonwealth Cup. The family is one that tends to improve with age and we can be sure Fanshawe will get the best out of this late-maturing four-year-old at some point this term.

KADAR

Karl Burke has had some high-class performers go through his hands – the most obvious being five-time Group 1-winning filly Laurens – and he seemed in no doubt last season that Kadar was a horse with a big future. Unfortunately, we only got to see him once when he overturned a Gosden hotpot on his debut at Haydock in September. That race arguably looked better on paper than it subsequently turned out to be, but Burke said he would have no hesitation going to the 2,000 Guineas as he thinks the colt would be competitive. That is high praise indeed, but Kadar was twice a non-runner from Group races in the autumn (Royal Lodge, Autumn Stakes, I backed him ante-post for both!) as the ground was considered too fast so he is short on experience. However, all being well with fitness and ground, we can expect him to start in a trial this spring and it will be interesting to see if he turns out as good as his trainer is hoping.

NAYEF ROAD

Mark Johnston has never been afraid to run his horses, so you could argue six runs for Nayef Road was a fairly light campaign as a two-year-old, even if he didn't make his debut until the end of June. He threw in a couple of stinkers, but overall he was a progressive performer, scoring twice and arguably running the best race of his life with a closing third in a Newmarket handicap when upped to 1m2f for the first time. That earned him a rise to a mark of 96, so he is going to need to improve again, but Johnston has won plenty of good handicaps with three-year-olds at the top end of the weights and there is every chance Nayef Road will continue to progress with racing.

QUORTO

It is very easy to view the 2,000 Guineas as a one-horse race as Too Darn Hot looked so good last year. However, it's also easy to forget there were a few other seriously talented horses yet to be really tested last term – John Gosden's Calyx was one and Quorto, for Godolphin and Charlie Appleby, is another. He began his career in June on the July course at Newmarket and he was a very impressive winner. Barely a month later he was back there to turn the Group 2 Superlative Stakes into a procession, winning by nearly four lengths. The form of that race is easy enough to crab, but that doesn't matter when the winner goes on to better things and Quorto did just that when next seen in September, running out a fairly comfortable winner of the Group 1 National Stakes at the Curragh from a quartet of Aidan O'Brien-trained blue bloods. Runner-up Anthony Van Dyck was beaten nearly three lengths further by Too Darn Hot in the Dewhurst later, as was third-placed Christmas and the fourth, Mohawk, so there is no need to argue with the pecking order in the 2,000 Guineas market, but Quorto has more to give too, and he was deliberately put away afterwards with a view to a Guineas challenge. Since then Appleby has been winning Group races all over the world and there is no doubt now he is one of the best trainers in Britain with a team to match his ambitions – and Quorto may give him another Classic winner after Masar's Derby success last term. The dam is a granddaughter of a Prix du Cadran winner, so there is some hope for more distance, but he's not in the

Derby (is in the Irish Derby) and a mile to 1m2f will probably be his trip.

ROCK EAGLE

Rock Eagle looked a horse of some potential when winning on his debut in a three-year-old novice contest from the previously experienced and now 109-rated Fajjaj at Windsor in April. Although he was getting 7lb from the runner-up, he ran green and was still well on top at the end. It was a bit disappointing he couldn't improve too much from that when beaten in a photo next time at Salisbury, and another Windsor success at odds of 1-4 hardly told us anything new. However, he was then a good fourth in a valuable handicap at Glorious Goodwood before closing his season with a win in the very valuable Old Rowley Cup Handicap over 1m4f at Newmarket, a race in which he was heavily backed into 3-1 favourite. Trainer Ralph Beckett believes the colt will develop into a decent stayer this season with the Ebor already being mentioned. After just five runs there should be a lot more to come.

UMMALNAR

Backward filly who didn't make her debut until July last year at the age of three when winning a Newmarket novice contest in comfortable fashion. We didn't really learn

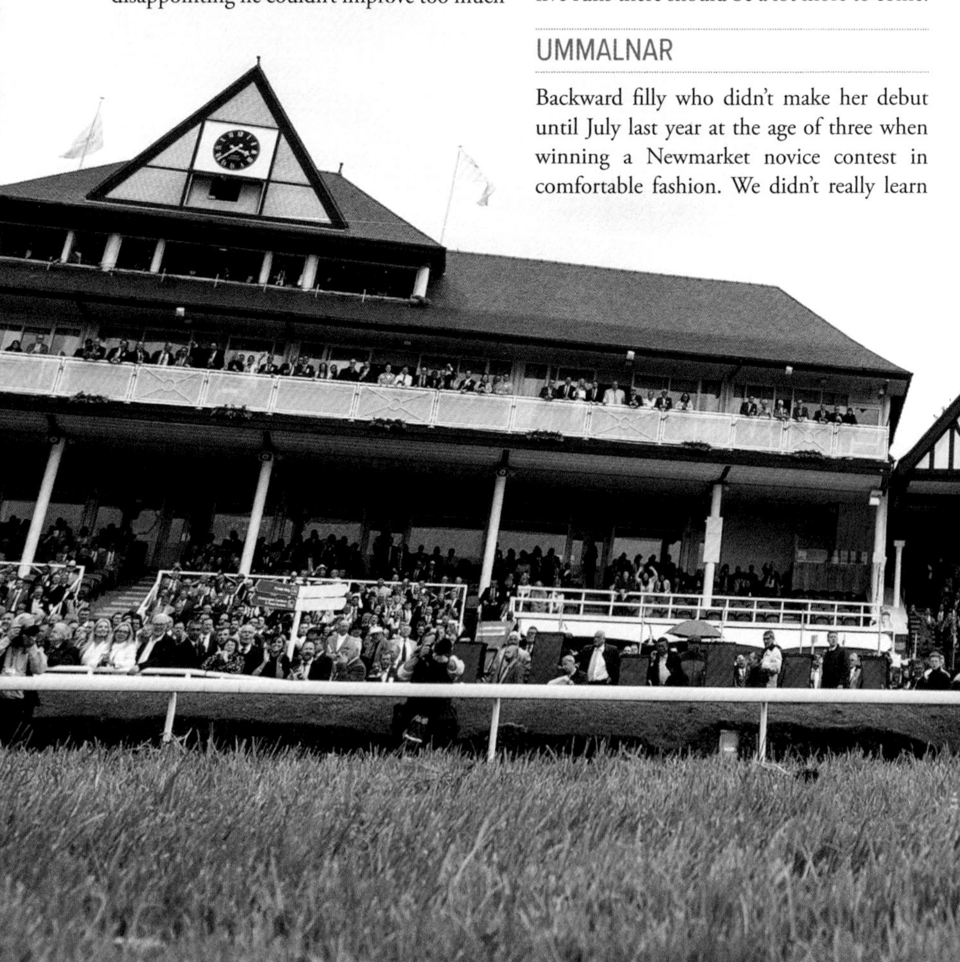

anything more about her when she won another novice at Chelmsford next time as it was a four-runner contest and she was 1-25, but her final third in Listed company at Saint-Cloud at least confirmed she could compete against decent rivals. Trainer's wife Maureen Haggas reckons she would "be a nice filly next year" when stepping up in trip from a mile could be an option. Given her connections it will be disappointing if this half-sister to globetrotting Sheikhzayedroad doesn't further enhance her paddock value as a four-year-old.

YOUNG RASCAL

William Haggas was always wary the Derby might come a bit too soon in his colt's career – and after he finished midfield in the Epsom Classic the trainer backed off him until the autumn. That strategy certainly paid off as he finished the campaign with a pair of wins at Newbury, first short-heading Mirage Dancer over 1m3f and then dead-heating with Morando over 1m4f. It might be that we see him drop to 1m2f this year, but the key to Young Rascal is almost certainly the ground so Haggas will be looking to see more rain this year than last. The four-year-old has the potential to be a player in decent Group company, perhaps even the highest level, and he really ought to be more of a man this year.

Expect to see Young Rascal climb the ranks this season

Pedigrees that suggest we can expect fireworks

DUBAI WARRIOR

3 b c Dansili - Mahbooba (Galileo)

This homebred colt for Sheikh Mohammed Bin Khalifa Al Maktoum shot to prominence in the Derby market with an easy success in a Chelmsford novice stakes in November. The Dansili colt is a brother to Mootasadir, who struck in the Group 3 Diamond Stakes at Dundalk in September, out of the South African Grade 1-winning juvenile Mahbooba, a daughter of Galileo like the dams of Magna Grecia, Saxon Warrior, The Autumn Sun and US Navy Flag.

ENTITLE

3 b f Dansili - Concentric (Sadler's Wells)

As a half-sister to dual Arc heroine Enable, hopes are high that her Dansili half-sister Entitle can build on a Lingfield novice stakes win in December and shine at three. Enable – who also lit up the Breeders' Cup when claiming the Turf at Churchill Downs in November – opened her account in a backend maiden on debut on the Newcastle all-weather, which suggests we can expect a lot more of Entitle this season.

IRIDESSA

3 b f Ruler Of The World - Senta's Dream (Danehill)

2013 Derby hero Ruler Of The World was one of two European first-season sires to supply a Group 1 winner last year – with his Coolmore studmate No Nay Never – when Iridessa sprung a 14-1 surprise in the Fillies' Mile at Newmarket. The Joseph O'Brien-trained filly is bred by his parents Aidan and Annemarie O'Brien's Whisperview Trading out of an unraced daughter of the 2002 Breeders' Cup Filly & Mare Turf winner Starine. Iridessa looks a prime candidate for the Oaks, for which she is a general 16-1 shot.

JAPAN

3 b c Galileo - Shastye (Danehill)

The third Book 1 millionaire out of Newsells Park Stud mare Shastye, Japan lived up to his lofty billing when landing the Beresford Stakes at Naas on just his third start and he should develop into a fine middle-distance performer this season. The 1.3 million gns yearling purchase is one of four runners with a Racing Post Rating over 100 out of Shastye, along with Middleton Stakes scorer Secret Gesture, Wolferton Handicap winner Sir Isaac Newton and Maurus, a talented runner in Australia.

LEGEND OF DUBAI

3 ch c Dubawi - Finsceal Beo (Mr Greeley)

Finsceal Beo, the champion two-year-old filly in Europe in 2006 who annexed the English and Irish Guineas a year later, is the equine equivalent of an ATM machine for owner Michael Ryan since her breeding career began. Her sixth foal Legend Of Dubai realised 650,000gns from Roger Varian at Book 1 of the 2017 Tattersalls

October Sale, and the Derby entry could be worth siding with this year. Finsceal Beo has produced four winners from five runners including the Group 2 Beresford Stakes scorer Ol' Man River and winning miler La Figlia.

MADHMOON

3 b c Dawn Approach - Aaraas (Haafhd)

"He'll keep me getting out of bed early over the winter," Kevin Prendergast told the Racing Post after this Dawn Approach colt downed Rekindling's half-brother Sydney Opera House in an August maiden at Leopardstown last year – and that was before the colt hacked up in the Champions Juvenile Stakes at the same course on Irish Champions Weekend a month later. The Classic contender shares his granddam with the Prendergast-trained Irish 2,000 Guineas winner Awtaad, which may be a clue as to his next target.

MARIA DANILOVA

3 b f Galileo - Dank (Dansili)

Chances are you're already familiar with Maria Danilova, after she sold under her previous name Gloam for four million guineas to top Book 1 of the 2017 Tattersalls October Sale. The filly, who is trained by John Gosden, is out of James Wigan's homebred mare Dank, winner of the Breeders' Cup Filly and Mare Turf and Beverley D. Stakes, so it would not surprise if she rises to the very top.

MIA MARIA

3 gr f Dansili - Majestic Silver (Linamix)

This filly hails from Moyglare Stud Farm's famous Aptostar family. She finished third on her juvenile debut at Gowran Park in September, a performance we can expect to be built upon this year. Reports suggest she has been working well and she is by Dansili, whose top-class daughters include Fallen For You, Passage Of Time, Queen's Trust and The Fugue, and out of Majestic Silver, a Listed-placed daughter of Linamix who has already produced dual Group 3 winner Carla Bianca and Listed-winning sprinter Joailliere.

NEWSPAPEROFRECORD

3 b f Lope De Vega - Sunday Times (Holy Roman Emperor)

What a treat it would be to see this filly on these shores after she won her first starts in the US by an aggregate of 20 lengths, culminating with a runaway victory in the Breeders' Cup Juvenile Fillies Turf at Churchill Downs in November. A general 10-1 shot for the Qipco 1,000 Guineas, Newspaperofrecord would not be the first Classic winner from breeder Allan Belshaw's Simply Times family as she shares her granddam Forever Times with last year's Irish Derby hero Latrobe.

UNNAMED

3 b g Intello - Galipette (Green Desert)

Gestut Zur Kuste's first batch of homebreds turned three last year and among them was Poule d'Essai des Pouliches heroine Teppal and the Poulains third Dice Roll.

The operation – which comprises a Swiss-based group of investors – also owns Galipette, a Green Desert three-parts sister to Showcasing, with her three-year-old Intello gelding in training with David Simcock.

His €65,000 yearling price tag at Arqana suggests he is a likeable sort who could help put Gestut Zur Kuste's name in lights in Britain.

DARK HORSES DAVE ORTON

The only way is up for this unexposed dozen

BALEFIRE

This three-year-old turned in an eyecatching debut when fourth in fair company at Leopardstown over 7f on good ground last October . Out of a 1m1f winner, he ought to be well up to winning races over a stiffer test for his shrewd trainer Mick Halford.

FOLLOW INTELLO

Although a beaten favourite on his handicap debut at Kempton last year, Follow Intello came out of that race leaving the clear impression there are races to be won with him when it all clicks. Trainer Chris Wall tends to get the best out of such late-developing sorts and it will be interesting to see if the four-year-old tries his luck as a stayer.

GOLD AT MIDNIGHT

She got off the mark at the third time of asking when scoring over 7f at Kempton in September and this filly has since left the care of Sir Michael Stoute. She is now with William Stone and, being bred to rate a lot higher than an opening handicap mark of 78, she should continue to do well.

HIGHJACKED

We've not seen the best of this son of Dick Turpin and a mark of 51 to kick off his three-year-old campaign is most attractive. Trainer John Davies has enjoyed success with Highjacked's very useful half-brother Alfred Richardson, and moving up beyond sprint trips this season should reap rewards.

INHALE

Inhale kicks off her Classic season somewhat under the radar having won a novice event at Kempton in November. After an eyecatching debut third at Lingfield, she relished a stiffer 7f at the Sunbury track next time and won impressively. Switching to turf won't be an issue and, although by a sprinter, there is real hope for middle distances on the dam's side of her pedigree. It will be a surprise if she's not at least Listed class.

KAFTAN

From a classic Juddmonte family, this Ger Lyons-trained filly caught the eye when fourth on her sole outing at two in a backend maiden at Leopardstown over 7f. It was a mixed campaign for Lyons last year, by his own usual standards anyway, and this is one who could ensure better fortunes for the stable in 2019. She ought to relish stepping up in trip and has a bright future.

KIMBERLEY GIRL

This speedily bred filly shaped better than the bare form in a couple of 6f novice contests at Newcastle last summer. She needs one more outing at three to quality for a handicap mark and, in canny hands with Mick Easterby, there is no doubt there are races to be won with her.

LINCOLN TALE

Although this filly failed to finish any closer than 12½ lengths behind the winner in three novice events around 7f as a juvenile, Lincoln Tale is a filly to keep onside. She will start in handicaps from an opening mark of 58 and is bred to enjoy going up in distance.

OMNIVEGA

Omnivega really caught the eye when doing plenty wrong on his introduction at Newmarket last season before being thrown in at the deep end back there in the Group 3 Autumn Stakes in October. He was predictably outclassed, but is very much a work in progress and the dam's side of his pedigree suggests he could peak when faced with a decent test at three.

QUOTE

An exciting and completely unexposed Galileo filly, Quote is giving out all the right vibes at Ballydoyle ahead of her Classic campaign. She popped out eyes when finishing fast all too late on her debut over a mile last autumn and, from a decent middle-distance family, she is one for an Oaks trial.

TURNBERRY ISLE

Having been set too much to do at Leopardstown last backend, Turnberry Isle made no mistake on his third run when signing off at Naas in November. He could stick at a mile early on as his dam was a crack sprinter, but further will surely suit as he develops and it will surprise if he doesn't bag a Group race along the way.

ZUBA

Zuba caused a turn-up when making it third time lucky switched to Chelmsford's Polytrack over 1m2f last October, but there was no fluke about his victory and the 210,000gns purchase is expected to make up into a very useful middle-distance handicapper this season. An opening mark of 75 should be a thing of the past come the end of the campaign.

Naas winner Turnberry Isle (right) could make mark at Group level

GLOBAL CHALLENGE NICHOLAS GODFREY

International stars who could strike in Britain

ALMOND EYE (Japan)
4f Lord Kanaloa - Fusaichi Pandora

Unbeaten since finishing second on her two-year-old debut, Japan's newest superstar had already become the fifth horse to claim that nation's fillies' Triple Crown (Oka Sho, Yushun Himba, Shuka Sho) before garnering worldwide acclaim when she smashed the Tokyo track record with a spectacular Japan Cup victory. A unanimous choice as her nation's Horse of the Year for 2018, she is set to run in the Dubai Turf before aiming to break the Japanese hoodoo in the Arc. Ascot's representatives will be doing everything they can to get her to Britain beforehand.

BEAT THE CLOCK (Hong Kong)
5g Hinchinbrook - Flion Fenena

Hong Kong sprinters rightly have a fearsome reputation on the world stage and their most likely candidate for a trip to Royal Ascot – where the region has struck with Cape Of Good Hope and Little Bridge – is this five-year-old, who has never finished outside the top three in 19 starts. After coming third to arch-rival Mr Stunning in the Hong Kong Sprint, he exacted revenge a month later to claim a much coveted Group 1 victory in the Centenary Sprint Cup at Sha Tin under regular partner Joao 'Magic Man' Moreira. Given that he also has decent form over 7f

Bulletin powers to victory in the Breeders' Cup Juvenile Sprint and could make the trip from the USA to Royal Ascot for the Commonwealth Cup

– twice beaten only by superstar Beauty Generation in Group 1 company – the stiff 6f of the Diamond Jubilee should be right up his street. First, though, he will contest the Chairman's Sprint on the Sha Tin Champions Day card on April 28.

BEAUTY GENERATION (Hong Kong)
6g Road To Rock - Stylish Bel

While the Royal Ascot team will admit it is odds against Beauty Generation's connections being tempted, rest assured they will be leaving no stone unturned in their efforts. Formerly known as Montaigne in Australia before being imported to Hong Kong, the highest-rated specialist miler on the planet produced a series of breathtaking performances in 2018 and early 2019 at Sha Tin, where he carries an air of invincibility. He broke the track record that had stood for a decade

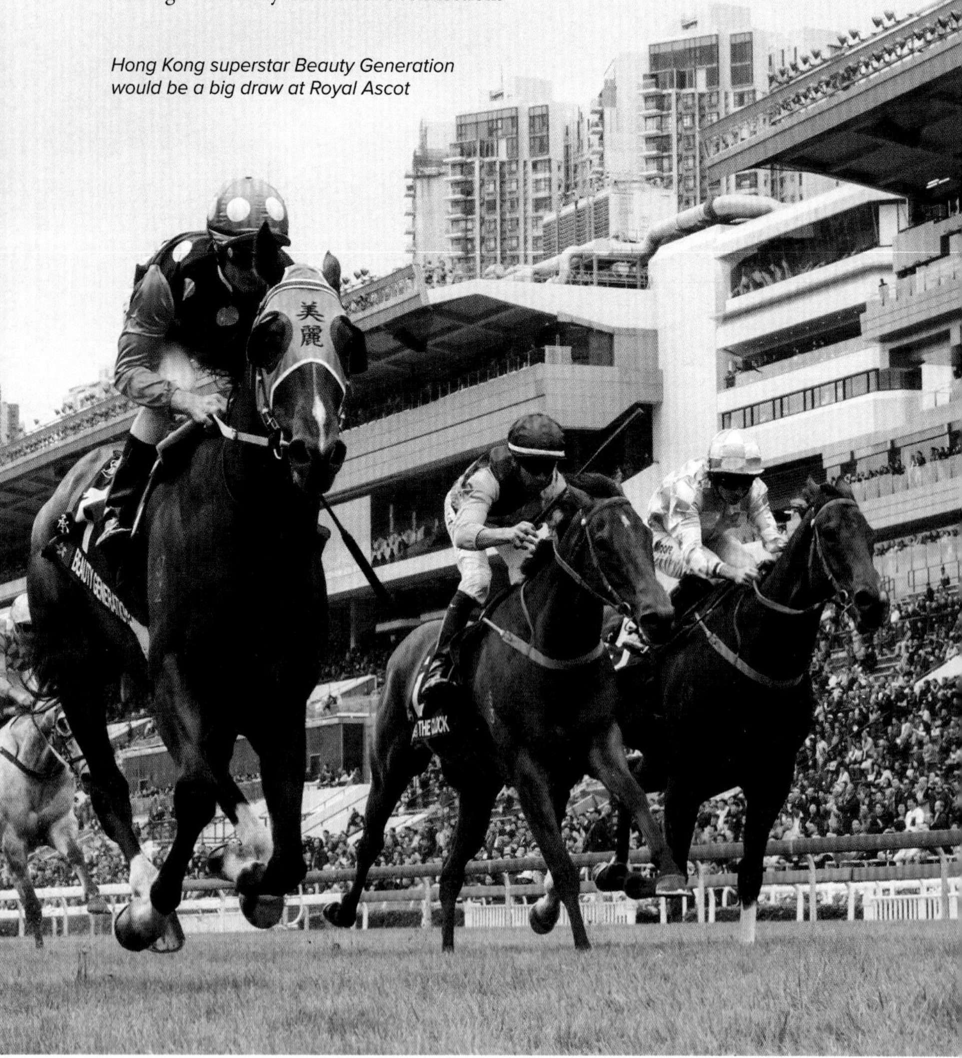

Hong Kong superstar Beauty Generation would be a big draw at Royal Ascot

before an imperious display for a repeat win in the Hong Kong Mile, overcoming a wide draw before being kicked clear at the top of the straight and then winning eased down. "So good it's scary" according to jockey Zac Purton, Beauty Generation is set to go abroad after the Champions Mile in April, with the Yasuda Kinen in Japan regarded the most probable target.

BLAST ONEPIECE (Japan)
4c Harbinger - Tsurumaru Onepiece

In the same ownership as star filly Almond Eye and catapulted himself to the top of last year's Japanese Classic generation when beating his elders in the season-ending grand prix, the Arima Kinen, at Nakayama in December, swooping late to collar the 2017 Japanese Derby victor Rey De Oro by a neck. A strong, staying type, he is a son of the spectacular 2010 King George winner Harbinger (who now stands at Shadai in Japan) and appeals as a possible contender for Ascot's midsummer showpiece. Almond Eye seems the owners' first-choice Arc candidate but this one would certainly not look out of place at ParisLongchamp as well.

BOUND FOR NOWHERE (USA)
5h The Factor - Fancy Deed

Shang Shang Shang's victory in last year's Norfolk Stakes took Wesley Ward's Royal Ascot tally into double figures and doubtless the royal meeting's adoptive American son can be relied upon to field his usual strong team of two-year-olds, which have provided seven of his ten successes. Also expected to return for his third visit is leading US turf sprinter-miler Bound For Nowhere, fourth in a red-hot Commonwealth Cup in 2017 before last year's third, beaten just three-quarters of a length, in the Diamond Jubilee. Ward also now handles former Brian Ellison-trained filly The Mackem Bullet, for whom a Royal Ascot homecoming must be considered highly likely.

BULLETIN (USA)
3c City Zip - Sue's Good News

Showed a clean pair of heels to a strong field full of fancied Europeans in the inaugural edition of the Breeders' Cup Juvenile Sprint over 5½f at Churchill Downs, where he broke like a shot from a gun before making all and going away again in a convincing effort. Given that was only the second run of his life it was especially impressive and, although it would be no surprise if he tried dirt at some stage, connections are said to be targeting the Commonwealth Cup.

EXULTANT (Hong Kong)
5g Teofilo - Contrary

Known as Irishcorrespondent when he was trained in Ireland by Mick Halford, this tough gelding has gone from strength to strength over middle distances in Hong Kong, where he was driven out to beat an international field in the Hong Kong Vase in December. Described as an "out-and-out stayer" by jockey Zac Purton although in our terms he probably meant a 1m4f horse, as they don't see that distance very often at Sha Tin, where he rubber-stamped his status towards the head of the local colony with a dominant performance in the Citi Hong Kong Gold Cup over 1m2f, a distance over which he needs a strong gallop. The Hardwicke, or Prince of Wales's Stakes, and King George could be on his summer agenda.

HOUTZEN (Australia)
4f I Am Invincible - Set To Unleash

After an initial flurry where it seemed Australian sprinters could do little wrong at Royal Ascot, there hasn't been a winner from down under since Black Caviar in 2012. Among those set to try their luck this time around is top Queensland filly Houtzen, winner of the 2017 Magic Millions 2YO Classic who flew down the track at Doomben in Brisbane to break the track record over

1,050 metres (about 5f) in a Listed handicap. Below form subsequently on what her trainer slammed as a "rock-hard track" at Gold Coast, she is a regular at home at the top level and could make them all go blasting off in the King's Stand. Expected to arrive in Newmarket for her preparation at the end of March.

NEWSPAPEROFRECORD (USA)
3f Lope De Vega - Sunday Times

At the very top of the Royal Ascot hit list after a spectacular performance to win the Breeders' Cup Juvenile Fillies' Turf, where she smashed her rivals by nearly seven lengths. Unbeaten in three races at two, her cumulative winning margin was about 20 lengths and BHA handicapper Graeme Smith suggested she stood "head and shoulders above what we saw in Europe" in the same division. European observers suggested a possible tilt at the 1,000 Guineas, while US counterparts were talking about the Kentucky Derby. However, a more conventional campaign on grass is planned, with the Coronation Stakes among possible options after a prep race on Kentucky Oaks day at Churchill Downs.

SANTA ANA LANE (Australia)
6g Lope De Vega - Fast Fleet

An audacious global campaign featuring races on three different continents is envisaged for a gelding who went into the Australian autumn campaign with four Group 1 successes already under his belt after landing the VRC Sprint Classic at Flemington and the Premiere Stakes at Randwick in the spring. Connections are eyeing a probable three-race programme at home focusing on the TJ Smith Stakes in Sydney before travelling abroad for the Chairman's Sprint Prize at Sha Tin on April 28 then a crack at the Diamond Jubilee Stakes at Royal Ascot. He could then stay in England for the July Cup or return to Australia for the Everest. Among other Aussie sprinters who could show up in England are Brave Smash, Zousain and Godolphin's Osborne Bulls.

THE AUTUMN SUN (Australia)
3c Redoute's Choice - Azmiyna

With Winx embarking on her lap of honour, her younger stablemate is next in line to take up her mantle as Australia's star performer thanks to a series of brilliant successes at a mile culminating in a display of total arrogance to win the Caulfield Guineas in October. After sitting three wide throughout, he eased away from the nation's best three-year-olds to score by more than four lengths, despite being eased right down – prompting trainer Chris Waller to say: "The Autumn Sun is one of the horses that make you go 'wow!'" The three-time Group 1 winner, who made an impressive winning start to his autumn campaign in February, has been inoculated ready for a trip to Royal Ascot, where the Queen Anne Stakes would be his target – although part-owner John Messara has warned he might just be too valuable as a stallion prospect for the arduous trip to be contemplated.

YOSHIDA (USA)
5h Heart's Cry - Hilda's Passion

A rare beast indeed in that he is a top-level winner on turf and dirt. Produced a solid effort at Royal Ascot last year when beaten just a length and a quarter in the Queen Anne, after which he went home to the States to win a Grade 1 on dirt at Saratoga and was then beaten less than two lengths in the Breeders' Cup Classic. Has to be rated one of the leading dirt performers in North America on that basis, yet he was also sent off favourite before a lacklustre display in the inaugural Pegasus World Cup Turf in January. All options, including the Dubai World Cup, are open for this versatile performer, but his legendary trainer Bill Mott has enjoyed his recent visits to Royal Ascot and might not take much persuading.

VIEW FROM FRANCE SCOTT BURTON

Persian leads way to be crowned Classic king

MOST two-year-old crops in Britain and Ireland will be a better-known group of horses than their French contemporaries, given the more measured approach to developing Classic potential taken by leading trainers such as Andre Fabre and Jean-Claude Rouget.

But even judged by that standard, the disparity seems particularly exaggerated heading into 2019, with Too Darn Hot, Quorto and Calyx heralding a potentially vintage crop in Newmarket, while France produced just three juveniles to warrant a rating of 110+ in the end of year classifications.

There may have been additional factors at play which exaggerated the waiting game played by the leading French trainers, notably the parched summer which affected the whole of north-western Europe and which condemned Chantilly to weeks of temperatures in the mid to high 30s, just as the best-bred two-year-old prospects should have been taking their first serious steps on the grass gallops.

Both during August at Deauville and in the early stages of the resumption in Paris, some traditionally informative races restricted to newcomers were perhaps not quite as rich in promise as we have become used to.

You have to go back to 2012 and Valyra to find the last winner of the Prix de Diane Longines not to have raced at two, while a year before that Reliable Man achieved the same feat in the Prix du Jockey Club.

It would not be the biggest surprise to see a major Group 1 prize fall to a horse with a

Anodor (white cap) finishes third in the Lagardere

similar background in 2019, while the profile of last year's Jockey Club winner – Study Of Man won a maiden on his only start at two – also looks a likely starting place given the curtailed campaigns many trainers settled for.

Having laid out all the caveats, the two French-trained colts to showcase real Classic potential last year raced a total of seven times and finished first and second in a Deauville maiden which more than lived up to its billing.

Persian King ended up on the wrong side of the result behind Anodor in the Prix de Crevecoeur but went on to build a huge reputation with two wide-margin conditions wins at Chantilly before fully justifying all the hype at Newmarket with victory in the Autumn Stakes.

His immediate victim on the Rowley Mile was the Aidan O'Brien-trained Magna Grecia, who further boosted the form when taking the Group 1 Vertem Futurity Stakes at Doncaster the following month.

Fabre has made a virtue of giving his leading two-year-olds experience of Newmarket down the years and, while his distaste for the racing surface at Longchamp last October was also a factor in choosing this assignment over the Group 1 Prix Jean-Luc Lagardere, the lights are green if the 2,000 Guineas becomes the target of choice for this tall and rangy son of Kingman.

Godolphin bought a 50 per cent share in Persian King over the winter and, while they also have Quorto as a major player for the Guineas, Sheikh Mohammed and his team are likely to take plenty of heed as to where Fabre wants to go.

The way Persian King travelled through the race, as well as the way he galloped out over the horizon with Pierre-Charles Boudot, suggests a mile should not be the limit of his range.

By Freddy Head's own admission **Anodor** was pretty straight for his racecourse debut against Persian King but the son of another first-season sire in Anodin made a fine impression when making virtually all, one he backed up with a straightforward success in the Group 3 Prix des Chenes.

The official handicapper raised Anodor another 3lb for his staying-on third behind Royal Marine and Broome in the Prix Jean-Luc Lagardere, a performance which visually didn't quite live up to what might have been hoped for.

Co-owner Jean-Louis Bouchard has made no secret of his increased ambitions when it comes to tackling the big races in Britain and a near miss at Royal Ascot with City Light is only likely to have made that particular fire burn more brightly.

While no conclusions should be drawn as to where Anodor's next Group 1 assignment comes, it would be a major surprise if Head doesn't at least give him an entry at Newmarket.

Anodor may have come up short on Arc day but Head can now count the winner of the Prix Marcel Boussac among his potential stars for 2019, even though **Lily's Candle** was trained by Fabrice Vermeulen when scoring at Longchamp.

Bought on the eve of her Boussac triumph by US-based Martin Schwartz, the daughter of Style Vendome cut little ice behind the extraordinary Newspaperofrecord at the Breeders' Cup and then passed through the Arqana sales ring for a third time, this time bought for €1.1 million by Katsumi Yoshida, who has chosen Head to train her at three.

In recent years placed horses from the Boussac have been worth following as keenly as the winners – Ervedya and Senga won Classics at three – and outside of the scope of this article, Richard Hannon and the Barnett family must have high hopes for Star Terms.

Arguably the filly to take out of the race was **Matematica**, who Carlos Laffon-Parias pitched into Group 1 company despite a narrow defeat on her Longchamp debut and who may have been beaten by inexperience when run down late on by Lily's Candle.

Matematica is a half-sister by Rock Of Gibraltar to the Wertheimers' Prix d'Aumale winner Soustraction and, although Laffon-Parias has spoken about shedding her maiden tag as an early season priority, she has already done more than enough to justify her Classic entries.

It will also be worth keeping an eye on the Fabrice Chappet-trained **Rocques**, whose unbeaten record was abruptly ended when a slightly one-paced sixth in the Boussac but who had previously looked smart.

Also carrying the cream and violet silks of Gerard Augustin-Normand, **Graignes** was a close-up third to Royal Meeting and Hermosa in the Criterium International, a third defeat in Group company but still good enough to make the son of Zoffany the third French-trained colt to join the 110+ club on official ratings.

The Criterium de Saint-Cloud has a mixed record when it comes to unearthing future stars but there was plenty to like about the way **Wonderment** battled past Sydney Opera House and Fox Tal, with trainer Nicolas Clement eyeing a potential tilt at the Investec Oaks.

Also among the fillies who gained more than a passing acquaintance with the racecourse last autumn was the well-bought **Suphala**, who made a big impression at the same two Chantilly meetings as Persian King for Fabre and Lady Bamford, disposing of the highly regarded Commes in the process.

Connections passed up the opportunity to test her Newmarket credentials in the Oh So Sharp Stakes but it is fairly short odds that the daughter of Frankel's next public appearance will be in a recognised Group-level Classic trial.

Returning to the theme of unexposed maiden winners, there are any number of likely candidates to throw into the mix. Any such list can only provide a snapshot of the potential talent waiting to be unleashed so we'll limit the number to four.

Avaitress (Alain de Royer-Dupre) holds only the Poule d'Essai des Pouliches entry and looked a miler in her backend success on the Chantilly Polytrack.

Vazirabad (second right) will build up gradually for the Ascot Gold Cup

Her form is tied in through runner-up Tifosa (a winner in February on the all-weather at Chantilly) and with **Olympe**, who took three attempts to get off the mark for Jean-Claude Rouget but who could still develop into a stakes performer.

In common with Olympe, **Shendam** is by Charm Spirit but has a stamina-laden female side to her Aga Khan pedigree and could develop into a Jockey Club or Derby hopeful for Mikel Delzangles off the back of an all-the-way maiden win at Longchamp over 1m1f.

And it will be Diane dreams that have kept the Australian connections of **Merimbula** awake over the southern summer after her striking win on the same Longchamp card for Freddy Head.

OLDER HORSES

Head produced a fine crop of three-year-old fillies last season and, while the talented Tantheem and Luminate have been retired, Group 1 winners Polydream and With You both return in 2019.

Head believes **Polydream** has unfinished business after getting badly impeded in the Prix de la Foret, before worse was to befall her when withdrawn by Kentucky state vets on the eve of the Breeders' Cup Mile.

The priority this season will be to establish whether the Oasis Dream four-year-old properly stays a mile and, given her scintillating performances at Deauville in each of the last two years, it would be no surprise to see her attempt the same Prix Maurice de Gheest / Prix Jacques le Marois double that Moonlight Cloud carried off over the space of eight days in 2013.

The Prix d'Ispahan looks the ideal test for **With You** and has already been mentioned as a likely early season target for George Strawbridge's homebred.

Further up the distance scale, Head and Strawbridge also race on with Prix du Cadran winner **Call The Wind** (a half-brother to We Are), one of a clutch of French-trained stayers being aimed at the Gold Cup in June.

While Dubai may be Call The Wind's starting point, Pia Brandt has mentioned Ascot's Sagaro Stakes as a potential reconnaissance mission for **Called To The Bar**.

Alain de Royer-Dupre has elected not to rush **Vazirabad** for Dubai this year and

Olmedo is likely to be in action early in the season

instead has targeted the Prix de Barbeville at the end of April as a potential comeback for last year's Gold Cup runner-up, with all roads leading back to Ascot.

It should also be noted that the Group 2 Prix Vicomtesse-Vigier has been added to the list of qualifying races for the second year of the Weatherbys Hamilton Stayers' Million.

As ever, Fabre is well served in the ranks of older horses, with Grand Prix de Saint-Cloud winner **Waldgeist** back again at the age of five, as will be his exciting year-younger sister **Waldlied**.

The 29-time French champion has interesting options at around a mile, with **Plumatic** and **Inns Of Court** back for more, while the potentially very exciting **Mer Et Nuages** returns from injury, the memory of an effortless Listed win at Longchamp last May still very much alive.

Both colts' Classic winners from last season are set to return. Jean-Claude Rouget hopes to have Poule d'Essai des Poulains hero **Olmedo** out early in the season following his recovery from a suspensory injury incurred in last season's Prix Jean Prat. And Pascal Bary could target the Prix Ganay early on for **Study Of Man** as he and the Niarchos family go in search of more Group 1 titles for their Jockey Club-winning son of Deep Impact.

THIS SEASON'S KEY HORSES

By Weekender editor Dylan Hill

Accidental Agent

5 b h Delegator - Roodle (Xaar)

Eve Johnson Houghton — Mrs RF Johnson Houghton

PLACINGS: 6121/5712148/36105- — RPR **118**

Starts	1st	2nd	3rd	4th	Win & Pl
16	5	2	1	1	£603,950

	6/18	Asct	1m Cls1 Gp1 gd-fm	£367,197
104	10/17	Asct	7f Cls2 98-109 Hcap gd-sft	£112,050
85	9/17	Kemp	7f Cls4 77-87 Hcap std-slw	£5,822
	10/16	NmkR	6f Cls2 Auct 2yo gd-fm	£81,165
	7/16	Chep	7f Cls4 Mdn Auct 2yo good	£5,175

Got up late to win messy Queen Anne at Royal Ascot last season, underlining effectiveness at the track after winning a big handicap in 2017; hasn't come close to another Group win, but was unlucky not to finish much closer in the Lockinge.

Addeybb (Ire)

5 ch g Pivotal - Bush Cat (Kingmambo)

William Haggas — Sheikh Ahmed Al Maktoum

PLACINGS: 41131/11803- — RPR **121+**

Starts	1st	2nd	3rd	4th	Win & Pl
10	5	-	2	1	£161,473

	4/18	Sand	1m Cls1 Gp2 gd-sft	£56,710
99	3/18	Donc	1m Cls2 97-107 Hcap soft	£62,250
93	9/17	NmkR	1m1f Cls2 65-93 Hcap gd-sft	£18,675
88	7/17	Asct	1m Cls3 74-88 3yo Hcap good	£9,704
	6/17	Hayd	1m Cls4 Mdn 3yo gd-sft	£4,690

Quickly moved from handicap to Group company last season when winning the Lincoln and the Sandown Mile; failed to build on that subsequently but missed much of the season due to unsuitable conditions having flopped on quicker ground in the Lockinge.

Advertise

3 b c Showcasing - Furbelow (Pivotal)

Martyn Meade — Phoenix Thoroughbred

PLACINGS: 12112- — RPR **118**

Starts	1st	2nd	3rd	4th	Win & Pl
5	3	2	-	-	£317,693

8/18	Curr	6f Gp1 2yo good	£126,106
7/18	NmkJ	6f Cls1 Gp2 2yo gd-fm	£45,368
5/18	Newb	6f Cls4 Mdn 2yo gd-fm	£6,469

Won three times over 6f last season, including the Group I Phoenix Stakes, and suffered only defeats behind potential superstars Calyx and Too Darn Hot; comprehensively beaten by the latter in the Dewhurst but proved he stays 7f and seems sure to get a mile.

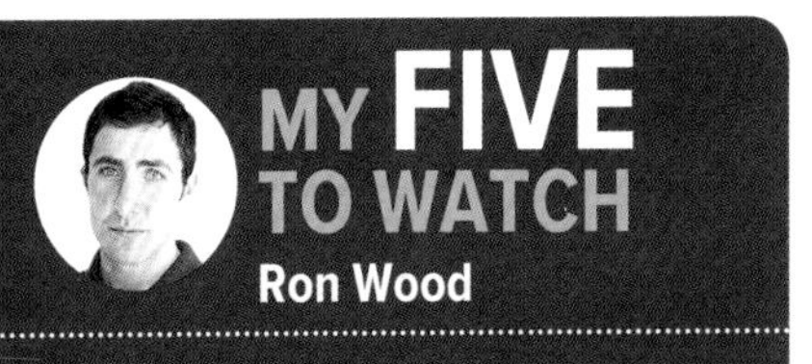

•Chablis •Hermosa •Lord North •San Andreas •Sucellus

Alpha Delphini

8 b g Captain Gerrard - Easy To Imagine (Cozzene)

Bryan Smart — The Alpha Delphini Partnership

PLACINGS: 12/836928711/232210- — RPR **117**

Starts	1st	2nd	3rd	4th	Win & Pl
27	8	6	3	-	£366,666

	8/18	York	5f Cls1 Gp1 gd-fm	£198,485
	10/17	Muss	5f Cls3 soft	£12,938
	9/17	Bevl	5f Cls3 soft	£12,450
	8/16	Bevl	5f Cls1 List good	£28,355
88	7/16	Asct	5f Cls2 85-109 Hcap gd-fm	£28,013
83	7/16	York	5f Cls3 81-94 Hcap good	£11,644
79	4/16	Muss	5f Cls4 67-80 Hcap gd-fm	£5,175
	8/15	Bevl	5f Cls4 Mdn good	£5,175

Shock winner of last season's Nunthorpe Stakes when pipping Mabs Cross; that was a clear career-best but had been a close third behind the same rival in the Palace House Stakes and had been prolific over the trip at a much lower level in previous seasons.

Amedeo Modigliani (Ire)

4 b c Galileo - Gooseberry Fool (Danehill Dancer)

Aidan O'Brien (Ir) — Mrs J Magnier, M Tabor, D Smith & MJ Jooste

PLACINGS: 31/ — RPR **94**

Starts	1st	2nd	3rd	4th	Win & Pl
2	1	-	1	-	£11,032

8/17	Gway	1m½f Mdn 2yo soft	£9,477

Well backed for the Derby last spring but suffered a setback and ended up missing the whole campaign despite reportedly being close to a return several times; had run away with a Galway maiden on his last run as a two-year-old and should be suited by middle distances.

Angel's Hideaway (Ire)

3 gr f Dark Angel - The Hermitage (Kheleyf)

John Gosden — Cheveley Park Stud

PLACINGS: 31421982- — RPR **105**

Starts	1st	2nd	3rd	4th	Win & Pl
8	2	2	1	1	£68,900

7/18	Asct	6f Cls1 Gp3 2yo gd-fm	£28,355
6/18	Hayd	6f Cls4 Mdn 2yo gd-fm	£4,852

Took a long time to build on early-season promise last year but bounced back to form when second to Mot Juste on first run over 7f in the Oh So Sharp Stakes; unlucky that day as forced to switch and carrying a penalty for previous Group 3 win in the Princess Margaret.

Anodor (Fr)

3 ch c Anodin - Decize (Kentucky Dynamite)

Freddy Head (Fr) — Ecurie Jean-Louis Bouchard

PLACINGS: 113- — RPR **111**

Starts	1st	2nd	3rd	4th	Win & Pl
3	2	-	1	-	£87,805

9/18	Lonc	1m Gp3 2yo good	£35,398
8/18	Deau	7½f 2yo good	£11,947

Won first two starts last season, beating the high-class Persian King first time out before following up in a Group 3; only third when odds-on for the Prix Jean-Luc Lagardere but perhaps undone by moderate gallop; remains a leading prospect for French Classics.

Anthony Van Dyck (Ire)

3 b c Galileo - Believe'N'Succeed (Exceed And Excel)

Aidan O'Brien (Ir) Mrs John Magnier, Michael Tabor & Derrick Smith

PLACINGS: 7111239- RPR **118**

Starts	1st	2nd	3rd	4th	Win & Pl
7	3	1	1	-	£220,030

	Date	Course	Race	Prize
	8/18	Curr	7f Gp2 2yo yield	£67,876
	7/18	Leop	7f Gp3 2yo gd-fm	£31,327
	7/18	Klny	1m Mdn 2yo good	£8,177

Smart colt who won three times last season, most notably in the Group 2 Futurity Stakes, before a good second behind Quorto in the National Stakes; beaten further when only third behind Too Darn Hot in the Dewhurst and well below his best when sent to the Breeders' Cup.

Antonia De Vega (Ire)

3 b f Lope De Vega - Witches Brew (Duke Of Marmalade)

Ralph Beckett Waverley Racing

PLACINGS: 118- RPR **100**

Starts	1st	2nd	3rd	4th	Win & Pl
3	2	-	-	-	£36,117

	Date	Course	Race	Prize
	8/18	Gdwd	7f Cls1 Gp3 2yo good	£28,355
	7/18	NmkJ	7f Cls3 Mdn 2yo gd-fm	£7,763

Finished lame when stepped up in class for the Fillies' Mile and remains a hugely exciting filly on evidence of first two wins; claimed a notable scalp in Zagitova first time out and powered home when following up in the Group 3 Prestige Stakes at Goodwood.

Arctic Sound

3 b c Poet's Voice - Polar Circle (Royal Academy)

Mark Johnston Saeed Bin Mohammed Al Qassimi

PLACINGS: 211611- RPR **108**

Starts	1st	2nd	3rd	4th	Win & Pl
6	4	1	-	-	£52,972

	Date	Course	Race	Prize
	9/18	NmkR	7f Cls1 Gp3 2yo good	£28,355
91	9/18	Donc	7f Cls2 72-91 2yo Hcap gd-sft	£11,644
	7/18	Bevl	7½f Cls5 2yo gd-sft	£4,140
	7/18	Sand	7f Cls4 2yo gd-fm	£6,469

Won four times last season, most notably in the Group 3 Tattersalls Stakes at Newmarket, though perhaps benefited from coming late off an overly strong gallop; had disappointed under more prominent tactics when up in grade previously (only run over a mile).

Arthur Kitt

3 b c Camelot - Ceiling Kitty (Red Clubs)

Tom Dascombe Chasemore Farm

PLACINGS: 11254- RPR **108**

Starts	1st	2nd	3rd	4th	Win & Pl
5	2	1	-	1	£108,892

	Date	Course	Race	Prize
	6/18	Asct	7f Cls1 List 2yo gd-fm	£51,039
	5/18	Hayd	6f Cls4 2yo good	£6,469

Won last season's Chesham Stakes at Royal Ascot and went on to perform well in other good races, finishing second (clear of the rest) behind Too Darn Hot in the Solario and fourth in the Breeders' Cup Juvenile Turf; only disappointing run in the Royal Lodge at Newmarket.

Auxerre (Ire)

4 b g Iffraaj - Roscoff (Daylami)

Charlie Appleby Godolphin

PLACINGS: 2111- RPR **106aw**

Starts	1st	2nd	3rd	4th	Win & Pl
4	3	1	-	-	£22,390

	Date	Course	Race	Prize
93	10/18	Kemp	1m Cls3 83-97 Hcap std-slw	£9,338
	9/18	Chmt	1m Cls4 stand	£6,469
	7/18	Hayd	1m Cls5 gd-fm	£4,852

Won last three races last season, culminating in a decent handicap at Kempton against another useful Godolphin horse with the pair clear; aimed at the Lincoln this spring and should be a leading contender before potentially stepping up to Pattern level.

Bacchus

5 ch g Kheleyf - Rumbled (Halling)

Brian Meehan GPM Morland, DJ Erwin & John GS Woodman

PLACINGS: 51268/1395314/1400- RPR **114**

Starts	1st	2nd	3rd	4th	Win & Pl
16	4	1	2	2	£171,858

	Date	Course	Race	Prize
105	6/18	Asct	6f Cls2 98-109 Hcap gd-fm	£108,938
100	8/17	NmkJ	6f Cls2 84-105 3yo Hcap soft	£28,013
92	4/17	Newb	7f Cls2 79-92 3yo Hcap gd-fm	£12,450
	6/16	Hayd	7f Cls4 2yo soft	£4,270

Progressive handicapper in 2017 and maintained that improvement to win the Wokingham first

time out last season at Royal Ascot; fair effort when fourth in a Group 3 next time but then beat only one home in two Group 1 sprints; stays 7f well.

Baghdad (Fr)

4 b c Frankel - Funny Girl (Darshaan)

Mark Johnston — Mohammed Bin Hamad Khalifa Al Attiya

PLACINGS: 5041/311- — RPR **101**

Starts		1st	2nd	3rd	4th	Win & Pl
7		3	-	1	1	£73,647
90	6/18	Asct	1m4f Cls2 87-98 3yo Hcap gd-fm			£56,025
80	5/18	York	1m4f Cls4 66-80 3yo Hcap gd-fm			£12,031
74	11/17	Chmt	1m2f Cls5 64-75 2yo Hcap stand			£4,528

Sharply progressive in the first half of last season, following up a York win by landing the King George V Stakes at Royal Ascot when last seen; still on a fair mark for top middle-distance handicaps and could work his way up to Pattern company.

Battaash (Ire)

5 b g Dark Angel - Anna Law (Lawman)

Charlie Hills — Hamdan Al Maktoum

PLACINGS: 10333/11141/12144- — RPR **129**

Starts	1st	2nd	3rd	4th	Win & Pl
15	7	1	3	3	£826,772
8/18	Gdwd	5f Cls1 Gp2 gd-fm			£176,935
5/18	Hayd	5f Cls1 Gp2 good			£56,710
10/17	Chan	5f Gp1 soft			£170,932
8/17	Gdwd	5f Cls1 Gp2 soft			£176,992
7/17	Sand	5f Cls1 Gp3 gd-fm			£36,862
6/17	Sand	5f Cls1 List 3yo gd-fm			£20,983
5/16	Bath	5f Cls4 2yo good			£4,690

Lightning quick sprinter who has won the last two runnings of the King George Stakes at Goodwood and the 2017 Prix de l'Abbaye by wide margins; beaten three times at Group 1 level last season, though, including when below-par in the Nunthorpe for a second time.

Beat The Bank

5 b g Paco Boy - Tiana (Diktat)

Andrew Balding — King Power Racing

PLACINGS: 1101110/0615100- — RPR **120+**

Starts	1st	2nd	3rd	4th	Win & Pl
14	7	-	-	-	£335,411
8/18	Gdwd	1m Cls1 Gp2 good			£70,888
7/18	Asct	1m Cls1 Gp2 gd-fm			£76,559
9/17	NmkR	1m Cls1 Gp2 gd-sft			£56,710
8/17	Gdwd	1m Cls1 Gp3 3yo soft			£56,710
7/17	NmkJ	1m Cls1 List 3yo good			£22,684
4/17	NmkR	7f Cls3 3yo gd-fm			£9,057
2/17	Dund	7f Mdn Auct 3yo stand			£5,782

Three-time Group 2 winner, including in last season's Summer Mile and Celebration Mile; 0-6 in Group 1 races but would have gone close with a clear run in the Queen Anne Stakes and unsuited by soft ground in the last two runnings of the QEII.

Anthony Van Dyck (1) won three races last season, including the Group 2 Futurity Stakes

Beatboxer (USA)

3 b/br c Scat Daddy - Thmoruplathlesupay (Unbridled's Song)

John Gosden — Princess Haya of Jordan

PLACINGS: 117- RPR **95+**

Starts	1st	2nd	3rd	4th	Win & Pl
3	2	-	-	-	£12,291

8/18	Hayd	1m Cls4 2yo gd-fm	£7,116
7/18	Sand	7f Cls4 Mdn 2yo gd-fm	£5,175

Won two novice races in impressive fashion last season but blotted his copybook when favourite for the Royal Lodge Stakes, running no sort of race having been awkward and bumped at the start; no surprise to see him bounce back in good mile races.

Ben Vrackie

4 b c Frankel - Kinnaird (Dr Devious)

John Gosden — Princess Haya of Jordan

PLACINGS: 7212033- RPR **109**

Starts	1st	2nd	3rd	4th	Win & Pl
7	1	2	2	-	£36,750

7/18	Ling	1m4f Cls5 std-slw	£3,752

Took a while to build on impressive 11-length win in a Lingfield novice last season but finished off with a terrific third in a valuable 1m4f handicap at Newmarket; tried over further three times in between but below that level every time; likely to improve again.

Benbatl

5 b h Dubawi - Nahrain (Selkirk)

Saeed Bin Suroor — Godolphin

PLACINGS: 1325156/112101512- RPR **124**

Starts	1st	2nd	3rd	4th	Win & Pl
16	7	3	1	-	£3,952,944

10/18	Caul	1m2f Gp1 good	£348,410
7/18	Muni	1m2f Gp1 good	£88,496
3/18	Meyd	1m1f Gp1 good	£2,666,667
2/18	Meyd	1m1f Gp2 good	£88,889
1/18	Meyd	1m1f Gp3 good	£77,778
6/17	Asct	1m2f Cls1 Gp3 3yo gd-fm	£51,039
4/17	Donc	7f Cls5 Mdn 3yo good	£3,235

Won three times at Group 1 level last season in Dubai, Germany and Australia; hasn't won in Britain since the 2017 Hampton Court Stakes at Royal Ascot and well beaten in two runs here last season in the Queen Anne Stakes and Juddmonte International.

Best Solution (Ire)

5 b h Kodiac - Al Andalyya (Kingmambo)

Saeed Bin Suroor — Godolphin

PLACINGS: /48180251/319511118- RPR **119**

Starts	1st	2nd	3rd	4th	Win & Pl
23	9	2	3	2	£2,628,768

0	10/18	Caul	1m4f Gd1 Hcap gd-sft	£1,820,809
	9/18	Badn	1m4f Gp1 gd-sft	£132,743
	8/18	Hopp	1m4f Gp1 good	£97,345
	7/18	NmkJ	1m4f Cls1 Gp2 gd-fm	£56,710
115	2/18	Meyd	1m4f 97-115 Hcap good	£71,111
	10/17	Newb	1m4f Cls1 Gp3 soft	£34,026
	5/17	Ling	1m3½f Cls1 List 3yo good	£34,026
	10/16	NmkR	1m Cls1 Gp3 2yo good	£45,368
	7/16	Gdwd	6f Cls2 Mdn 2yo good	£12,938

Prolific and high-class middle-distance performer who won three times at the top level last season, twice in Europe before adding the Caulfield Cup in Australia; has also won his last two races in Britain, including last season's Princess of Wales's Stakes.

Beyond Reason (Ire)

3 b f Australia - No Explaining (Azamour)

Charlie Appleby — Godolphin

PLACINGS: 2141167- RPR **108**

Starts	1st	2nd	3rd	4th	Win & Pl
7	3	1	-	1	£114,316

8/18	Deau	7f Gp2 2yo gd-sft	£65,575
7/18	Deau	7f Gp3 2yo gd-sft	£35,398
6/18	Kemp	6f Cls5 2yo std-slw	£3,881

Showed best form last season when getting cut in the ground in France, winning two good races at Deauville including a Group 2 in most impressive fashion by three lengths; twice well beaten at Group 1 level subsequently, including when up in trip for the Fillies' Mile.

Billesdon Brook

4 ch f Champs Elysees - Coplow (Manduro)

Richard Hannon — Pall Mall Partners & Mrs RJ McCreery

PLACINGS: 32213115/41445- RPR **115**

Starts	1st	2nd	3rd	4th	Win & Pl
13	4	2	2	3	£435,569

	5/18	NmkR	1m Cls1 Gp1 3yo gd-fm	£310,487
	8/17	Gdwd	7f Cls1 Gp3 2yo good	£22,684
87	8/17	Gdwd	7f Cls2 70-87 2yo Hcap soft	£16,173
	7/17	Kemp	7f Cls5 2yo std-slw	£3,235

Became the biggest-priced winner in the history of the 1,000 Guineas when successful at 66-1 at Newmarket last May; yet to prove that performance wasn't a fluke, however, and disappointed in three subsequent runs; clearly suited by a strongly run mile, though, and didn't get those circumstances again.

Blue Point (Ire)

5 b h Shamardal - Scarlett Rose (Royal Applause)

Charlie Appleby — Godolphin

PLACINGS: 112123/1341/29173-1 — RPR **123**

Starts	1st	2nd	3rd	4th	Win & Pl
16	7	3	3	1	£897,287

Date	Course	Race	Prize
2/19	Meyd	5f Gp2 good	£118,110
6/18	Asct	5f Cls1 Gp1 gd-fm	£305,525
10/17	Asct	6f Cls1 Gp3 gd-sft	£39,697
5/17	Asct	6f Cls1 Gp3 3yo gd-fm	£45,368
8/16	York	6f Cls1 Gp2 2yo good	£124,762
7/16	Donc	6f Cls4 2yo gd-fm	£4,528
6/16	Nott	6f Cls5 2yo gd-fm	£3,235

Top-class sprinter who made Group 1 breakthrough when overhauling Battaash in last season's King's Stand Stakes; extended fine record at Ascot having also gained previous two victories at the track over 6f; beaten in the July Cup and the Nunthorpe subsequently.

Boitron (Fr)

3 b c Le Havre - Belliflore (Verglas)

Richard Hannon — Augustin-Normand & Middleham Park

PLACINGS: 1114- — RPR **107**

Starts	1st	2nd	3rd	4th	Win & Pl
4	3	-	-	1	£43,212

Date	Course	Race	Prize
8/18	Newb	7f Cls1 List 2yo good	£14,461
8/18	Donc	7f Cls4 Auct 2yo gd-fm	£4,787
7/18	Newb	6f Cls5 Auct 2yo gd-fm	£3,752

Won first three starts last season, including a Listed race at Newbury in commanding fashion, although there was little quality behind; lost his unbeaten record when only fourth in the Group 1 Prix Jean-Luc Lagardere but unsuited by run of the race (hard to make up ground).

Brando

7 ch g Pivotal - Argent Du Bois (Silver Hawk)

Kevin Ryan — Mrs Angie Bailey

PLACINGS: 913/1031976/1242824- — RPR **119**

Starts	1st	2nd	3rd	4th	Win & Pl
30	8	8	3	3	£863,566

Rating	Date	Course	Race	Prize
	4/18	NmkR	6f Cls1 Gp3 good	£34,026
	8/17	Deau	6½f Gp1 good	£185,583
	4/17	NmkR	6f Cls1 Gp3 gd-fm	£34,026
110	9/16	Ayr	6f Cls2 98-110 Hcap gd-sft	£124,500
	7/16	Sand	5f Cls1 Gp3 soft	£36,862
88	4/16	NmkR	5f Cls3 81-89 Hcap gd-sft	£9,057
84	9/15	Hayd	6f Cls3 80-89 Hcap soft	£8,086
	8/15	Haml	6f Cls5 Mdn good	£3,235

Won the Group 1 Prix Maurice de Gheest in 2017 and went close at the top level last season, finishing second in the July Cup at Newmarket and Sprint Cup at Haydock; kicked off the campaign with a second successive win in the Abernant Stakes.

Broome (Ire)

3 b c Australia - Sweepstake (Acclamation)

Aidan O'Brien (Ir) — Michael Tabor, Derrick Smith & Mrs John Magnier

PLACINGS: 51622- — RPR **112**

Starts	1st	2nd	3rd	4th	Win & Pl
5	1	2	-	-	£117,516

Date	Course	Race	Prize
8/18	Gway	1m½f Mdn 2yo yld-sft	£9,812

Came up short in Group company after winning a maiden last season; improved on easy defeat by Madhmoon at Leopardstown when a neck second in the Prix Jean-Luc Lagardere, though perhaps helped by setting a stop-start gallop; could progress over further.

Brundtland (Ire)

4 b c Dubawi - Future Generation (Hurricane Run)

Charlie Appleby — Godolphin

PLACINGS: 1/1114- — RPR **116**

Starts	1st	2nd	3rd	4th	Win & Pl
5	4	-	-	1	£214,951

Date	Course	Race	Prize
10/18	Lonc	1m7f Gp2 3yo good	£100,885
9/18	Lonc	1m4f Gp2 3yo good	£65,575
8/18	Claf	1m4f List 3yo gd-sft	£24,336
10/17	NmkR	1m2f Cls3 Mdn 2yo gd-fm	£6,469

Quickly developed into a high-class middle-distance/staying performer last season, winning three out of four starts including the Prix Niel; followed up in the Prix Chaudenay over 1m7f and unlucky when a length fourth in the Prix Royal-Oak having been carried very wide.

Call The Wind

5 ch g Frankel - In Clover (Inchinor)

Freddy Head (Fr) — George Strawbridge

PLACINGS: 3543111- — RPR **112+**

Starts	1st	2nd	3rd	4th	Win & Pl
7	3	-	2	1	£186,261

Date	Course	Race	Prize
10/18	Lonc	2m4f Gp1 good	£151,699
8/18	Deau	1m5½f gd-sft	£14,602
8/18	Claf	1m4f soft	£12,389

Improved rapidly when back from a break in the second half of last season and completed a hat-trick when winning the Prix du Cadran; had stamina to prove over 2m4f trip having never run beyond 1m6f but did well to beat subsequent Prix Royal-Oak winner Holdthasigreen.

Calyx

3 b c Kingman - Helleborine (Observatory)

John Gosden — K Abdullah

PLACINGS: 11- — RPR **116+**

Starts	1st	2nd	3rd	4th	Win & Pl
2	2	-	-	-	£90,240

Date	Course	Race	Prize
6/18	Asct	6f Cls1 Gp2 2yo gd-fm	£85,065
6/18	NmkJ	6f Cls4 2yo gd-fm	£5,175

Brilliant winner of last season's Coventry Stakes when beating high-class pair Advertise and Sergei Prokofiev by a length and potentially value for far more (streaked six lengths clear on his side); missed rest of the year with a bone injury and return is hugely anticipated.

Cape Byron

5 ch g Shamardal - Reem Three (Mark Of Esteem)

Roger Varian — Sheikh Mohammed Obaid Al Maktoum

PLACINGS: 21/13/9404227- RPR **110**

Starts	1st	2nd	3rd	4th	Win & Pl
11	2	3	1	2	£66,080

	Date	Course	Race	Prize
	9/17	Asct	1m Cls3 soft	£9,704
	10/16	NmkR	7f Cls4 Mdn 2yo gd-sft	£4,528

Long held in high regard and yet to quite live up to expectations but did better after being gelded last season; ran well in several big handicaps, finishing second at Goodwood and Ascot, and not helped by a bad draw when a beaten favourite back at Ascot on final run.

Cape Of Good Hope (Ire)

3 b c Galileo - Hveger (Danehill)

Aidan O'Brien (Ir) — Mrs John Magnier, Michael Tabor & Derrick Smith

PLACINGS: 74123- RPR **105**

Starts	1st	2nd	3rd	4th	Win & Pl
5	1	1	1	1	£40,948

	Date	Course	Race	Prize
	7/18	Tipp	7½f 2yo gd-fm	£8,722

Full brother to Highland Reel and Idaho; Aidan O'Brien's first string in last season's Royal Lodge Stakes according to the market but below his best after 77-day absence when third behind two stablemates; had bumped into a real star when second to Quorto in the Superlative.

Capri (Ire)

5 gr h Galileo - Dialafara (Anabaa)

Aidan O'Brien (Ir) — Derrick Smith, Mrs John Magnier & Michael Tabor

PLACINGS: 21113/436110/15540- RPR **119**

Starts	1st	2nd	3rd	4th	Win & Pl
16	6	1	2	2	£1,499,631

	Date	Course	Race	Prize
	4/18	Naas	1m2f Gp3 sft-hvy	£32,894
	9/17	Donc	1m6½f Cls1 Gp1 3yo gd-sft	£396,970
	7/17	Curr	1m4f Gp1 3yo good	£730,769
	9/16	Curr	1m Gp2 2yo heavy	£52,059
	8/16	Tipp	7½f List 2yo yld-sft	£23,860
	7/16	Gway	1m½f Mdn 2yo yield	£7,688

Dual Classic winner in 2017, landing the Irish Derby and the St Leger; missed much of last season after a reappearance win at Naas and not quite at his best during a busy autumn; still ran well when fifth in the Arc and found drop to 1m2f against him in the Champion Stakes.

Century Dream (Ire)

5 b h Cape Cross - Salacia (Echo Of Light)

Simon Crisford — Abdulla Belhabb

PLACINGS: 31/3411611/011443d3-2 RPR **119**

Starts	1st	2nd	3rd	4th	Win & Pl
18	7	1	3	4	£371,576

	Date	Course	Race	Prize
	6/18	Epsm	1m½f Cls1 Gp3 good	£51,039
	5/18	Asct	1m Cls1 List soft	£20,983
101	10/17	Newb	1m2f Cls2 83-102 Hcap soft	£12,938
98	9/17	Hayd	1m Cls2 89-99 Hcap heavy	£12,450
93	7/17	Ayr	1m Cls2 82-94 Hcap good	£15,563
87	6/17	Donc	1m Cls3 80-94 3yo Hcap soft	£7,763
	10/16	Nott	1m½f Cls5 Mdn 2yo gd-sft	£3,235

Prolific winner for much of the last two seasons, improving from a handicapper into a genuine Group 1 miler; not beaten far in the Queen Anne Stakes and the QEII on Ascot's straight

Dual Classic winner Capri (grey) wins a Group 3 at Naas last season

mile having also won a Listed race there in May; goes on any ground.

Chablis (Ire)

3 b f Galileo - Vadawina (Unfuwain)

Aidan O'Brien (Ir) Mrs John Magnier & John C Oxley

PLACINGS: 1- RPR **83+**

Starts	1st	2nd	3rd	4th	Win & Pl
1	1	-	-	-	£6,541

10/18	Gowr	7f Mdn 2yo yield	£6,542

Cost 1.55 million gns and made a winning start last season when taking a 7f maiden at Gowran Park in October; likely to prove best over much further (half-brother Vadamar effective over staying trips) and should have much more to offer.

Chairmanoftheboard (Ire)

3 b c Slade Power - Bound Copy (Street Cry)

Mick Channon David Kilburn, David Hudd & Chris Wright

PLACINGS: 16- RPR **94+**

Starts	1st	2nd	3rd	4th	Win & Pl
2	1	-	-	-	£5,327

10/18	Gdwd	6f Cls5 Auct 2yo soft	£4,787

Stunning eight-length debut winner at Goodwood last season, at which point only Calyx and Ten Sovereigns had been awarded a higher RPR of any first-time-out two-year-olds all year; only sixth when 11-8 for the Horris Hill next time but will surely prove much better than that.

Circus Maximus (Ire)

3 b c Galileo - Duntle (Danehill Dancer)

Aidan O'Brien (Ir) Flaxman Stables, Mrs Magnier, M Tabor & D Smith

PLACINGS: 5134- RPR **112**

Starts	1st	2nd	3rd	4th	Win & Pl
4	1	-	1	1	£28,080

9/18	Gowr	1m Mdn 2yo heavy	£8,995

Twice ran well in top juvenile races after winning a maiden last season; third in the Autumn Stakes before getting much closer to Magna Grecia when a length fourth in the Vertem Futurity Trophy on softer ground (had also won maiden on heavy); should get middle distances.

City Light (Fr)

5 b h Siyouni - Light Saber (Kendor)

Stephane Wattel (Fr) Ecurie Jean-Louis Bouchard

PLACINGS: 174/2222102/1112520- RPR **121**

Starts	1st	2nd	3rd	4th	Win & Pl
17	5	7	-	1	£371,348

5/18	Lonc	5f Gp3 good	£35,398
3/18	Ling	6f Cls2 stand	£93,375
3/18	Chan	6½f stand	£17,699
10/17	Chan	6f 3yo v soft	£14,060
9/16	StCl	1m 2yo gd-sft	£9,926

Developed into a top-class sprinter last season, kicking off on the all-weather before coming within a short head of winning the Diamond Jubilee Stakes at Royal Ascot; yet to prove quite as effective over the minimum trip but did win a 5f Group 3 at Longchamp.

Communique (Ire)

4 ch c Casamento - Midnight Line (Kris S)

Mark Johnston Sheikh Hamdan Bin Mohammed Al Maktoum

PLACINGS: 22/32105114481125- RPR **113**

Starts	1st	2nd	3rd	4th	Win & Pl
16	5	4	1	2	£208,429

	9/18	NmkR	1m4f Cls1 List gd-fm	£22,684
103	9/18	Newb	1m4f Cls2 96-103 Hcap gd-sft	£16,173
97	8/18	Gdwd	1m2f Cls2 85-105 3yo Hcap good	£46,688
92	7/18	NmkJ	1m2f Cls2 86-104 3yo Hcap gd-fm	£49,800
84	5/18	Newb	1m2f Cls2 82-101 3yo Hcap gd-fm	£43,575

Kept extremely busy last season but progressed virtually all year, producing a career-best run when second in the Cumberland Lodge Stakes in October after successive wins in a Newbury handicap off 103 and a Newmarket Listed race; still unexposed over 1m4f.

Constantinople (Ire)

3 b c Galileo - One Moment In Time (Danehill)

Aidan O'Brien (Ir) Derrick Smith, Mrs John Magnier & Michael Tabor

PLACINGS: 531- RPR **95+**

Starts	1st	2nd	3rd	4th	Win & Pl
3	1	-	1	-	£7,751

10/18	Thur	1m Mdn 2yo gd-fm	£6,542

Made rapid progress in three maidens last season and signed off with a ten-length victory at Thurles; imposing colt with a giant stride and seems sure to get at least 1m4f; looks a likely sort to start off in a Derby trial.

Coronet

5 gr m Dubawi - Approach (Darshaan)

John Gosden Denford Stud

PLACINGS: 11/3514253/12322- RPR **116**

Starts	1st	2nd	3rd	4th	Win & Pl
14	4	4	3	1	£859,161

5/18	York	1m2½f Cls1 Gp2 gd-fm	£70,888
6/17	Asct	1m4f Cls1 Gp2 3yo gd-fm	£121,927
10/16	NmkR	1m2f Cls1 List 2yo good	£28,355
9/16	Leic	1m Cls4 Mdn 2yo gd-sft	£5,175

Has finished second four times at Group 1 level

in the last two seasons, coming closest when beaten a nose by Waldgeist in the Grand Prix de Saint-Cloud; has dropped below that grade only twice in that time, winning the 2017 Ribblesdale Stakes and last year's Middleton Stakes.

Cross Counter

4 b g Teofilo - Waitress (Kingmambo)

Charlie Appleby — Godolphin

PLACINGS: **1/1241121-** — RPR **118**

Starts	1st	2nd	3rd	4th	Win & Pl
8	5	2	-	1	£2,622,562

0	11/18	Flem	2m Gd1 Hcap gd-sft	£2,456,647
	8/18	Gdwd	1m4f Cls1 Gp3 3yo gd-fm	£85,065
101	7/18	Asct	1m4f Cls2 82-101 3yo Hcap gd-fm	£31,125
	1/18	Wolv	1m1½f Cls5 3yo stand	£3,752
	12/17	Wolv	1m½f Cls5 2yo stand	£3,881

Hugely progressive last season and signed off with a memorable win in the Melbourne Cup; also has the speed for top 1m4f races judging by runaway win in the Group 3 Gordon Stakes at Glorious Goodwood and had Kew Gardens back in third when just beaten in the Great Voltigeur.

Crystal Ocean

5 b h Sea The Stars - Crystal Star (Mark Of Esteem)

Sir Michael Stoute — Sir Evelyn de Rothschild

PLACINGS: **2/13312/111222-** — RPR **127**

Starts	1st	2nd	3rd	4th	Win & Pl
12	5	5	2	-	£1,043,480

	6/18	Asct	1m4f Cls1 Gp2 gd-fm	£127,598
	5/18	Newb	1m4f Cls1 Gp3 gd-fm	£56,710
	4/18	Sand	1m2f Cls1 Gp3 gd-sft	£39,697
	8/17	Gdwd	1m4f Cls1 Gp3 3yo soft	£56,710
	4/17	Nott	1m2f Cls5 Mdn 3yo gd-fm	£3,235

Progressed well in 2017 (second in the St Leger) and continued to flourish early last season, winning the Hardwicke Stakes and beaten a neck in the King George; beaten more comprehensively the next twice but unsuited by drop to 1m2f in the Champion Stakes.

D'Bai (Ire)

5 b g Dubawi - Savannah Belle (Green Desert)

Charlie Appleby — Godolphin

PLACINGS: **031365/14521656423-1** — RPR **115+**

Starts	1st	2nd	3rd	4th	Win & Pl
24	6	4	4	2	£392,367

	1/19	Meyd	7f Gp2 good	£118,110
	6/18	Hayd	7f Cls1 Gp3 gd-fm	£35,727
110	1/18	Meyd	7f 102-113 Hcap good	£71,111
105	7/17	Asct	1m Cls2 84-105 3yo Hcap gd-sft	£28,013
	10/16	Pont	1m Cls1 List 2yo soft	£19,849
	7/16	NmkJ	7f Cls4 Mdn 2yo gd-fm	£4,528

Gained his first Group win in last season's John of Gaunt Stakes at Haydock and went on to run well in several better races later in the year, especially back at the same 7f trip; placed in the Park and Challenge Stakes before winning at Meydan for the second year in a row.

Dancing Vega (Ire)

3 ch f Lope De Vega - We Can Say It Now (Starcraft)

Ralph Beckett — Waverley Racing

PLACINGS: **1-** — RPR **92+**

Starts	1st	2nd	3rd	4th	Win & Pl
1	1	-	-	-	£3,752

	10/18	Donc	1m Cls5 Mdn 2yo gd-sft	£3,752

Very impressive when making a winning debut by four lengths at Doncaster last October and form looks strong after runner-up won a Listed race next time out; should progress with racing (both half-siblings produced career-best efforts on their final run).

Dandhu

3 ch f Dandy Man - Poldhu (Cape Cross)

David Elsworth — Mrs A Coughlan & D Elsworth

PLACINGS: **6412-** — RPR **105+**

Starts	1st	2nd	3rd	4th	Win & Pl
4	1	1	-	1	£33,712

	9/18	Kemp	7f Cls3 2yo std-slw	£11,828

Improved with every run last season, getting off the mark on her third run at Kempton before a fine effort when second in the Rockfel Stakes behind Just Wonderful; always strongest at the finish and seems sure to improve over a mile despite being by a sprinter.

Danehill Kodiac (Ire)

6 b h Kodiac - Meadow (Green Desert)

Richard Hannon — Davies, Smith, Carr, Brown & Govier

PLACINGS: **1/4354123/142130/22-** — RPR **114**

Starts	1st	2nd	3rd	4th	Win & Pl
19	5	5	3	4	£177,161

	10/17	Asct	1m4f Cls1 Gp3 gd-sft	£34,026
97	8/17	NmkJ	1m4f Cls2 96-108 Hcap soft	£16,173
84	8/16	Asct	1m4f Cls3 79-91 3yo Hcap gd-fm	£22,131
82	9/15	Donc	1m Cls2 75-88 2yo Hcap good	£9,338
	8/15	Chmt	1m Cls4 Mdn 2yo stand	£5,175

Missed most of last season after finishing second behind high-class pair Defoe and Idaho in early-season Group 3 races; has now lost penalty for win in that grade in the 2017 Cumberland Lodge Stakes, beating subsequent Group 1 winner Waldgeist.

Dark Vision (Ire)

3 b c Dream Ahead - Black Dahlia (Dansili)

Mark Johnston — Godolphin

PLACINGS: **1116-** — RPR **110+**

Starts	1st	2nd	3rd	4th	Win & Pl
4	3	-	-	-	£129,052

	7/18	Gdwd	7f Cls1 Gp2 2yo good	£113,420
	7/18	York	6f Cls3 Auct 2yo gd-fm	£9,704
	7/18	Yarm	6f Cls4 2yo gd-fm	£4,916

Won first three starts last season, completing the hat-trick in stunning fashion when sweeping from last to first in the Vintage Stakes at Goodwood, albeit perhaps helped by a pace collapse up front; well below his best when last of six next time in the Champagne Stakes.

Dash Of Spice

5 br h Teofilo - Dashiba (Dashing Blade)

David Elsworth — JC Smith

PLACINGS: 421/22110- RPR **109+**

Starts	1st	2nd	3rd	4th	Win & Pl
8	3	3	-	1	£103,620

98	6/18	Asct	1m4f Cls2 96-105 Hcap gd-fm	£56,025
87	6/18	Epsm	1m4f Cls2 85-104 Hcap good	£31,125
	12/17	Ling	1m2f Cls5 Mdn stand	£2,911

Progressed well early last season and won the Duke of Edinburgh at Royal Ascot; disappointing favourite when down in trip for the John Smith's Cup and missed the rest of the year; held a Winter Derby entry but trainer mindful not to ruin mark with the Ebor a possible target.

Dee Ex Bee

4 b c Farhh - Dubai Sunrise (Seeking The Gold)

Mark Johnston — Sheikh Hamdan Bin Mohammed Al Maktoum

PLACINGS: 16312/32273243- RPR **119**

Starts	1st	2nd	3rd	4th	Win & Pl
13	2	4	4	1	£539,835

	10/17	Epsm	1m½f Cls2 2yo heavy	£12,450
	8/17	Gdwd	7f Cls2 Mdn 2yo soft	£19,407

Ran consistently well in top three-year-old middle-distance races last season, most notably when second to Masar in the Derby; couldn't quite build on that but still finished second in the Gordon Stakes, third in the Grand Prix de Paris and fourth in the St Leger.

Defoe (Ire)

5 gr g Dalakhani - Dulkashe (Pivotal)

Roger Varian — Sheikh Mohammed Obaid Al Maktoum

PLACINGS: 120/11110/113202- RPR **117+**

Starts	1st	2nd	3rd	4th	Win & Pl
14	7	3	1	-	£334,940

	5/18	NmkR	1m4f Cls1 Gp2 good	£59,546
	4/18	Newb	1m4f Cls1 Gp3 gd-sft	£34,026
	8/17	Newb	1m5½f Cls1 Gp3 soft	£34,026
	7/17	Haml	1m3f Cls1 List 3yo good	£23,818
98	7/17	York	1m2½f Cls2 77-98 3yo Hcap good	£31,125
88	5/17	Newb	1m2f Cls2 77-95 3yo Hcap soft	£43,575
	9/16	Ffos	1m Cls5 Mdn 2yo soft	£3,235

Impressive winner of last season's Jockey Club Stakes to make it six wins out of seven; found the ground too quick when third in the Tattersalls Gold Cup but still came up short at the top level on softer ground in the autumn; has since been gelded.

Desert Encounter (Ire)

7 b g Halling - La Chicana (Invincible Spirit)

David Simcock — Abdulla Al Mansoori

PLACINGS: 132/123615/93726131- RPR **117**

Starts	1st	2nd	3rd	4th	Win & Pl
23	8	4	5	1	£575,725

	10/18	Wood	1m4f Gd1 good	£282,353
	8/18	Wind	1m3½f Cls1 List good	£20,983
	9/17	Newb	1m3f Cls1 Gp3 good	£34,026
	5/17	Asct	1m4f Cls1 List gd-fm	£25,520
91	6/16	Wind	1m3½f Cls2 85-96 Hcap soft	£12,938
89	5/16	NmkR	1m6f Cls2 86-97 Hcap gd-fm	£18,675
82	4/16	Donc	1m4f Cls4 72-82 App Hcap soft	£5,175
	10/15	Muss	1m4f Cls6 Auct Mdn 3-4yo good	£2,264

Enjoyed his finest hour when winning the Canadian International at Woodbine last season from Thundering Blue; hasn't quite looked up to that level in Britain but was third in the 2017 Eclipse and won a Group 3 at Newbury that year (beaten half a length in the same race last year).

Desert Skyline (Ire)

5 ch g Tamayuz - Diamond Tango (Acatenango)

David Elsworth — C Benham, D Whitford L Quinn & K Quinn

PLACINGS: 1/23623219/32964458- RPR **116**

Starts	1st	2nd	3rd	4th	Win & Pl
19	3	4	3	2	£261,121

	9/17	Donc	2m2f Cls1 Gp2 gd-sft	£56,710
83	10/16	NmkR	1m1f Cls4 69-83 2yo Hcap gd-sft	£4,528
	9/16	Yarm	1m Cls4 Mdn 2yo gd-fm	£4,658

Relished an extreme test of stamina when winning the Doncaster Cup in 2017 on good to soft ground; generally below that level last season, occasionally over inadequate trips, but ran a big race when beaten only three lengths on soft ground in the Long Distance Cup.

Donjuan Triumphant (Ire)

6 b h Dream Ahead - Mathuna (Tagula)

Andrew Balding — King Power Racing

PLACINGS: 332/039118/55249431- RPR **115**

Starts	1st	2nd	3rd	4th	Win & Pl
30	6	7	5	3	£448,860

	11/18	Donc	6f Cls1 List soft	£22,684
109	9/17	Hayd	6f Cls2 98-109 Hcap heavy	£56,025
	9/17	Hayd	7f Cls3 gd-sft	£9,704
	10/15	MsnL	6f Gp2 2yo soft	£83,953
	10/15	York	6f Cls1 List 2yo gd-sft	£28,355
88	9/15	Ayr	6f Cls2 71-92 2yo Hcap good	£15,563

Lost his way having once looked a Group I sprinter for Richard Fahey (second in the 2016 Prix Maurice de Gheest) but has steadily come back to form for Andrew Balding; finished last season on a high with a Listed win at Doncaster after two fine runs back at the top level.

Dream Castle

5 b g Frankel - Sand Vixen (Dubawi)

Saeed Bin Suroor — Godolphin

PLACINGS: 125572/7350-11 — RPR **116**

Starts	1st	2nd	3rd	4th	Win & Pl
12	3	2	1	-	£360,985

	Date	Course	Race	Prize
	1/19	Meyd	1m1f Gp2 good	£118,110
	1/19	Meyd	1m1f Gp3 good	£94,488
	4/17	Donc	7f Cls5 Mdn 3yo good	£3,235

Looked a real talent early in his three-year-old campaign in 2017, finishing second in the Greenham and an unlucky fifth in the 2,000 Guineas, but lost his way and was barely sighted until Meydan this year; back on track after a gelding operation there and retains big potential.

Dreamfield

5 b h Oasis Dream - Izzi Top (Pivotal)

John Gosden — Godolphin

PLACINGS: 11/1267- — RPR **113**

Starts	1st	2nd	3rd	4th	Win & Pl
6	3	1	-	-	£59,423

	Date	Course	Race	Prize
95	5/18	Asct	6f Cls3 81-96 Hcap gd-fm	£7,763
	10/16	NmkR	7f Cls2 2yo gd-sft	£9,057
	10/16	Nott	6f Cls5 Mdn 2yo gd-sft	£3,235

Very nearly landed a huge gamble in last season's Wokingham when backed down to 2-1 but beaten a neck by Bacchus; had come into the race unbeaten in three runs (punctuated by missing 2017 through injury) but well beaten twice subsequently.

Dubai Warrior

3 b c Dansili - Mahbooba (Galileo)

John Gosden — Sheikh Mohammed Bin Khalifa Al Maktoum

PLACINGS: 1- — RPR **87+aw**

Starts	1st	2nd	3rd	4th	Win & Pl
1	1	-	-	-	£4,787

Date	Course	Race	Prize
11/18	Chmt	1m Cls5 2yo stand	£4,787

Impressive winner of sole start last season, easing home by four and a half lengths at Chelmsford in November; full of scope for improvement and bred to thrive over middle distances (full brother Mootasadir progressed throughout last year to win a 1m2½f Group 3).

East

3 ch f Frankel - Vital Statistics (Indian Ridge)

Kevin Ryan — East Partners

PLACINGS: 112- — RPR **110+**

Starts	1st	2nd	3rd	4th	Win & Pl
3	2	1	-	-	£166,758

Date	Course	Race	Prize
10/18	StCl	7f Gp3 2yo good	£35,398
9/18	Haml	6f Cls4 2yo soft	£5,434

Cost €315,000 and justified that price tag in just three starts last season, winning a Group 3 at Saint-Cloud and running on really well from the rear for a distant second in the Breeders' Cup Juvenile Fillies Turf; looks an out-and-out miler on pedigree.

Dash Of Spice lands last season's Duke of Edinburgh Stakes at Royal Ascot

El Astronaute (Ire)

6 ch g Approve - Drumcliffe Dancer (Footstepsinthesand)

John Quinn — Ross Harmon Racing

PLACINGS: 701225/231234424121- RPR **111**

Starts	1st	2nd	3rd	4th	Win & Pl
39	10	9	4	6	£245,757

	10/18	MsnL	5½f List soft	£23,009
101	8/18	York	5½f Cls2 88-105 Hcap gd-fm	£43,575
98	5/18	York	5f Cls2 84-101 Hcap gd-fm	£18,675
91	8/17	Gdwd	5f Cls2 85-104 Hcap good	£19,407
90	5/17	Ches	5f Cls2 84-95 Hcap good	£18,675
88	4/17	NmkR	5f Cls3 83-95 Hcap gd-fm	£9,057
84	8/16	Epsm	5f Cls2 84-98 Hcap good	£12,450
85	9/15	Ches	5½f Cls2 78-99 2yo Hcap gd-sft	£16,173
77	8/15	Leic	5f Cls4 68-84 2yo Hcap good	£3,946
	7/15	Thsk	5f Cls5 Mdn 2yo gd-fm	£3,235

Hugely progressive sprinter last season; placed in several big handicaps before finally landing a good prize at York in August; went on to prove himself at Listed level, finishing a head second at Doncaster before winning at Maisons-Laffitte.

Elarqam

4 b c Frankel - Attraction (Efisio)

Mark Johnston — Hamdan Al Maktoum

PLACINGS: 11/4634- RPR **116**

Starts	1st	2nd	3rd	4th	Win & Pl
6	2	-	1	2	£84,354

9/17	NmkR	7f Cls1 Gp3 2yo gd-sft	£28,355
9/17	York	7f Cls3 2yo gd-sft	£7,763

Unbeaten as a two-year-old and began last season with a solid effort when fourth in the 2,000 Guineas; bitterly disappointing in three subsequent runs (favourite every time), doing best when stepped up in trip to finish a half-length third in the York Stakes; talented but plenty to prove.

Elwazir

4 ch c Frankel - Dash To The Front (Diktat)

Owen Burrows — Hamdan Al Maktoum

PLACINGS: 24/115- RPR **109+**

Starts	1st	2nd	3rd	4th	Win & Pl
5	2	1	-	1	£17,803

96	7/18	Asct	1m2f Cls3 81-96 Hcap gd-fm	£9,704
	6/18	Sand	1m2f Cls5 good	£4,528

Began last season with two notable victories, easily beating subsequent Melbourne Cup hero Cross Counter at Sandown and comfortably following up on his handicap debut at Ascot; below par when stepped up to Group 3 level at Haydock next time.

Emaraaty Ana

3 b c Shamardal - Spirit Of Dubai (Cape Cross)

Kevin Ryan — Sheikh Mohammed Obaid Al Maktoum

PLACINGS: 1315- RPR **110**

Starts	1st	2nd	3rd	4th	Win & Pl
4	2	-	1	-	£142,525

8/18	York	6f Cls1 Gp2 2yo gd-fm	£127,598
4/18	Wind	5f Cls4 2yo good	£4,787

Narrow winner of last season's Gimcrack Stakes at York having disappointed when third behind Natalie's Joy on return from short layoff; only fifth in the Middle Park after that but bred for much further (dam won a 1m4f Listed race) and should progress.

Emblazoned (Ire)

4 b c Invincible Spirit - Sendmylovetorose (Bahamian Bounty)

John Gosden — Princess Haya of Jordan

PLACINGS: **21133-** RPR **110**

Starts	1st	2nd	3rd	4th	Win & Pl
5	2	1	2	-	£72,913

5/18	Yarm	6f Cls5 gd-fm	£3,752
4/18	Ling	7f Cls5 3yo stand	£3,752

Unraced as a two-year-old but made rapid progress in the first half of last season and finished third in the Commonwealth Cup at Royal Ascot on just his fifth run; missed the rest of the year but expected to return in top sprints.

Enable

5 b m Nathaniel - Concentric (Sadler's Wells)

John Gosden — K Abdullah

PLACINGS: **1/3111111/111-** RPR **122+**

Starts	1st	2nd	3rd	4th	Win & Pl
11	10	-	1	-	£8,007,025

11/18	Chur	1m4f Gd1 good	£1,629,630
10/18	Lonc	1m4f Gp1 good	£2,528,319
9/18	Kemp	1m4f Cls1 Gp3 std-slw	£39,697
10/17	Chan	1m4f Gp1 soft	£2,441,880
8/17	York	1m4f Cls1 Gp1 gd-sft	£198,485
7/17	Asct	1m4f Cls1 Gp1 gd-sft	£652,165
7/17	Curr	1m4f Gp1 3yo gd-fm	£194,872
6/17	Epsm	1m4f Cls1 Gp1 3yo good	£283,550
5/17	Ches	1m3½f Cls1 List 3yo good	£34,026
11/16	Newc	1m Cls5 Mdn 2yo stand	£2,911

Outstanding mare who has won her last nine races, including seven at Group 1 level; missed much of last season but returned in the autumn and won a second successive Prix de l'Arc de Triomphe before stepping up on that form to add the Breeders' Cup Turf.

Eqtidaar (Ire)

4 b c Invincible Spirit - Madany (Acclamation)

Sir Michael Stoute — Hamdan Al Maktoum

PLACINGS: **14/24190-** RPR **115**

Starts	1st	2nd	3rd	4th	Win & Pl
7	2	1	-	2	£310,148

6/18	Asct	6f Cls1 Gp1 3yo gd-fm	£283,550
8/17	Nott	6f Cls5 Mdn 2yo gd-sft	£3,235

Lived up to big home reputation when winning last season's Commonwealth Cup at Royal Ascot; patchy record otherwise and most disappointing when ninth in the July Cup but perhaps unsuited by soft and heavy ground when twice below best in those conditions.

Marvellous mare Enable storms home at Longchamp to pull off an Arc repeat last autumn

Equilateral

4 b c Equiano - Tarentaise (Oasis Dream)

Charlie Hills | K Abdullah

PLACINGS: 16/108144- | RPR **111**

Starts	1st	2nd	3rd	4th	Win & Pl
8	3	-	-	2	£21,578

	9/18	Leic	5f Cls3 gd-fm	£9,452
	5/18	Donc	6f Cls5 gd-fm	£3,752
	8/17	Bath	5f Cls5 Mdn 2yo gd-sft	£2,911

Made a massive impression with an eight-length win at Doncaster first time out last season (sent off just 6-1 for the Commonwealth Cup next time) but didn't quite go on from there, with only subsequent win at 1-2 in a three-runner race; still held in high regard at home.

Fabricate

7 b g Makfi - Flight Of Fancy (Sadler's Wells)

Michael Bell | The Queen

PLACINGS: 5381/**3446115**/124013- | RPR **115**

Starts	1st	2nd	3rd	4th	Win & Pl
22	7	2	5	3	£218,918

	8/18	Wind	1m2f Cls1 Gp3 good	£34,026
	3/18	Kemp	1m2f Cls1 List stand	£25,520
	8/17	Wind	1m2f Cls1 Gp3 gd-fm	£34,026
102	8/17	Gdwd	1m2f Cls2 92-108 Hcap good	£31,125
97	10/16	Leic	1m4f Cls2 96-102 Hcap gd-sft	£15,753
87	5/15	Hayd	1m4f Cls3 80-92 3yo Hcap gd-sft	£12,450
	5/15	Sals	1m4f Cls5 Mdn 3yo gd-fm	£4,205

Has won the Group 3 Winter Hill Stakes at Windsor for the last two years; gained first Group win in that race in 2017 and built on that

Fabricate (right) is a smart operator at Listed and Group 3 level

In 2019 the Injured Jockeys Fund will open its third Rehabilitation and Fitness Centre Peter O'Sullevan House in Newmarket. This will complete the national coverage of care and support we can offer our sports men and women in the UK.

We provide appropriate support in a prompt and sympathetic manner to those jockeys, past or present, who are injured, unable to ride, or generally in need.

As a not-for-profit, self funding organisation we are reliant on the support and generosity of our supporters.

To find out how you can become involved and support the Injured Jockeys Fund or make a donation please visit us at:

www.ijf.org.uk or call: **01638 662246**

Compassion • Care • Support

The Injured Jockeys Fund (Registered Charity No. 1107395)

last season in several similar races, also winning a Listed race at Kempton and running Crystal Ocean close in the Gordon Richards Stakes.

Fairyland (Ire)

3 b f Kodiac - Queenofthefairies (Pivotal)

Aidan O'Brien (Ir) Mrs EM Stockwell, Michael Tabor & Derrick Smith

PLACINGS: 11311- RPR **112**

Starts	1st	2nd	3rd	4th	Win & Pl
5	4	-	1	-	£353,723

9/18	NmkR	6f Cls1 Gp1 2yo gd-fm	£174,758
8/18	York	6f Cls1 Gp2 2yo gd-fm	£127,598
5/18	Curr	6f List 2yo gd-fm	£31,327
5/18	Naas	6f Mdn 2yo gd-yld	£10,358

Won four out of five last season and was best in her group when third in the Albany Stakes at Royal Ascot; scraped home when returning from a subsequent break in the Lowther but more impressive when adding the Cheveley Park; not certain to get a mile.

Feliciana De Vega

3 b f Lope De Vega - Along Came Casey (Oratorio)

Ralph Beckett Waverley Racing

PLACINGS: 11- RPR **101+aw**

Starts	1st	2nd	3rd	4th	Win & Pl
2	2	-	-	-	£31,723

12/18	Deau	7½f List 2yo stand	£26,549
11/18	NmkR	7f Cls4 2yo soft	£5,175

Out of a dual Listed winner and soon lived up to her pedigree by winning a Listed race on the all-weather track at Deauville in December; had run away with a novice stakes at Newmarket on her debut by six lengths on soft ground; should stay 1m2f.

First Eleven

4 b c Frankel - Zenda (Zamindar)

John Gosden K Abdullah

PLACINGS: 962/213513- RPR **112+**

Starts	1st	2nd	3rd	4th	Win & Pl
9	2	2	2	-	£91,110

97	9/18	Asct	1m4f Cls2 83-98 3yo Hcap gd-fm	£62,250
77	5/18	Newb	1m3f Cls4 72-86 3yo Hcap gd-fm	£6,728

Beautifully bred colt (half-brother to Kingman) who progressed well in handicaps last season, doing best when winning a valuable heat at Ascot in September; twice a beaten favourite at Group 3 level but perhaps unsuited by soft ground when third in the Cumberland Lodge.

Flag Of Honour (Ire)

4 b c Galileo - Hawala (Warning)

Aidan O'Brien (Ir) Mrs John Magnier, Michael Tabor & Derrick Smith

PLACINGS: 9151/35011145- RPR **116**

Starts	1st	2nd	3rd	4th	Win & Pl
12	5	-	1	1	£440,407

9/18	Curr	1m6f Gp1 good	£252,212
8/18	Curr	1m6f Gp3 good	£32,894
7/18	Curr	1m6f Gp2 gd-fm	£62,655
10/17	Leop	1m1f Gp3 2yo yield	£31,769
10/17	Naas	7f Mdn 2yo yield	£8,687

Flourished when stepped up to staying trips last season and completed a hat-trick when winning the Irish St Leger; only fourth behind Stradivarius in the Long Distance Cup but ran another cracker when fifth in the Prix Royal-Oak despite losing many lengths in an in-running incident.

Flaming Spear (Ire)

7 ch g Lope De Vega - Elshamms (Zafonic)

Dean Ivory Tony Bloom

PLACINGS: /20001/19180/501501- RPR **116**

Starts	1st	2nd	3rd	4th	Win & Pl
20	6	1	-	-	£195,501

	11/18	Kemp	1m Cls1 List std-slw	£25,520
104	8/18	Gdwd	7f Cls2 85-104 Hcap good	£62,250
101	8/17	York	1m Cls2 92-109 Hcap gd-sft	£52,913
97	1/17	Newc	7f Cls2 87-100 Hcap stand	£28,013
92	12/16	Newc	1m Cls3 82-95 Hcap stand	£7,246
	7/14	York	6f Cls3 Auct Mdn 2yo gd-fm	£7,439

Has won valuable summer handicaps at York and Goodwood in the last two years despite steadily climbing in the weights; still capable off higher marks judged on fast-finishing fifth at Ascot last autumn (given too much to do) and left unchanged after Listed win at Kempton.

Fleeting (Ire)

3 b f Zoffany - Azafata (Motivator)

Aidan O'Brien (Ir) Mrs John Magnier, Michael Tabor & Derrick Smith

PLACINGS: 1731- RPR **107**

Starts	1st	2nd	3rd	4th	Win & Pl
4	2	-	1	-	£54,245

9/18	Donc	1m Cls1 Gp2 2yo good	£39,697
6/18	Limk	7f Mdn 2yo gd-fm	£8,177

Seemingly exposed as below the best Irish-trained juvenile fillies last season when twice well beaten after debut win but then won the May Hill Stakes at Doncaster (runner-up unlucky in Prix Marcel Boussac); dam won over 1m6f so should get much further.

Forest Ranger (Ire)

5 b g Lawman - Alava (Anabaa)

Richard Fahey | Mrs H Steel

PLACINGS: 13/1652328/117552- | RPR **116**

Starts	1st	2nd	3rd	4th	Win & Pl
15	4	3	2	-	£269,988

	Date	Course	Race	Prize
	5/18	Ches	1m2½f Cls1 Gp2 good	£70,888
	4/18	NmkR	1m1f Cls1 Gp3 good	£34,026
	4/17	Newc	1m Cls2 3yo stand	£62,250
	9/16	Rdcr	7f Cls5 Mdn 2yo gd-fm	£3,235

Improved early last season after being gelded and won two Group races, including the Huxley Stakes at Chester; quietly fancied for the Eclipse after that (sent off 11-1) but went off the boil until a better final run when a neck second at Newmarket.

Fox Tal

3 b c Sea The Stars - Maskunah (Sadler's Wells)

Andrew Balding | King Power Racing

PLACINGS: 3143- | RPR **110**

Starts	1st	2nd	3rd	4th	Win & Pl
4	1	-	2	1	£33,425

	Date	Course	Race	Prize
	7/18	Ffos	7½f Cls4 2yo gd-fm	£5,434

Nearly pulled off a 33-1 shock in the Criterium de Saint-Cloud, relishing more prominent ride over 1m2f trip having been only fourth in a Listed race at Salisbury; had scrambled home when gaining sole win on good to firm and later withdrawn at Newmarket because of quick ground.

Frosty (Ire)

3 gr f Galileo - Laddies Poker Two (Choisir)

Aidan O'Brien (Ir) | Mrs John Magnier, Michael Tabor & Derrick Smith

PLACINGS: 17- | RPR **84+aw**

Starts	1st	2nd	3rd	4th	Win & Pl
2	1	-	-	-	£8,176

	Date	Course	Race	Prize
	9/18	Dund	7f Mdn 2yo stand	£8,177

Sister to same connections' brilliant four-time Group 1 winner Winter; made a winning debut at Dundalk last season but struggled when only seventh in the Oh So Sharp Stakes; sent off just 9-4 that day, though, and seems sure to leave that form well behind in time.

Ghaiyyath (Ire)

4 b c Dubawi - Nightime (Galileo)

Charlie Appleby | Godolphin

PLACINGS: 311/1- | RPR **113+**

Starts	1st	2nd	3rd	4th	Win & Pl
4	3	-	1	-	£76,042

	Date	Course	Race	Prize
	9/18	Lonc	1m2f Gp3 3yo gd-sft	£35,398
	10/17	NmkR	1m Cls1 Gp3 2yo good	£34,026
	9/17	NmkR	1m Cls4 Mdn 2yo gd-sft	£5,175

Ran only once last season because of injury but still added to glowing reputation with a smooth Group 3 win at Longchamp; had also won last two starts as a two-year-old, including the Autumn Stakes; had been seen as a Derby horse and should get 1m4f.

Ghostwatch (Ire)

4 b g Dubawi - Nature Spirits (Beat Hollow)

Charlie Appleby | Godolphin

PLACINGS: 33/13152121- | RPR **109+**

Starts	1st	2nd	3rd	4th	Win & Pl
10	4	2	3	-	£157,692

	Date	Course	Race	Prize
	10/18	Asct	1m6f Cls1 List 3yo good	£36,862
92	8/18	York	1m6f Cls2 81-100 3yo Hcap gd-fm	£77,813
82	6/18	Sand	1m6f Cls4 67-82 3yo Hcap good	£9,587
	4/18	Wolv	1m4f Cls5 Mdn stand	£3,752

Much improved after a gelding operation midway through last season, winning the Melrose at York on his next run and adding a Listed race at Ascot when stepped back up to 1m6f (good effort in defeat over 1m4f in between); should stay further and could be a Cup horse.

Gifted Master (Ire)

6 b g Kodiac - Shobobb (Shamardal)

Hugo Palmer | Dr Ali Ridha

PLACINGS: 029/4971181/6140155- | RPR **120**

Starts	1st	2nd	3rd	4th	Win & Pl
28	11	2	2	3	£749,062

	Date	Course	Race	Prize
111	8/18	Gdwd	6f Cls2 89-111 Hcap gd-fm	£155,625
109	5/18	NmkR	6f Cls2 85-109 Hcap gd-fm	£31,125
	11/17	Ling	6f Cls1 List stand	£20,983
	8/17	NmkJ	6f Cls1 List gd-fm	£20,983
	8/17	Donc	6f Cls3 good	£9,338
	4/16	Asct	6f Cls1 Gp3 3yo gd-sft	£45,368
	4/16	NmkR	6f Cls2 3yo gd-sft	£54,100
	10/15	NmkR	1m Cls1 Gp3 2yo good	£45,368
	10/15	NmkR	7f Cls2 2yo gd-fm	£270,550
	6/15	Newc	6f Cls4 2yo gd-fm	£4,528
	4/15	NmkR	5f Cls3 2yo gd-fm	£8,410

Without a win in a Group race since April 2016 (beaten 11 times) but has shown a very smart level of form at a lower level, especially when handicapping last season; did brilliantly to defy a mark of 111 in the Stewards' Cup to follow up previous big-field win at Newmarket.

Glorious Journey

4 b g Dubawi - Fallen For You (Dansili)

Charlie Appleby | Sheikha Al Jalila Racing

PLACINGS: 11/439419- | RPR **112**

Starts	1st	2nd	3rd	4th	Win & Pl
8	3	-	1	2	£93,310

	Date	Course	Race	Prize
	8/18	Deau	1m Gp3 3yo gd-sft	£35,398
	9/17	StCl	7f Gp3 2yo good	£34,188
	6/17	NmkJ	6f Cls4 2yo good	£4,528

Didn't quite progress as hoped last season

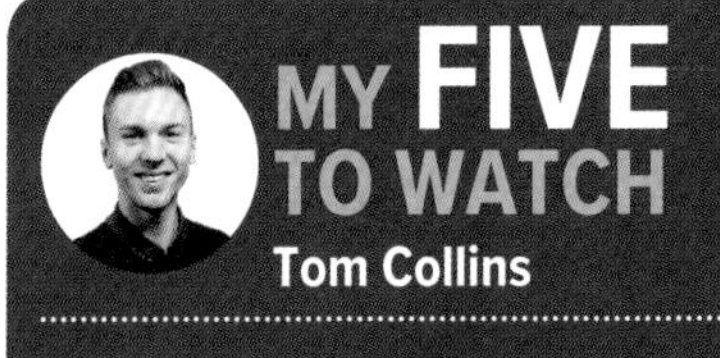

- Dubai Warrior
- Elwazir
- Jack Yeats
- Japan
- Supernova

after winning both starts as a two-year-old but managed to run out a convincing winner of a Group 3 at Deauville on his penultimate run; reportedly needed to grow up mentally and retains potential over a mile.

Goddess (USA)

3 b f Camelot - Cherry Hinton (Green Desert)

Aidan O'Brien (Ir) — Mrs John Magnier & John G Sikura

PLACINGS: 916- — RPR **96+**

Starts	1st	2nd	3rd	4th	Win & Pl
3	1	-	-	-	£10,070

7/18	Leop	7f Mdn 2yo gd-fm	£9,540

Installed favourite for the fillies' Classics after romping home by ten lengths in a maiden at Leopardstown last July but finished last of six when 4-9 for a Group 3 back there next time and missed the rest of the season; full sister to 1m2f Grade 1 winner Athena.

Great Scot

3 b c Requinto - La Rosiere (Mr Greeley)

Tom Dascombe — Empire State Racing Partnership

PLACINGS: 11315- — RPR **111**

Starts	1st	2nd	3rd	4th	Win & Pl
5	3	-	1	-	£49,190

9/18	Hayd	1m Cls1 List 2yo heavy	£14,461
7/18	Hayd	7f Cls4 2yo good	£6,469
6/18	Ches	7f Cls4 Mdn Auct 2yo gd-fm	£5,852

Won three out of five races last season and slightly unlucky not to come into the Vertem Futurity Trophy unbeaten after a head defeat in France; ran another fine race at Doncaster when a close fifth having been hampered; versatile having won on good to firm and heavy ground.

Guaranteed (Ire)

3 b c Teofilo - Gearanai (Toccet)

Jim Bolger (Ir) — Mrs J S Bolger & Rectory Road Holdings

PLACINGS: 215721- — RPR **105**

Starts	1st	2nd	3rd	4th	Win & Pl
6	2	2	-	-	£59,566

10/18	Leop	1m1f Gp3 2yo good	£32,894
7/18	Curr	7f Mdn 2yo good	£10,903

Beaten three times at Pattern level after winning his maiden but improved for the step up to 1m1f when landing the Eyrefield Stakes at Leopardstown, relishing a proper stamina test; should stay at least 1m4f and has the Ballysax and the Derrinstown on his agenda.

Hazapour (Ire)

4 ch c Shamardal - Hazarafa (Daylami)

Dermot Weld (Ir) — Aga Khan

PLACINGS: 713/153- — RPR **112+**

Starts	1st	2nd	3rd	4th	Win & Pl
6	2	-	2	-	£111,639

5/18	Leop	1m2f Gp3 3yo good	£52,212
9/17	Gway	1m½f Mdn 2yo soft	£9,214

Won last season's Derrinstown Derby Trial but didn't quite last home over the longer trip at Epsom despite finishing a creditable fifth;

suffered a setback when beaten at odds-on next time and missed the rest of the season; will have top 1m2f races on his agenda.

Hello Youmzain (Fr)

3 b c Kodiac - Spasha (Shamardal)

Kevin Ryan — Jaber Abdullah

PLACINGS: 121- — RPR **114**

Starts	1st	2nd	3rd	4th	Win & Pl
3	2	1	-	-	£101,970

10/18	MsnL	6f Gp2 2yo soft	£95,841
8/18	Carl	6f Cls5 Mdn 2yo gd-sft	£4,205

Took a big step forward to win the Group 2 Criterium de Maisons-Laffitte on final run last season; had been beaten a short head by subsequent Listed winner San Donato at Haydock; helped by soft ground and likely to stay at least 7f according to rider.

Herculean

4 ch c Frankel - African Rose (Observatory)

Roger Charlton — K Abdullah

PLACINGS: 1/213- — RPR **97**

Starts	1st	2nd	3rd	4th	Win & Pl
4	2	1	1	-	£14,552

7/18	Pont	1m2f Cls5 gd-fm	£4,528
9/17	Asct	7f Cls3 Mdn 2yo soft	£7,763

Extremely well-bred colt who didn't quite live up to high expectations last season, albeit in just three runs; only third when 6-4 on handicap debut at Doncaster on final run but may have found 1m2f on good to soft ground too far (out of a Sprint Cup winner); should do better.

Hermosa (Ire)

3 b f Galileo - Beauty Is Truth (Pivotal)

Aidan O'Brien (Ir) — Michael Tabor, Derrick Smith & Mrs John Magnier

PLACINGS: 4163122- — RPR **111**

Starts	1st	2nd	3rd	4th	Win & Pl
7	2	2	1	1	£232,369

9/18	Naas	7f Gp3 2yo good	£35,243
7/18	Gway	7f Mdn 2yo soft	£9,540

Progressed nicely last season and finished second twice at Group 1 level in the Fillies' Mile and Criterium International (favourite both times in potentially modest races for the grade); could be effective from a mile to a mile and a half (sister Hydrangea a Group 1 winner at both trips).

Hey Gaman

4 b c New Approach - Arsaadi (Dubawi)

James Tate — Sultan Ali

PLACINGS: 2910112/327530- — RPR **112**

Starts	1st	2nd	3rd	4th	Win & Pl
13	3	3	2	-	£202,384

8/17	Newb	7f Cls1 List 2yo soft	£14,461
7/17	NmkJ	6f Cls3 2yo gd-sft	£9,057
7/17	Yarm	6f Cls4 2yo gd-fm	£4,658

Ran mostly in France last season, doing best when a close second in the Poule d'Essai des Poulains; won on good to firm as a two-year-

Hello Youmzain (left) makes a winning start to his career by scoring at Carlisle last season

old but hasn't run in such conditions since and reportedly found good ground quicker than ideal when only fifth in the Prix Jean Prat.

Highgarden

4 b f Nathaniel - Regalline (Green Desert)

John Gosden — Mrs CR Philipson & Mrs H Lascelles

PLACINGS: 1/346251- RPR **109**

Starts	1st	2nd	3rd	4th	Win & Pl
7	2	1	1	1	£57,899

	Date	Course	Race	Prize
	9/18	NmkR	1m4f Cls1 Gp3 gd-fm	£34,026
	10/17	Newb	1m Cls4 2yo soft	£5,175

Slow to live up to two-year-old promise last season (had been sent off favourite when fourth in the Musidora Stakes) but came good after a break with a narrow Listed win at Newmarket on her final run; expected to prove even better on softer ground and will get further.

Holdthasigreen (Fr)

7 ch g Hold That Tiger - Greentathir (Muhtathir)

Bruno Audouin (Fr) — Jean Gilbert

PLACINGS: 13/19123231/1711221- RPR **115+**

Starts	1st	2nd	3rd	4th	Win & Pl
23	11	4	4	-	£575,315

	Date	Course	Race	Prize
	10/18	Chan	1m7f Gp1 gd-sft	£176,982
	8/18	Deau	1m7f Gp2 good	£65,575
	7/18	MsnL	1m7½f List good	£23,009
	3/18	Chan	1m7f List heavy	£23,009
	12/17	Toul	1m4f List v soft	£25,641
	6/17	Pari	1m4f List good	£25,641
	3/17	MsnL	1m7½f List good	£22,222
	10/16	Nant	1m4f List v soft	£22,059
	7/16	Vich	1m4f List good	£19,118
0	5/16	Deau	1m4½f 4yo Hcap stand	£9,559
	2/16	Porn	1m4f 4yo stand	£5,515

Prolific Listed winner in France who flourished when campaigned more ambitiously towards the end of last season, winning Group 1 and Group 2 races; possibly flattered by Prix Royal-Oak win in an incident-packed race but had also come second in the Prix du Cadran.

I Can Fly (left) finished second in the QEII and has plenty of promise

I Can Fly

4 b f Fastnet Rock - Madonna Dell'Orto (Montjeu)

Aidan O'Brien (Ir) Derrick Smith, Mrs John Magnier & Michael Tabor

PLACINGS: 13/3084151420- RPR **117**

Starts	1st	2nd	3rd	4th	Win & Pl
12	3	1	2	2	£416,233

9/18	Leop	1m Gp2 gd-fm	£104,425
8/18	Klny	1m List good	£26,106
9/17	Dund	7f Mdn 2yo stand	£7,897

Ran a huge race when second at 33-1 behind Roaring Lion in the QEII at Ascot last October; had shown glimpses of that ability before, notably when winning a Group 2 at Leopardstown; patent non-stayer when tried over 1m4f in the Oaks; acts on any going.

Idaho (Ire)

6 b h Galileo - Hveger (Danehill)

Aidan O'Brien (Ir) Michael Tabor, Derrick Smith & Mrs John Magnier

PLACINGS: 1U5/6136845/8145335- RPR **116+**

Starts	1st	2nd	3rd	4th	Win & Pl
23	4	2	5	3	£1,196,472

5/18	Ches	1m5½f Cls1 Gp3 good	£56,710
6/17	Asct	1m4f Cls1 Gp2 gd-fm	£127,598
8/16	York	1m4f Cls1 Gp2 3yo gd-fm	£90,736
10/15	Curr	1m Mdn 2yo gd-fm	£8,826

Has failed to win in 12 attempts at Group level but has won three lesser Group races, most recently last season's Ormonde Stakes at Chester over 1m5½f; has started to look short of pace over shorter but didn't quite get home in two runs over 2m.

Imaging

4 b c Oasis Dream - Mirror Lake (Dubai Destination)

Dermot Weld (Ir) K Abdullah

PLACINGS: 21/12152- RPR **106**

Starts	1st	2nd	3rd	4th	Win & Pl
7	3	3	-	-	£65,761

5/18	Naas	7f List 3yo gd-yld	£30,022
3/18	Cork	1m½f 3yo heavy	£9,267
10/17	Limk	7f Mdn 2yo heavy	£6,318

Particularly impressive early last season, winning twice either side of a good second to Gustav Klimt; may have needed first run back from a break and improved when second under a penalty in a Listed race at Leopardstown; capable of better back on softer ground.

Invincible Army (Ire)

4 b c Invincible Spirit - Rajeem (Diktat)

James Tate Saeed Manana

PLACINGS: 2142212/1299- RPR **114**

Starts	1st	2nd	3rd	4th	Win & Pl
11	3	5	-	1	£181,603

5/18	Asct	6f Cls1 Gp3 3yo soft	£45,368
9/17	Kemp	6f Cls1 Gp3 2yo std-slw	£25,520
6/17	NmkJ	6f Cls4 2yo gd-fm	£4,528

Closely matched with Commonwealth Cup one-two Eqtidaar and Sands Of Mali on impressive form early last season but finished only ninth when well fancied for the Royal Ascot Group 1; ninth again in a Group 3 at Newbury next time and missed the rest of the season.

Iridessa (Ire)

3 b f Ruler Of The World - Senta's Dream (Danehill)

Joseph O'Brien (Ir) Mrs CC Regalado-Gonzalez

PLACINGS: 1531- RPR **114**

Starts	1st	2nd	3rd	4th	Win & Pl
4	2	-	1	-	£304,452

10/18	NmkR	1m Cls1 Gp1 2yo gd-fm	£283,550
7/18	Klny	1m 2yo good	£10,903

Surprise winner of last season's Fillies' Mile, relishing return to the distance having twice been well held since her debut victory, although possibly flattered by coming from off the pace in a strongly run race; seems sure to stay at least 1m4f and prominent in the Oaks market.

Jackfinbar (Fr)

4 b c Whipper - Anna Simona (Slip Anchor)

Harry Dunlop Haven't A Pot Partnership

PLACINGS: 501/46211- RPR **107**

Starts	1st	2nd	3rd	4th	Win & Pl
8	3	1	-	1	£64,418

	9/18	Lonc	1m7f Gp3 3yo good	£35,398
91	7/18	Sand	1m6f Cls3 82-91 3yo Hcap gd-fm	£18,675
	12/17	Wolv	1m1½f Cls5 Auct 2yo stand	£3,881

Improved rapidly last season; defied 13lb rise for narrow defeat in France when beating subsequent Listed winner Ghostwatch at Sandown and comfortably followed up in a Group 3 at Longchamp; could progress into a top stayer.

Japan

3 b c Galileo - Shastye (Danehill)

Aidan O'Brien (Ir) Derrick Smith, Mrs John Magnier & Michael Tabor

PLACINGS: 711- RPR **109+**

Starts	1st	2nd	3rd	4th	Win & Pl
3	2	-	-	-	£66,973

9/18	Naas	1m Gp2 2yo good	£57,434
9/18	List	7f Mdn 2yo heavy	£9,540

Showed plenty of promise in three runs last

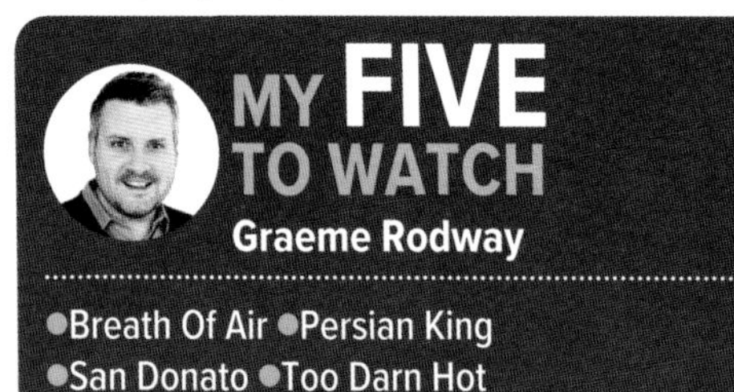

season, notably when getting up close home in the Beresford Stakes having been stuck in a pocket; looks a fine middle-distance prospect and interesting that Coolmore paid 3.4 million gns for his yearling brother last September.

Jash (Ire)

3 b c Kodiac - Miss Azeza (Dutch Art)

Simon Crisford — Hamdan Al Maktoum

PLACINGS: 112- — RPR **119**

Starts	1st	2nd	3rd	4th	Win & Pl
3	2	1	-	-	£69,087

9/18	Sals	6f Cls4 2yo gd-fm	£4,787
8/18	NmkJ	6f Cls4 2yo gd-fm	£5,175

Won first two starts in novices by wide margins and confirmed himself a smart colt when a half-length second behind Ten Sovereigns in the Middle Park; enhanced reputation in defeat that day (pulled well clear of the third) and could still be a Group 1 sprinter/miler.

Just Wonderful (USA)

3 b f Dansili - Wading (Montjeu)

Aidan O'Brien (Ir) — Michael Tabor, Derrick Smith & Mrs John Magnier

PLACINGS: 1031714- — RPR **110**

Starts	1st	2nd	3rd	4th	Win & Pl
7	3	-	1	1	£150,233

9/18	NmkR	7f Cls1 Gp2 2yo gd-fm	£56,710
9/18	Curr	1m Gp3 2yo gd-yld	£41,770
5/18	Curr	6f Mdn 2yo gd-fm	£9,540

Patchy record last season but proved a high-class filly on her day, notably when showing a smart turn of foot in the Rockfel Stakes to put herself in 1,000 Guineas contention; well below that level in four defeats, though forgiven Breeders' Cup effort having blown the start.

Kachy

6 b h Kyllachy - Dubai Bounty (Dubai Destination)

Tom Dascombe — David Lowe

PLACINGS: 00/450202/11213951-1 — RPR **117aw**

Starts	1st	2nd	3rd	4th	Win & Pl
24	8	4	1	1	£309,424

	2/19	Ling	6f Cls1 List stand	£25,520
	12/18	Wolv	6f Cls2 stand	£12,450
	5/18	Ches	5f Cls3 good	£11,828
	2/18	Ling	6f Cls1 List stand	£25,520
105	1/18	Ling	6f Cls2 86-105 Hcap stand	£11,828
105	5/16	Ches	5f Cls2 86-105 3yo Hcap good	£18,675
	7/15	Gdwd	5f Cls1 Gp3 2yo good	£42,533
	6/15	Ches	5f Cls4 2yo gd-fm	£6,469

Seems to have found his niche on the all-weather over the last two years but also produced some good form on turf last season; proved particularly well suited to Chester's tight turns when winning by nine lengths in May and then finished a neck third in the Temple Stakes.

Kadar (USA)

3 b/br c Scat Daddy - Kaloura (Sinndar)

Karl Burke — Phoenix Thoroughbred

PLACINGS: 1- — RPR **86+**

Starts	1st	2nd	3rd	4th	Win & Pl
1	1	-	-	-	£6,469

9/18	Hayd	1m Cls4 2yo gd-sft	£6,469

Very impressive when winning sole start at Haydock last season and immediately hailed a 2,000 Guineas horse by his trainer, though ultimately likely to prove best over at least 1m2f; twice a non-runner later in the season due to unsuitably quick ground.

Kew Gardens (Ire)

4 b c Galileo - Chelsea Rose (Desert King)

Aidan O'Brien (Ir) — Derrick Smith, Mrs John Magnier & Michael Tabor

PLACINGS: 71241/32911317- — RPR **121**

Starts	1st	2nd	3rd	4th	Win & Pl
13	5	2	2	1	£924,592

9/18	Donc	1m6½f Cls1 Gp1 3yo good	£421,355
7/18	Lonc	1m4f Gp1 3yo good	£303,398
6/18	Asct	1m6f Cls1 Gp2 3yo gd-fm	£113,420
10/17	NmkR	1m2f Cls1 List 2yo good	£22,684
8/17	Klny	1m Mdn 2yo soft	£7,897

Progressed throughout last season and showed stamina is his forte with comfortable St Leger victory, adding to earlier Queen's Vase success; form not quite as strong over 1m4f but still won an admittedly weak Grand Prix de Paris and was third in the Great Voltigeur.

Khaadem (Ire)

3 br c Dark Angel - White Daffodil (Footstepsinthesand)

Charlie Hills — Hamdan Al Maktoum

PLACINGS: 311- — RPR **103+**

Starts	1st	2nd	3rd	4th	Win & Pl
3	2	-	1	-	£17,149

9/18	Donc	6f Cls2 2yo gd-sft	£11,205
8/18	NmkJ	6f Cls4 2yo good	£5,175

Promising sprinter who won last two races in good fashion last season, most notably a novice stakes at Doncaster; was being aimed at the Middle Park Stakes until getting cast in his box a week beforehand; could be a Commonwealth Cup horse.

CHELMSFORDCITY
RACECOURSE

Quality Racing and Great Prize Money

ass 1 – 4 races made up 43% of the programme at Chelmsford City Racecourse in 8 with over £5million prize money – higher quality and more reward than any other AWT venue in the UK.

Principal CCR Races in 2019

lmsford City Racecourse stages top racing throughout the traditional Flat racing on. Feature races include:

11th April
he £60,000 Cardinal Conditions Stakes

1 mile race for 3 year olds
New for 2019
Final leg of European Road to Kentucky Derby qualifiers
Most qualifying points and possible gateway a slot in the 2019 Kentucky Derby line-up

2nd May
The £55,000 Chelmer Stakes (Listed)

- 6f race for 3 year old fillies
- Recent addition to Chelmsford City Racecourse's fixture list
- Will suit progressive fillies heading to Royal Ascot and beyond

19th June
The £75,000 Queen Charlotte Stakes (Listed)

7f Listed race for fillies & mares of 4 years and older
Centrepiece of the UK's richest ever evening ture, held at Chelmsford City Racecourse in 2018

31st August
The £100,000 Chelmsford City Cup

- 7f race for 3 year olds and older
- Highly competitive handicap race will be as fast and furious as ever

14th September

- 7f handicap with prize fund of £60,000
- ITV1 coverage

Kick On

3 b c Charm Spirit - Marika (Marju)

John Gosden — Qatar Racing

PLACINGS: 216- — RPR **107+**

Starts	1st	2nd	3rd	4th	Win & Pl
3	1	1	-	-	£11,127

	Date	Course	Race	Prize
	9/18	NmkR	1m Cls4 Mdn 2yo good	£6,469

Missed much of last season with a foot abscess but returned with a good maiden win at Newmarket and acquitted himself well when sixth in the Vertem Futurity Trophy at Doncaster, beaten around three lengths; sire's record suggests he could improve on quick ground.

King Ottokar (Fr)

3 b c Motivator - Treasure (Anabaa)

Charlie Fellowes — Mrs Susan Roy

PLACINGS: 19- — RPR **97**

Starts	1st	2nd	3rd	4th	Win & Pl
2	1	-	-	-	£5,530

	Date	Course	Race	Prize
	9/18	Newb	7f Cls4 2yo soft	£5,531

Highly regarded colt who made a winning debut at Newbury last season; only ninth when stepped up in class for the Vertem Futurity Trophy at Doncaster but hugely progressive young trainer reiterates he looks like the best horse he's had.

Knight To Behold (Ire)

4 b c Sea The Stars - Angel Of The Gwaun (Sadler's Wells)

Harry Dunlop — L Neil Jones

PLACINGS: 21/10018- — RPR **117**

Starts	1st	2nd	3rd	4th	Win & Pl
7	3	1	-	-	£245,247

	Date	Course	Race	Prize
	8/18	Deau	1m2f Gp2 3yo gd-sft	£201,770
	5/18	Ling	1m3½f Cls1 List 3yo gd-fm	£34,026
	10/17	NmkR	1m Cls4 2yo gd-fm	£6,469

Inconsistent last season but proved very smart when allowed to dominate from the front, beating Kew Gardens in the Lingfield Derby Trial and adding a Group 2 at Deauville by four lengths; hadn't been felt to stay 1m4f when disappointing in the Irish Derby.

La Pelosa (Ire)

3 b f Dandy Man - Lauren's Girl (Bushranger)

Charlie Appleby — Godolphin

PLACINGS: 1253210- — RPR **106**

Starts	1st	2nd	3rd	4th	Win & Pl
7	2	2	1	-	£129,537

	Date	Course	Race	Prize
	9/18	Wood	1m Gd1 2yo firm	£88,235
	5/18	Kemp	6f Cls4 2yo std-slw	£5,822

Twice second to Main Edition last season, getting closest when beaten a neck in the Albany Stakes at Royal Ascot; returned to form when back on a similarly fast surface to win a Grade I in Canada but disappointed at the Breeders' Cup next time.

Lady Kaya (Ire)

3 b f Dandy Man - Kayak (Singspiel)

Sheila Lavery (Ir) — Joanne Lavery

PLACINGS: 31426- — RPR **107**

Starts	1st	2nd	3rd	4th	Win & Pl
5	1	1	1	1	£84,817

	Date	Course	Race	Prize
	8/18	Curr	7f 2yo good	£16,327

Impressive ten-length winner of a Curragh maiden last season and proved herself a high-class filly when second in the Moyglare Stud Stakes; just outstayed that day and dropped to 6f next time when a below-par sixth in the Cheveley Park.

Lah Ti Dar

4 b f Dubawi - Dar Re Mi (Singspiel)

John Gosden — Lord Lloyd-Webber

PLACINGS: 11123- — RPR **117+**

Starts	1st	2nd	3rd	4th	Win & Pl
5	3	1	1	-	£297,887

	Date	Course	Race	Prize
	8/18	York	1m4f Cls1 List gd-fm	£39,697
	5/18	NmkR	1m2f Cls1 List 3yo gd-fm	£28,355
	4/18	Newb	1m2f Cls4 Mdn 3yo gd-sft	£5,531

Missed much of last season due to illness having been a leading fancy for the Oaks but returned with a stunning ten-length win in a Listed race at York in August; ran two fair races in defeat subsequently, particularly when second in the St Leger.

Laraaib (Ire)

5 b h Pivotal - Sahool (Unfuwain)

Owen Burrows — Hamdan Al Maktoum

PLACINGS: 1113/2961- — RPR **114**

Starts	1st	2nd	3rd	4th	Win & Pl
8	4	1	1	-	£79,199

	Date	Course	Race	Prize
	10/18	Asct	1m4f Cls1 Gp3 soft	£34,026
95	7/17	Asct	1m2f Cls3 83-97 Hcap good	£9,704
83	5/17	Hayd	1m2f Cls3 83-95 3yo Hcap gd-fm	£7,439
	5/17	Chep	1m2f Cls5 Mdn gd-fm	£4,852

Initially disappointing when stepped up to Group company after winning first three starts in 2017; finally delivered on early promise when winning the Cumberland Lodge Stakes at Ascot in October, proving stamina for 1m4f and effectiveness on all types of ground.

Latrobe (Ire)

4 br c Camelot - Question Times (Shamardal)

Joseph O'Brien (Ir) — NC Williams & Mr & Mrs LJ Williams

PLACINGS: 2/22117220- — RPR **116**

Starts	1st	2nd	3rd	4th	Win & Pl
9	2	5	-	-	£1,072,377

	Date	Course	Race	Prize
	6/18	Curr	1m4f Gp1 3yo gd-fm	£756,637
	6/18	Curr	1m4f Mdn gd-fm	£7,087

Surprise winner of last season's Irish Derby, taking advantage of Saxon Warrior's below-par run; no real threat in two more runs at the top level in Europe, though still finished second behind Flag Of Honour in the Irish St Leger and went close in a 1m2f Group 1 in Australia.

Laurens (Fr)

4 b f Siyouni - Recambe (Cape Cross)

Karl Burke — John Dance

PLACINGS: 1211/2116118- — RPR **117**

Starts	1st	2nd	3rd	4th	Win & Pl
11	7	2	-	-	£1,466,717

Date	Course	Race	Prize
10/18	NmkR	1m Cls1 Gp1 good	£151,345
9/18	Leop	1m Gp1 gd-fm	£182,743
6/18	Chan	1m2½f Gp1 3yo gd-sft	£505,664
5/18	Lonc	1m2f Gp1 3yo gd-sft	£126,416
10/17	NmkR	1m Cls1 Gp1 2yo good	£321,829
9/17	Donc	1m Cls1 Gp2 2yo gd-sft	£39,697
7/17	Donc	7f Cls5 Mdn 2yo good	£2,911

Five-time Group 1 winner who proved in her element when dropped back to a mile towards the end of last season, winning the Matron and Sun Chariot Stakes; had also won twice at the top level in France up to 1m2½f but failed to stay 1m4f in the Yorkshire Oaks.

Le Brivido (Fr)

5 b h Siyouni - La Bugatty (Dr Fong)

Aidan O'Brien (Ir) — Prince Faisal Bin Khaled & Mrs Magnier

PLACINGS: 1/121/6- — RPR **107**

Starts	1st	2nd	3rd	4th	Win & Pl
5	3	1	-	-	£193,066

Date	Course	Race	Prize
6/17	Asct	7f Cls1 Gp3 3yo gd-fm	£51,039
4/17	Chan	6f 3yo good	£14,060
11/16	Chan	6½f 2yo stand	£9,926

Looked to have a huge future when winning the Jersey Stakes in 2017 after a close second in the Poule d'Essai des Poulains but has run only once since when well beaten in last season's Abernant Stakes; has since left Andre Fabre.

Librisa Breeze

7 gr g Mount Nelson - Bruxcalina (Linamix)

Dean Ivory — Tony Bloom

PLACINGS: /121416/4921/994808- — RPR **109**

Starts	1st	2nd	3rd	4th	Win & Pl
22	6	3	-	3	£694,093

OR	Date	Course	Race	Prize
	10/17	Asct	6f Cls1 Gp1 soft	£340,260
108	10/16	Asct	7f Cls2 98-109 Hcap soft	£112,050
100	7/16	Asct	7f Cls2 87-109 Hcap gd-fm	£93,375
92	4/16	Wolv	1m½f Cls3 87-95 Hcap stand	£7,246
85	9/15	Kemp	1m Cls4 75-85 Hcap std-slw	£4,690
	3/15	Ling	1m2f Cls5 Mdn 3yo stand	£3,235

Bitterly disappointing last season (only decent effort when fourth in the Prix Maurice de Gheest) but had been a top-class performer at 6f/7f before that; won the Group 1 Champions Sprint at Ascot in 2017 for a third victory at that track after two big 7f handicaps in 2016.

Lily's Candle (Fr)

3 gr f Style Vendome - Golden Lily (Dolphin Street)

Freddy Head (Fr) — Martin S Schwartz Racing

PLACINGS: 611410- — RPR **109**

Starts	1st	2nd	3rd	4th	Win & Pl
6	3	-	-	1	£243,858

Date	Course	Race	Prize
10/18	Lonc	1m Gp1 2yo good	£202,265
8/18	Vich	7f List 2yo soft	£26,549
7/18	Mars	1m 2yo good	£7,965

Bought for €390,000 before surprise win in last season's Prix Marcel Boussac; perhaps favoured by being delivered last that day as leaders fell in a heap but had still won twice previously, including a Listed race at Vichy; well beaten at the Breeders' Cup.

Limato (Ire)

7 b g Tagula - Come April (Singspiel)

Henry Candy — Paul G Jacobs

PLACINGS: 41216/03241/0001119- — RPR **118**

Starts	1st	2nd	3rd	4th	Win & Pl
26	12	5	1	2	£1,328,317

Date	Course	Race	Prize
10/18	NmkR	7f Cls1 Gp2 gd-fm	£68,052
9/18	York	6f Cls1 List gd-sft	£28,355
8/18	NmkJ	6f Cls1 List gd-fm	£22,684
10/17	NmkR	7f Cls1 Gp2 good	£68,052
10/16	Chan	7f Gp1 good	£126,044
7/16	NmkJ	6f Cls1 Gp1 gd-fm	£302,690
9/15	Donc	7f Cls1 Gp2 good	£56,710
4/15	Asct	6f Cls1 Gp3 3yo gd-fm	£45,368
10/14	Rdcr	6f Cls1 List 2yo good	£117,220
7/14	Newb	6f Cls1 List 2yo gd-fm	£14,461
6/14	Kemp	6f Cls3 2yo stand	£6,225
6/14	Kemp	6f Cls5 Mdn 2yo stand	£2,588

Dual Group 1 winner in 2016 when landing the July Cup and Prix de la Foret; not far off that level last season, winning three times including a second successive Challenge Stakes at Newmarket, but no better than ninth in four runs in Group 1 races.

Line Of Duty (Ire)

3 ch c Galileo - Jacqueline Quest (Rock Of Gibraltar)

Charlie Appleby — Godolphin

PLACINGS: 22111- — RPR **114+**

Starts	1st	2nd	3rd	4th	Win & Pl
5	3	2	-	-	£462,408

Date	Course	Race	Prize
11/18	Chur	1m Gd1 2yo yield	£407,407
10/18	Chan	1m1f Gp3 2yo gd-sft	£35,398
9/18	Gdwd	1m Cls2 Mdn 2yo good	£15,753

Went from strength to strength in the second half of last season, culminating in a tense Breeders' Cup victory when surviving a stewards' enquiry; completed a hat-trick that day after taking a Goodwood maiden and a Chantilly Group 3; should get middle distances.

MY FIVE TO WATCH

Justin O'Hanlon

• Gustavus Weston • Mount Everest • Tankerville • Trethias • Who's Steph

Lord Glitters (Fr)

6 gr g Whipper - Lady Glitters (Homme De Loi)

David O'Meara — Geoff & Sandra Turnbull

PLACINGS: 11254/11212/2223166- — RPR **118**

Starts		1st	2nd	3rd	4th	Win & Pl
19		6	8	1	1	£629,564
	8/18	York	1m1f Cls1 Gp3 gd-fm			£56,710
102	10/17	Asct	1m Cls2 98-110 Hcap soft			£155,625
	5/17	StCl	1m soft			£11,966
	4/17	Chan	1m stand			£11,966
	6/16	Le L	1m2f 3yo heavy			£9,926
	5/16	Chat	1m2f 3yo soft			£5,882

Remarkably consistent since moving from France and was out of the first three for the first time in nine runs in Britain when not beaten far into sixth in the QEII (also sixth in Canada last season); came closest to a Group 1 win when second in the Queen Anne.

Low Sun

6 b g Champs Elysees - Winter Solstice (Unfuwain)

Willie Mullins (Ir) — Mrs S Ricci

PLACINGS: 2531/161- — RPR **108**

Starts		1st	2nd	3rd	4th	Win & Pl
7		3	1	1	-	£340,121
97	10/18	NmkR	2m2f Cls2 86-107 Hcap gd-fm			£307,250
89	6/18	Curr	2m 73-97 Hcap gd-fm			£16,327
	9/16	StCl	1m2½f 3yo gd-sft			£9,191

Smart dual-purpose performer who relished a stiff test of stamina when winning last season's Cesarewitch; had also won over 2m at the Curragh and was unsuited by drop to 1m4f when beaten in between; appreciates quick ground but has won on soft over hurdles.

Loxley (Ire)

4 b c New Approach - Lady Marian (Nayef)

Charlie Appleby — Godolphin

PLACINGS: 17/121102- — RPR **115**

Starts		1st	2nd	3rd	4th	Win & Pl
8		4	2	-	-	£206,428
	8/18	Deau	1m4½f Gp2 soft			£100,885
	8/18	Deau	1m2f List 3yo soft			£24,336
	6/18	NmkJ	1m2f Cls4 3yo gd-fm			£5,822
	10/17	Gdwd	1m1f Cls4 2yo soft			£4,197

Progressive over middle distances last season; peaked with a 1m4½f Group 2 win on soft ground in France and also effective on good to firm; didn't get home in the St Leger but did much better again back at 1m2f when narrowly beaten in the Prix Dollar.

Mabs Cross

5 b m Dutch Art - Miss Meggy (Pivotal)

Michael Dods — David W Armstrong

PLACINGS: 831111/2143321- — RPR **114**

Starts		1st	2nd	3rd	4th	Win & Pl
13		6	2	3	1	£399,714
	10/18	Lonc	5f Gp1 good			£176,982
	5/18	NmkR	5f Cls1 Gp3 good			£34,026
	10/17	Muss	5f Cls1 List gd-sft			£17,244
82	6/17	Hayd	5f Cls4 69-87 Hcap gd-fm			£6,469
74	6/17	Wind	5f Cls4 74-87 3yo Hcap gd-fm			£5,013
	5/17	Newc	5f Cls5 Mdn 3yo stand			£3,558

Developed into a top-class sprinter last season, signing off with a first Group 1 win in the Prix de l'Abbaye having come desperately close when a nose second in the Nunthorpe Stakes; has most of her form on quick ground but won a Listed race on good to soft in 2017.

Madhmoon (Ire)

3 b c Dawn Approach - Aaraas (Haafhd)

Kevin Prendergast (Ir) — Hamdan Al Maktoum

PLACINGS: 11- — RPR **114+**

Starts		1st	2nd	3rd	4th	Win & Pl
2		2	-	-	-	£87,858
	9/18	Leop	1m Gp2 2yo gd-fm			£78,319
	8/18	Leop	1m Mdn 2yo good			£9,540

Won both starts last season, including a really strong Group 2 at Leopardstown in commanding fashion; looks a genuine Classic contender on that evidence, though may prove more of a Guineas than Derby horse (little form over 1m4f in pedigree).

Lord Glitters (grey) grinds it out to win the Group 3 Strensall Stakes at York last summer

Magic Circle (Ire)

7 b g Makfi - Minkova (Sadler's Wells)

Ian Williams — Dr Marwan Koukash

PLACINGS: 11/20143/557150/110- **RPR 118**

Starts	1st	2nd	3rd	4th	Win & Pl
22	8	1	1	2	£230,905

	5/18	Sand	2m Cls1 Gp3 good	£39,697
101	5/18	Ches	2m2½f Cls2 97-108 Hcap good	£92,385
97	8/17	York	2m½f Cls2 91-105 Hcap gd-sft	£43,575
90	7/16	York	2m½f Cls3 83-95 Hcap good	£9,704
78	10/15	Donc	1m6½f Cls3 76-96 Hcap gd-sft	£7,439
72	10/15	Hayd	2m Cls4 65-80 Hcap gd-sft	£4,690
66	7/15	NmkJ	1m5f Cls4 66-80 3yo Hcap soft	£6,469
60	5/15	Donc	1m4f Cls5 60-70 3yo Hcap soft	£3,235

Progressive early last season, looking a top-class stayer when running away with the Chester Cup and the Henry II Stakes at Sandown; laid out for the Melbourne Cup (sent off favourite) but well beaten after breaking a blood vessel.

Magic Wand (Ire)

4 b f Galileo - Prudenzia (Dansili)

Aidan O'Brien (Ir) — Michael Tabor, Derrick Smith, Mrs John Magnier & MJ Jooste

PLACINGS: 7/314155224-2 **RPR 114**

Starts	1st	2nd	3rd	4th	Win & Pl
11	2	3	1	2	£1,124,601

	6/18	Asct	1m4f Cls1 Gp2 3yo gd-fm	£113,420
	5/18	Ches	1m3½f Cls1 List 3yo good	£42,533

Runaway winner of last season's Ribblesdale Stakes at Royal Ascot and has since finished second three times at Group 1 level, most notably when beaten a head in the Prix Vermeille; equally effective at 1m2f; has twice disappointed on soft ground or worse.

Magical (Ire)

4 b f Galileo - Halfway To Heaven (Pivotal)

Aidan O'Brien (Ir) — Derrick Smith, Mrs John Magnier & Michael Tabor

PLACINGS: 211244/414012- **RPR 121**

Starts	1st	2nd	3rd	4th	Win & Pl
12	4	3	-	4	£1,094,909

	10/18	Asct	1m4f Cls1 Gp1 soft	£340,260
	7/18	Curr	1m1f Gp2 gd-fm	£60,044
	8/17	Curr	7f Gp2 2yo soft	£57,991
	8/17	Cork	1m Mdn 2yo gd-yld	£8,687

Had tended to come up short at the top level until improving massively when stepped up in trip last autumn; won a 1m4f Group 1 at Ascot on Champions Day and pushed Enable to three-quarters of a length in the Breeders' Cup Turf.

Magna Grecia (Ire)

3 b c Invincible Spirit - Cabaret (Galileo)

Aidan O'Brien (Ir) — D Smith, Mrs J Magnier, M Tabor & Flaxman Stable

PLACINGS: 121- **RPR 114**

Starts	1st	2nd	3rd	4th	Win & Pl
3	2	1	-	-	£153,439

	10/18	Donc	1m Cls1 Gp1 2yo gd-sft	£131,000
	9/18	Naas	7f Mdn 2yo good	£9,540

Soon developed into a top juvenile having had all three runs in the space of just four weeks last autumn; narrow winner of the Vertem Futurity Trophy after a close second to Persian King in the Autumn Stakes; not certain to stay beyond 1m2f (wasn't even entered in the Derby).

Maid Up

4 gr f Mastercraftsman - Complexion (Hurricane Run)

Andrew Balding — Brightwalton Bloodstock

PLACINGS: 80/33111219- **RPR 107**

Starts	1st	2nd	3rd	4th	Win & Pl
10	4	1	2	-	£131,970

	8/18	Gdwd	1m6f Cls1 Gp3 3yo good	£42,533
82	7/18	Asct	1m4f Cls3 78-90 Hcap gd-fm	£12,938
76	6/18	Gdwd	1m4f Cls4 65-76 3yo Hcap gd-fm	£6,728
69	6/18	Donc	1m2f Cls5 61-70 3yo Hcap gd-fm	£3,752

Hugely progressive filly last season; supplemented for the St Leger having won four of her previous five races, with sole defeat by a short head to Pilaster in a 1m6f Group 2 at Doncaster; only ninth at Doncaster but could still do well again in good staying races.

Main Edition (Ire)

3 b f Zoffany - Maine Lobster (Woodman)

Mark Johnston — Saif Ali

PLACINGS: 1117153- RPR **107**

Starts	1st	2nd	3rd	4th	Win & Pl
7	4	-	1	-	£107,604

8/18	NmkJ	7f Cls1 Gp3 2yo gd-sft	£28,355
6/18	Asct	6f Cls1 Gp3 2yo gd-fm	£51,039
6/18	Gdwd	6f Cls5 2yo soft	£4,528
5/18	Wind	6f Cls4 2yo gd-fm	£6,728

Won four of her first five races last season, including the Albany Stakes at Royal Ascot and the Sweet Solera at Newmarket when stepped up to 7f for the first time; went too hard in front in the Moyglare and may have had enough for the year when third in the Rockfel.

Manuela De Vega (Ire)

3 b f Lope De Vega - Roscoff (Daylami)

Ralph Beckett — Waverley Racing

PLACINGS: 11- RPR **96+**

Starts	1st	2nd	3rd	4th	Win & Pl
2	2	-	-	-	£38,246

10/18	Pont	1m Cls1 List 2yo gd-sft	£22,684
9/18	Sals	7f Cls2 Mdn 2yo gd-fm	£15,563

Unbeaten in two races last season and stepped up to Listed level impressively at Pontefract despite still looking green; full sister to dual 1m4f Listed winner Isabel De Urbina so should relish going up in trip and could even be an Oaks filly.

Marie's Diamond (Ire)

3 br c Footstepsinthesand - Sindiyma (Kalanisi)

Mark Johnston — Middleham Park Racing LXXXVI

PLACINGS: 1361212940- RPR **107**

Starts	1st	2nd	3rd	4th	Win & Pl
10	3	2	1	1	£127,164

7/18	Curr	6½f Gp3 2yo good	£33,938
6/18	Ches	6f Cls4 Auct 2yo gd-fm	£5,852
4/18	Leic	5f Cls5 2yo heavy	£4,787

Tough colt who ran well in many top juvenile races at around 6f last season; won the Anglesey Stakes at the Curragh in between two runner-up finishes at Group 2 level and bounced back with a good fourth in the Middle Park; flopped over a mile at the Breeders' Cup.

Marmelo

6 b h Duke Of Marmalade - Capriolla (In The Wings)

Hughie Morrison — The Fairy Story Partnership & Aziz Kheir

PLACINGS: 621232/152169/21122- RPR **115**

Starts	1st	2nd	3rd	4th	Win & Pl
17	5	7	1	-	£1,002,313

7/18	Lonc	1m6f Gp2 good	£65,575
6/18	York	1m6f Cls1 List gd-fm	£28,355
8/17	Deau	1m7f Gp2 good	£63,333
4/17	Chan	1m7f Gp3 good	£34,188
7/16	Donc	1m4f Cls5 Mdn soft	£3,881

High-class stayer who ran a huge race to finish second in last year's Melbourne Cup; hadn't finished out of the first two in four runs in Europe, winning a Group 2 at Longchamp and a Listed race at York; has tried 2m only in Australia and trainer feels he has the speed for 1m4f.

Masar (Ire)

4 ch c New Approach - Khawlah (Cape Cross)

Charlie Appleby — Godolphin

PLACINGS: 13136/0131- RPR **122**

Starts	1st	2nd	3rd	4th	Win & Pl
9	4	-	3	-	£1,021,394

6/18	Epsm	1m4f Cls1 Gp1 3yo good	£850,650
4/18	NmkR	1m Cls1 Gp3 3yo good	£34,026
9/17	Sand	7f Cls1 Gp3 2yo good	£25,520
5/17	Gdwd	6f Cls4 2yo good	£6,469

Became Godolphin's first Derby winner with an impressive victory at Epsom, relishing step up to 1m4f as main rivals appeared weak stayers; had also shown plenty of speed to win the Craven and finish third in the 2,000 Guineas; missed rest of the season through injury.

Matematica (Ger)

3 b f Rock Of Gibraltar - Mathematicienne (Galileo)

Carlos Laffon-Parias (Fr) — Wertheimer & Frere

PLACINGS: 22- RPR **109**

Starts	1st	2nd	3rd	4th	Win & Pl
2	-	2	-	-	£85,699

Defied lack of experience to come within a short neck of winning last season's Prix Marcel Boussac when just pipped close home by Lily's Candle; had also been beaten narrowly on sole previous start at Longchamp; should be a smart middle-distance filly.

Mekong

4 b c Frankel - Ship's Biscuit (Tiger Hill)

Sir Michael Stoute — Philip Newton

PLACINGS: 64/1721412- RPR **108**

Starts	1st	2nd	3rd	4th	Win & Pl
9	3	2	-	2	£122,844

94	9/18	Hayd	1m6f Cls2 85-96 3yo Hcap heavy	£62,250
88	8/18	Chmt	1m6f Cls2 80-95 3yo Hcap stand	£31,125
	4/18	Leic	1m2f Cls5 3yo heavy	£4,528

Smart and progressive stayer last season; close fourth when favourite for the Melrose at York

and stepped up on that with a seven-length handicap win at Haydock and a half-length Listed second at Ascot; both turf wins on heavy ground but effective on much quicker.

Mildenberger

4 b c Teofilo - Belle Josephine (Dubawi)

Mark Johnston — Sheikh Hamdan Bin Mohammed Al Maktoum

PLACINGS: 11313/12- RPR **108**

Starts	1st	2nd	3rd	4th	Win & Pl
7	4	1	2	-	£118,449

4/18	NmkR	1m1f Cls1 List 3yo gd-sft	£22,684
8/17	Sals	1m Cls1 List 2yo good	£17,013
7/17	Newb	7f Cls4 2yo gd-sft	£6,469
7/17	Hayd	7f Cls4 2yo gd-fm	£4,528

Missed much of last season after a couple of setbacks but had already appeared to improve on solid juvenile form when stepping up in trip; won the Feilden Stakes at Newmarket and bumped into a superstar when second to Roaring Lion in the Dante.

Mirage Dancer

5 b h Frankel - Heat Haze (Green Desert)

Sir Michael Stoute — K Abdullah

PLACINGS: 1/4334/2152120- RPR **119**

Starts	1st	2nd	3rd	4th	Win & Pl
12	3	3	2	2	£169,239

8/18	Gdwd	1m4f Cls1 Gp3 gd-fm	£56,710
5/18	Gdwd	1m4f Cls1 List good	£28,355
10/16	Donc	7f Cls5 Mdn 2yo good	£4,528

One-time Derby hope who has taken much

Mirage Dancer (left) heads to Group 3 victory at Goodwood and is likely to do well over middle distances again this season

longer than expected to make the leap to Group 1 level but continued to get there steadily last season; won Group 3 and Listed races at Goodwood and came within a short head of defying a penalty in the St Simon Stakes.

Mitchum Swagger

7 b g Paco Boy - Dont Dili Dali (Dansili)

Ralph Beckett — The Anagram Partnership

PLACINGS: 932205/574150/36812- RPR **113**

Starts	1st	2nd	3rd	4th	Win & Pl
21	4	5	2	1	£114,169

	11/18	NmkR	1m Cls1 List soft	£20,983
	8/17	Thsk	7f Cls3 gd-sft	£9,057
87	9/15	Hayd	1m Cls3 77-89 Hcap soft	£8,086
	5/15	Newb	7f Cls4 Mdn 3yo good	£6,469

Missed much of last season having got injured when finishing third in the Lincoln; reportedly needed first two runs back to reach full fitness and proved much better when running away with a Listed race at Newmarket next time; seems best on soft ground.

Mohaather

3 b c Showcasing - Roodeye (Inchinor)

Marcus Tregoning — Hamdan Al Maktoum

PLACINGS: 211- RPR **107+**

Starts	1st	2nd	3rd	4th	Win & Pl
3	2	1	-	-	£28,490

10/18	Newb	7f Cls1 Gp3 2yo gd-sft	£22,684
10/18	Nott	6f Cls5 2yo good	£3,881

Surprise 33-1 winner of last season's Horris Hill Stakes at Newbury; form questionable as none of the first six had run in a Class 1 race but runner-up did pull 5l clear of the rest; out of the granddam of Queen Anne winner Accidental Agent and should also be a miler.

Mohawk (Ire)

3 b c Galileo - Empowering (Encosta De Lago)

Aidan O'Brien (Ir) — Derrick Smith, Mrs John Magnier & Michael Tabor

PLACINGS: 513417- RPR **112**

Starts	1st	2nd	3rd	4th	Win & Pl
6	2	-	1	1	£107,835

9/18	NmkR	1m Cls1 Gp2 2yo gd-fm	£75,850
6/18	Cork	7f Mdn 2yo gd-fm	£8,995

Won last season's Royal Lodge Stakes, relishing only chance to race over a mile, but probably made the most of a weak race for the grade and was well beaten on all three other runs at Pattern level; could do better when stepped up to middle distances.

Morando (Fr)

6 gr g Kendargent - Moranda (Indian Rocket)

Andrew Balding — King Power Racing

PLACINGS: 41117/1432/30521- RPR **116**

Starts	1st	2nd	3rd	4th	Win & Pl
14	5	2	2	2	£120,776

	10/18	Newb	1m4f Cls1 Gp3 gd-sft	£23,463
	7/17	Wind	1m Cls1 List gd-sft	£20,983
96	9/16	Ayr	1m Cls2 87-101 Hcap gd-sft	£15,563
86	6/16	Ches	7½f Cls3 62-86 3yo Hcap good	£12,450
	5/16	Wind	1m Cls5 Mdn 3-4yo good	£2,911

Twice disappointing on quick ground last summer but bounced back on softer in the autumn, going close in a Listed race at Ayr before staying on well on first run over 1m4f to force a dead-heat with Young Rascal in a Group 3 at Newbury; could have more to offer over that trip.

Mot Juste (USA)

3 b f Distorted Humor - Time On (Sadler's Wells)

Roger Varian — R Barnett

PLACINGS: 6411- RPR **104**

Starts	1st	2nd	3rd	4th	Win & Pl
4	2	-	-	1	£38,502

10/18	NmkR	7f Cls1 Gp3 2yo gd-fm	£34,026
9/18	Bevl	7½f Cls5 2yo good	£4,140

Followed up impressive seven-length Beverley novice win with a narrow success in the Oh So Sharp Stakes at Newmarket, albeit when getting the run of the race; should have no problem getting a mile and beyond (out of a Sadler's Wells mare who won a 1m4f Group 2).

Mount Everest (Ire)

3 b c Galileo - Six Perfections (Celtic Swing)

Aidan O'Brien (Ir) — Flaxman Stables, Mrs Magnier, M Tabor & D Smith

PLACINGS: 6212- RPR **109**

Starts	1st	2nd	3rd	4th	Win & Pl
4	1	2	-	-	£30,824

8/18	Curr	1m Mdn 2yo good	£9,540

Progressed nicely last season having twice been beaten in maidens, including at 4-9 on second occasion; off the mark at the Curragh next time and took a big step forward when a short-head second in the Beresford Stakes, perhaps idling in front; should thrive over middle distances.

Mr Lupton (Ire)

6 ch g Elnadim - Chiloe Wigeon (Docksider)

Richard Fahey — ND Kershaw & Partner

PLACINGS: 8925648/26187149712- RPR **115**

Starts	1st	2nd	3rd	4th	Win & Pl
38	7	7	5	2	£505,281

	9/18	Newb	5f Cls1 Gp3 soft	£34,026
	7/18	York	5f Cls1 List gd-fm	£28,355
103	5/18	York	5f Cls2 82-107 Hcap good	£31,125
107	5/17	NmkR	6f Cls2 93-108 Hcap gd-fm	£31,125
102	6/16	York	6f Cls2 89-102 3yo Hcap gd-sft	£62,250
	9/15	Donc	6½f Cls2 2yo good	£147,540
	6/15	Hayd	5f Cls5 Mdn 2yo gd-fm	£2,911

Smart sprinter who won three times last season, taking form to a new level with first wins at Group 3 and Listed level; gained all those victories over 5f but had previously produced best form in winning big-field 6f handicaps.

Mustashry

6 b/br g Tamayuz - Safwa (Green Desert)

Sir Michael Stoute — Hamdan Al Maktoum

PLACINGS: 4/210124/0117/12110- RPR **117**

Starts	1st	2nd	3rd	4th	Win & Pl
16	7	3	-	2	£296,241

	9/18	NmkR	1m Cls1 Gp2 gd-fm	£56,710
	9/18	Donc	7f Cls1 Gp2 good	£61,417
	7/18	Sand	1m2f Cls1 List gd-fm	£22,684
	8/17	York	1m1f Cls1 Gp3 good	£51,039
105	8/17	Chmt	1m Cls2 93-105 Hcap stand	£32,345
95	7/16	Asct	1m Cls2 80-98 3yo Hcap gd-fm	£28,013
	5/16	Thsk	1m Cls5 Mdn good	£3,235

Proved himself a high-class and versatile horse last season; won the Group 2 Joel Stakes over a mile at Newmarket, defying a penalty for winning over 7f at the same level in the Park Stakes having earlier won a 1m2f Listed race; needs good ground or quicker.

Natalie's Joy

3 b f Lope De Vega - Semaphore (Zamindar)

Mark Johnston — Merriebelle Stable & S Chappell

PLACINGS: 171- RPR **99**

Starts	1st	2nd	3rd	4th	Win & Pl
3	2	-	-	-	£21,188

7/18	Newb	6f Cls1 List 2yo gd-fm	£14,461
5/18	Gdwd	6f Cls4 Mdn 2yo good	£6,728

Hugely impressive winner of two of her three starts last season; disappointing seventh when favourite for the Chesham Stakes in between but had Gimcrack winner Emaraaty Ana behind her when back on track in a Listed race at Newbury; likely to go for a Guineas trial.

Norway (Ire)

3 ch c Galileo - Love Me True (Kingmambo)

Aidan O'Brien (Ir) — Derrick Smith, Mrs John Magnier & Michael Tabor

PLACINGS: 53114- RPR **105**

Starts	1st	2nd	3rd	4th	Win & Pl
5	2	-	1	1	£43,550

10/18	NmkR	1m2f Cls1 List 2yo gd-fm	£22,684
10/18	Naas	1m Mdn 2yo good	£6,542

Proved himself a strong and high-class stayer when easily winning the Zetland Stakes last season and could follow a similar path as 2017 winner Kew Gardens; held up that day and

below his best when switched to front-running tactics in the Criterium de Saint-Cloud.

Oasis Charm

5 b g Oasis Dream - Albaraka (Selkirk)

Charlie Appleby — Godolphin

PLACINGS: 21602/11-15 — RPR **110**

Starts	1st	2nd	3rd	4th	Win & Pl
9	4	2	-	-	£146,314

104	1/19	Meyd	1m2f 97-111 Hcap good	£82,677
96	5/18	NmkR	1m1f Cls2 85-109 Hcap good	£31,125
91	4/18	Chmt	1m2f Cls3 78-96 Hcap stand	£9,704
	4/17	Leic	1m2f Cls5 Mdn gd-fm	£3,881

Looked a progressive handicapper early last season when winning at Chelmsford and Newmarket but missed most of the year; still seemed to have more to offer when enjoying a winning campaign in Meydan this winter.

Old Glory (Ire)

3 b c Frankel - Belesta (Xaar)

Aidan O'Brien (Ir) — Zayat Stables, Mrs Magnier, M Tabor & D Smith

PLACINGS: 123- — RPR **102**

Starts	1st	2nd	3rd	4th	Win & Pl
3	1	1	1	-	£23,861

	9/18	Naas	7f Mdn 2yo good	£8,995

Cost €1.6 million and looked a high-class prospect when making a winning debut at Naas; beaten at odds-on in a Listed race before also coming up just short in a Group 3 but may have found 7f too sharp both times and should do better over middle distances.

Old Persian

4 b c Dubawi - Indian Petal (Singspiel)

Charlie Appleby — Godolphin

PLACINGS: 3117/1211615- — RPR **118**

Starts	1st	2nd	3rd	4th	Win & Pl
11	6	1	1	-	£316,278

	8/18	York	1m4f Cls1 Gp2 3yo gd-fm	£96,407
	6/18	Asct	1m4f Cls1 Gp2 3yo gd-fm	£127,598
	5/18	NmkR	1m2f Cls1 List 3yo gd-fm	£22,684
94	4/18	NmkR	1m2f Cls3 79-94 3yo Hcap good	£12,938
	10/17	NmkR	1m Cls4 2yo good	£4,528
	9/17	Chmt	1m Cls4 2yo stand	£7,439

Twice disappointed in the Classics last season (sixth in the Irish Derby and fifth in the St Leger) but Great Voltigeur win in between couldn't have worked out better with Cross Counter and Kew Gardens behind; also carried a penalty that day for King Edward VII Stakes win.

Olmedo (Fr)

4 b c Declaration Of War - Super Pie (Pivotal)

Jean-Claude Rouget (Fr) — Ecurie Antonio Caro & Gerard Augustin-Normand

PLACINGS: 122/2107- — RPR **113+**

Starts	1st	2nd	3rd	4th	Win & Pl
7	2	3	-	-	£411,155

	5/18	Lonc	1m Gp1 3yo good	£303,398
	8/17	Deau	7½f 2yo good	£11,538

Pounced late to win last season's Poule d'Essai des Poulains but looked a non-stayer in the Prix du Jockey Club; suffered a serious injury in the Prix Jean Prat next time but on the comeback trail this spring and being aimed at early return.

Oasis Charm (right) scores at Newmarket last May and is open to further improvement

One Master

5 b m Fastnet Rock - Enticing (Pivotal)

William Haggas — Lael Stable

PLACINGS: 311/4341158- — RPR **112**

Starts	1st	2nd	3rd	4th	Win & Pl
10	4	-	2	2	£294,609

	Date	Course	Race	Prize
	10/18	Lonc	7f Gp1 good	£176,982
	8/18	Tipp	7½f Gp3 gd-yld	£33,938
	10/17	Asct	7f Cls1 List gd-sft	£22,684
	9/17	Yarm	6f Cls5 Mdn soft	£3,558

Surprise winner of last season's Prix de la Foret at 33-1; looked flattered by that win (many hard-luck stories behind in rough race) but had been progressive prior to that, winning a Group 3 at Tipperary on her previous start, and then beaten only a length in the Breeders' Cup Mile.

Ostilio

4 ch c New Approach - Room Three (Mark Of Esteem)

Simon Crisford — Sheikh Mohammed Obaid Al Maktoum

PLACINGS: 22/2211211- — RPR **116**

Starts	1st	2nd	3rd	4th	Win & Pl
9	4	5	-	-	£225,434

	Date	Course	Race	Prize
	10/18	Lonc	1m Gp2 good	£100,885
104	9/18	Donc	1m Cls2 96-110 Hcap good	£15,563
90	6/18	Asct	1m Cls2 90-102 3yo Hcap gd-fm	£74,700
84	5/18	NmkR	1m Cls4 80-84 3yo Hcap gd-fm	£7,763

Improved with every run last season, graduating from big handicap wins at Royal Ascot and Doncaster to a Group 2 breakthrough at Longchamp's Arc meeting; already not far off level of recent Group 1 mile winners and open to further progress.

Peach Tree (Ire)

3 ch f Galileo - Pikaboo (Pivotal)

Aidan O'Brien (Ir) — Michael Tabor Derrick Smith & Mrs John Magnier

PLACINGS: 518201- — RPR **104**

Starts	1st	2nd	3rd	4th	Win & Pl
6	2	1	-	-	£49,058

	Date	Course	Race	Prize
	10/18	Navn	1m List 2yo yield	£26,106
	6/18	Curr	7f Mdn 2yo gd-fm	£9,267

Has a middle-distance pedigree (full sister Flattering won last year's Munster Oaks) and did well over a mile last season, winning a Listed race at Navan and finishing second to Just Wonderful in a Group 3 either side of a below-par effort in the May Hill.

●Goddess ●Just Wonderful ●Madhmoon ●Mount Everest ●Ten Sovereigns

Persian King (Ire)

3 b c Kingman - Pretty Please (Dylan Thomas)

Andre Fabre (Fr) — Ballymore Thoroughbred

PLACINGS: 2111- — RPR **115**

Starts	1st	2nd	3rd	4th	Win & Pl
4	3	1	-	-	£70,220

	Date	Course	Race	Prize
	10/18	NmkR	1m Cls1 Gp3 2yo gd-fm	£34,026
	9/18	Chan	1m 2yo good	£19,469
	9/18	Chan	1m 2yo gd-sft	£11,947

Completed a hat-trick with victory in a red-hot Autumn Stakes at Newmarket last season (Vertem Futurity Trophy first, third and fourth behind); trainer has used juvenile races on the Rowley Mile to prepare his Guineas winners and likely to return to Newmarket a leading contender.

Phoenix Of Spain (Ire)

3 gr c Lope De Vega - Lucky Clio (Key Of Luck)

Charlie Hills — Tony Wechsler & Ann Plummer

PLACINGS: 41122- — RPR **114**

Starts	1st	2nd	3rd	4th	Win & Pl
5	2	2	-	1	£126,733

	Date	Course	Race	Prize
	8/18	York	7f Cls1 Gp3 2yo gd-fm	£56,710
	7/18	Wolv	7f Cls5 2yo std-slw	£3,752

Smart juvenile last season who won the Acomb Stakes at York and progressed in defeat in last two runs; just edged out by Magna Grecia in the Vertem Futurity Trophy after bumping into Too Darn Hot in the Champagne Stakes; should stay at least 1m2f.

Pilaster

4 b f Nathaniel - Portal (Hernando)

Roger Varian — Cheveley Park Stud

PLACINGS: 7/11138- — RPR **109**

Starts	1st	2nd	3rd	4th	Win & Pl
6	3	-	1	-	£203,531

	Date	Course	Race	Prize
	8/18	Gdwd	1m6f Cls1 Gp2 good	£170,130
	7/18	Kemp	1m4f Cls3 stand	£9,704
	5/18	Chmt	1m2f Cls3 stand	£12,938

Won first two starts last season on the all-weather before flourishing when stepped up in class, adding a Group 2 at Glorious Goodwood; arguably unlucky not to follow up in the Park Hill Stakes when a half-length third having been given plenty to do off a slow pace.

Pink Dogwood (Ire)

3 br f Camelot - Question Times (Shamardal)

Aidan O'Brien (Ir) — Derrick Smith, Mrs John Magnier & Michael Tabor

PLACINGS: 2215- — RPR **105**

Starts	1st	2nd	3rd	4th	Win & Pl
4	1	2	-	-	£27,120

	Date	Course	Race	Prize
	9/18	Gowr	1m Mdn 2yo heavy	£8,995

Sent off just 3-1 for last season's Prix Marcel Boussac but seemed to get racing too far out in front and finished only fifth; had been progressing sharply with experience and got off the mark with a seven-length win on heavy ground at Gowran.

Plumatic

5 b h Dubawi - Plumania (Anabaa)

Andre Fabre (Fr) — Wertheimer & Frere

PLACINGS: 12020/31144- — RPR **116**

Starts	1st	2nd	3rd	4th	Win & Pl
10	3	2	1	2	£138,267

Date	Course	Race	Prize
8/18	Sals	1m Cls1 Gp3 gd-sft	£43,383
7/18	Chan	1m gd-sft	£12,389
3/17	StCl	1m2½f 3yo soft	£12,051

Campaigned as a middle-distance horse in 2017 (finished 11th in the Arc) but did better over a mile last season, winning a Group 3 and finishing a close fourth in the Prix du Moulin; below-par fourth behind Ostilio when 6-4 favourite for a Group 2 on final run.

Polydream (Ire)

4 b f Oasis Dream - Polygreen (Green Tune)

Freddy Head (Fr) — Wertheimer & Frere

PLACINGS: 112/0117- — RPR **119+**

Starts	1st	2nd	3rd	4th	Win & Pl
7	4	1	-	-	£331,892

Date	Course	Race	Prize
8/18	Deau	6½f Gp1 good	£192,152
6/18	Lonc	7f Gp3 soft	£35,398
8/17	Deau	7f Gp3 2yo gd-sft	£34,188
7/17	Deau	6f 2yo good	£11,538

Top-class juvenile in 2017 who finished last in the Poule d'Essai des Pouliches but restored her reputation when winning the Prix Maurice de Gheest; had no luck in running in the Prix de la Foret before being controversially withdrawn from the Breeders' Cup Mile.

Pretty Baby (Ire)

4 b f Orpen - Premiere Danseuse (Gold Away)

William Haggas — Sheikh Rashid Dalmook Al Maktoum

PLACINGS: 21/1121- — RPR **105+**

Starts	1st	2nd	3rd	4th	Win & Pl
6	4	2	-	-	£93,393

Date	Course	Race	Prize
8/18	Gdwd	7f Cls1 Gp3 gd-fm	£45,368
5/18	Nott	6f Cls1 List gd-fm	£22,684
5/18	Rdcr	6f Cls5 gd-fm	£4,528
10/17	Chmt	6f Cls5 2yo stand	£4,528

Has won four times in six races and beaten no more than half a length in other two; gained most notable success in a 7f Group 3 at Glorious Goodwood last season when relishing step up beyond 6f for the first time and could have even more to offer over a mile.

Pretty Pollyanna

3 b f Oasis Dream - Unex Mona Lisa (Shamardal)

Michael Bell — WJ & TCO Gredley

PLACINGS: 151143- — RPR **115**

Starts	1st	2nd	3rd	4th	Win & Pl
6	3	-	1	1	£298,905

Date	Course	Race	Prize
8/18	Deau	6f Gp1 2yo good	£176,982
7/18	NmkJ	6f Cls1 Gp2 2yo gd-fm	£45,368
6/18	Yarm	6f Cls5 Mdn 2yo gd-fm	£3,817

Looked the leading juvenile filly for much of last season and beat some decent colts handsomely in the Prix Morny; disappointing in the autumn when only fourth in the Cheveley Park and third in the Fillies' Mile (did too much in front over longer trip).

Prince Eiji

3 ch c Dubawi - Izzi Top (Pivotal)

Roger Varian — Sheikh Mohammed Obaid Al Maktoum

PLACINGS: 135- — RPR **102+**

Starts	1st	2nd	3rd	4th	Win & Pl
3	1	-	1	-	£15,797

Date	Course	Race	Prize
9/18	Asct	7f Cls3 Mdn 2yo good	£7,763

Cost 2.6 million guineas and showed plenty of promise in first two runs last season, winning at Ascot and finishing third in the Tattersalls Stakes at Newmarket when much the best of those who helped to force an overly strong pace; below par when fifth in France next time.

Prince Of Arran

6 b g Shirocco - Storming Sioux (Storming Home)

Charlie Fellowes — Saeed Bel Obaida

PLACINGS: 3528085/21886323138- — RPR **114aw**

Starts	1st	2nd	3rd	4th	Win & Pl
30	5	6	4	2	£620,501

OR	Date	Course	Race	Prize
0	11/18	Flem	1m4½f Gd3 Hcap good	£104,913
104	2/18	Meyd	2m 98-107 Hcap good	£71,111
83	11/16	Kemp	1m4f Cls3 82-95 Hcap std-slw	£7,159
80	4/16	Kemp	1m3f Cls3 77-81 3yo Hcap stand	£7,159
	11/15	Kemp	1m Cls6 Auct Mdn 2yo stand	£2,264

Smart stayer who proved a money-spinner for connections in 2018 with big wins in Dubai and Australia before finishing a terrific third in the Melbourne Cup; hasn't won in Britain since 2016 but finished second in last year's Ebor and the 2017 Sagaro Stakes.

Projection

6 b g Acclamation - Spotlight (Dr Fong)

Roger Charlton — The Royal Ascot Racing Club

PLACINGS: 41/453/6302/3352316- — RPR **115**

Starts	1st	2nd	3rd	4th	Win & Pl
19	3	2	5	2	£168,853

10/18	Asct	6f Cls1 Gp3 soft	£39,697
9/15	Sals	6f Cls2 2yo gd-sft	£9,704
8/15	Wind	6f Cls5 Mdn 2yo gd-fm	£2,911

Gained a long-overdue victory when winning a 6f Group 3 on soft ground at Ascot in October; had been unlucky not to win a big handicap in previous campaigns and continued to knock on the door in Group/Listed races last season; acts on any ground.

Psychedelic Funk

5 ch g Choisir - Parabola (Galileo)

Ger Lyons (Ir) — Sean Jones

PLACINGS: 11326/0231431/19- — RPR **113+**

Starts	1st	2nd	3rd	4th	Win & Pl
14	5	2	3	1	£147,174

4/18	Naas	7f Gp3 sft-hvy	£31,327
10/17	Tipp	7½f Gp3 heavy	£34,038
7/17	Naas	1m good	£7,897
5/16	Naas	6f 2yo yld-sft	£6,783
4/16	Naas	6f Mdn 2yo good	£7,009

Hugely impressive when a wide-margin Group 3 winner at Naas first time out last season; trainer's Group 1 ambitions thwarted by quick ground (twice a non-runner due to unsuitable conditions) and ran only once subsequently when well below best; has since been gelded.

Quorto (Ire)

3 b c Dubawi - Volume (Mount Nelson)

Charlie Appleby — Godolphin

PLACINGS: 111- — RPR **121**

Starts	1st	2nd	3rd	4th	Win & Pl
3	3	-	-	-	£227,091

9/18	Curr	7f Gp1 2yo gd-yld	£176,549
7/18	NmkJ	7f Cls1 Gp2 2yo gd-fm	£45,368
6/18	NmkJ	6f Cls4 2yo gd-fm	£5,175

Won all three starts last season and most impressive when beating Anthony Van Dyck in the Group 1 National Stakes; connections opted against running in the Dewhurst, citing the 2,000 Guineas as his long-term aim; could get further (dam was third in the Oaks).

Raakib Alhawa (Ire)

3 b c Kingman - Starlet (Sea The Stars)

David Simcock — Khalifa Dasmal

PLACINGS: 10- — RPR **95+**

Starts	1st	2nd	3rd	4th	Win & Pl
2	1	-	-	-	£9,960

9/18	Newb	1m Cls2 2yo gd-sft	£9,960

Did really well to win a traditionally strong conditions race at Newbury first time out last season, edging out a previous winner with the others well strung out; beat only one home when sent off just 6-1 for the Vertem Futurity Trophy but may well prove up to that level in time.

Rainbow Heart (Ire)

3 b f Born To Sea - Sea Of Heartbreak (Rock Of Gibraltar)

William Haggas — Sunderland Holding

PLACINGS: 31- — RPR **96+**

Starts	1st	2nd	3rd	4th	Win & Pl
2	1	-	1	-	£4,843

10/18	NmkR	7f Cls5 Auct 2yo good	£3,881

Runaway eight-length winner of a 7f Newmarket maiden last October; had been too keen first time out according to his trainer when third over the same course and distance; bred for middle distances and earmarked for an Oaks trial if learning to settle better.

Rakan

3 b c Sea The Stars - Tarfasha (Teofilo)

Dermot Weld (Ir) — Hamdan Al Maktoum

PLACINGS: 31- — RPR **86**

Starts	1st	2nd	3rd	4th	Win & Pl
2	1	-	1	-	£10,506

10/18	Leop	1m Mdn 2yo gd-yld	£9,540

First foal of same connections' Oaks runner-up Tarfasha; fair third on his debut last season before taking a big step forward when winning at Leopardstown, seeing out a mile strongly; sure to get further and trainer immediately nominated the Derrinstown Derby Trial.

Raymond Tusk (Ire)

4 b c High Chaparral - Dancing Shoes (Danehill)

Richard Hannon — Middleham Park Racing XXXI & K Sohi

PLACINGS: 1261261-6 — RPR **111**

Starts	1st	2nd	3rd	4th	Win & Pl
8	3	2	-	-	£168,792

10/18	Siro	1m4f Gp2 good	£103,540
7/18	Haml	1m3f Cls1 List 3yo gd-fm	£24,385
4/18	Newb	1m Cls4 Mdn 3yo gd-sft	£5,531

Held in high regard at home and campaigned accordingly last season, even running in the Eclipse on just his third run; justified connections' faith by winning Group 2 and Listed races as well as finishing second in the Geoffrey Freer Stakes.

Red Impression

3 gr f Dark Angel - Purissima (Fusaichi Pegasus)

Roger Charlton — K Abdullah

PLACINGS: 11- — RPR **91+aw**

Starts	1st	2nd	3rd	4th	Win & Pl
2	2	-	-	-	£7,633

11/18	Ling	6f Cls5 2yo stand	£3,752
10/18	Kemp	6f Cls5 Mdn 2yo std-slw	£3,881

Looked a potential star on the all-weather this

winter, including when winning her second start under a penalty at Kempton by six lengths; not certain to get a mile on pedigree but could prove a smart filly either way.

Regal Reality

4 b c Intello - Regal Realm (Medicean)

Sir Michael Stoute — Cheveley Park Stud

PLACINGS: 1/6133- RPR **111**

Starts	1st	2nd	3rd	4th	Win & Pl
5	2	-	2	-	£79,317

	8/18	Gdwd	1m Cls1 Gp3 3yo gd-fm	£56,710
	9/17	Yarm	7f Cls4 Mdn 2yo soft	£4,528

Excellent winner of a good Group 3 at Goodwood last season, beating Ostilio; disappointing he could finish no better than third on next two runs, though may have found heavy ground against him on one occasion; looks the type to make a better four year-old.

Rock Eagle

4 ch g Teofilo - Highland Shot (Selkirk)

Ralph Beckett — JC Smith

PLACINGS: 12141- RPR **101**

Starts	1st	2nd	3rd	4th	Win & Pl
5	3	1	-	1	£87,123

92	10/18	NmkR	1m4f Cls2 85-106 3yo Hcap gd-fm	£74,700
	6/18	Wind	1m2f Cls5 gd-fm	£3,752
	4/18	Wind	1m2f Cls5 3yo good	£3,752

Lightly raced and progressive middle-distance performer; came within a head of winning first three starts and finished strongly when fourth over 1m2f at Glorious Goodwood; relished step up to 1m4f when winning a valuable three-year-old handicap at Newmarket on final run.

Rocques (Fr)

3 b f Lawman - Regina Mundi (Montjeu)

Fabrice Chappet (Fr) — G Augustin-Normand, Ecurie Du Gave & A Jathiere

PLACINGS: 1116- RPR **104**

Starts	1st	2nd	3rd	4th	Win & Pl
4	3	-	-	-	£66,814

9/18	Lonc	1m Gp3 2yo good	£35,398
7/18	Claf	7f 2yo soft	£19,469
7/18	Chan	7f 2yo good	£11,947

Favourite for last season's Prix Marcel Boussac after winning first three starts but finished a two-length sixth, staying on having been outpaced and short of room in the straight; should benefit from stepping up to middle distances.

Romanised (Ire)

4 b c Holy Roman Emperor - Romantic Venture (Indian Ridge)

Ken Condon (Ir) — Robert Ng

PLACINGS: 1762/61759- RPR **121**

Starts	1st	2nd	3rd	4th	Win & Pl
9	2	1	-	-	£252,512

5/18	Curr	1m Gp1 3yo gd-fm	£206,195
4/17	Navn	6f Mdn 2yo good	£8,687

Patchy record overall but managed to pull off a 25-1 upset when coming from last to first off

Romanised springs a surprise for a 25-1 success in the Irish 2,000 Guineas

a strong gallop in the Irish 2,000 Guineas last season; otherwise 0-7 outside maiden company and has made the frame just once, with three poor runs following Curragh success.

Royal Intervention (Ire)

3 ch f Exceed And Excel - Exciting Times (Jeune Homme)

Ed Walker | Lord Lloyd Webber & WS Farish

PLACINGS: 212- | RPR **101**

Starts	1st	2nd	3rd	4th	Win & Pl
3	1	2	-	-	£28,879

	6/18	**NmkJ**	6f Cls1 List 2yo gd-fm	£17,013

Went wrong when a beaten favourite in the Princess Margaret Stakes and missed the rest of the season but had looked a hugely exciting filly when running away with a Listed race at Newmarket prior to that; form questionable but has lots of potential.

Royal Line

5 ch h Dubawi - Melikah (Lammtarra)

John Gosden | Hh Sheikha Al Jalila Racing

PLACINGS: 1137/311- | RPR **115+**

Starts	1st	2nd	3rd	4th	Win & Pl
7	4	-	2	-	£75,202

105	**11/18**	**Donc**	1m4f Cls2 91-107 Hcap soft	£43,575
95	**4/18**	**Epsm**	1m4f Cls3 81-96 Hcap good	£15,563
88	**9/17**	**Hayd**	1m4f Cls3 80-94 Hcap heavy	£9,338
	9/17	**Wind**	1m3½f Cls5 Mdn 3yo gd-sft	£2,976

Impressive winner of last season's November Handicap at Doncaster; very lightly raced for his age and had been off the track since winning at Epsom in April but overcame his absence to win off 105; appreciated cut in the ground but has also shown smart form on good.

Royal Marine (Ire)

3 b c Raven's Pass - Inner Secret (Singspiel)

Saeed Bin Suroor | Godolphin

PLACINGS: 611-4 | RPR **113**

Starts	1st	2nd	3rd	4th	Win & Pl
4	2	-	-	1	£215,905

10/18	**Lonc**	1m Gp1 2yo good	£202,265
9/18	**Donc**	7f Cls3 Mdn 2yo gd-sft	£9,704

Ran away with a strong Doncaster maiden and followed up in the Prix Jean-Luc Lagardere at Longchamp; possibly flattered by the way that race was run (always prominent as those behind found it hard to make up ground) but open to further progress.

Royal Meeting (Ire)

3 b c Invincible Spirit - Rock Opera (Lecture)

Saeed Bin Suroor — Godolphin

PLACINGS: 11- — RPR **116+**

Starts	1st	2nd	3rd	4th	Win & Pl
2	2	-	-	-	£131,202

10/18	Chan	7f Gp1 2yo gd-sft	£126,416
9/18	Yarm	7f Cls4 Mdn 2yo gd-fm	£4,787

Left the form of narrow Yarmouth debut win a long way behind when beating Hermosa in the Criterium International at Chantilly in October; suspicion that will prove a very weak Group I but still did remarkably well to win on just his second start and could be a top miler.

Rumble Inthejungle (Ire)

3 ch c Bungle Inthejungle - Guana (Dark Angel)

Richard Spencer — Rebel Racing Premier & Cheveley Park Stud

PLACINGS: 14193- — RPR **109+**

Starts	1st	2nd	3rd	4th	Win & Pl
5	2	-	1	1	£82,593

8/18	Gdwd	5f Cls1 Gp3 2yo good	£42,533
5/18	Sals	5f Cls4 2yo gd-fm	£5,111

High-class juvenile sprinter last season and seemed to get stronger as the year went on bar one below-par effort in the Flying Childers; had previously run away with the Molecomb Stakes at Glorious Goodwood and was a good third in the Middle Park on first run over 6f.

Salouen (Ire)

5 ch h Canford Cliffs - Gali Gal (Galileo)

Sylvester Kirk — H Balasuriya

PLACINGS: 2123/207823/3234369- — RPR **118**

Starts	1st	2nd	3rd	4th	Win & Pl
22	2	6	6	2	£426,005

9/16	Sals	1m Cls4 2yo gd-fm	£5,822
8/16	Wind	1m Cls5 Mdn 2yo gd-fm	£3,235

Hasn't won since 2016 but has been very highly tried in that time and came within a head of winning last season's Coronation Cup when nearly turning over Cracksman; also ran a big race when sixth in the Arc but below that level when given more winnable opportunities.

San Donato (Ire)

3 b c Lope De Vega - Boston Rocker (Acclamation)

Roger Varian — Sheikh Mohammed Obaid Al Maktoum

PLACINGS: 28111- — RPR **102+**

Starts	1st	2nd	3rd	4th	Win & Pl
5	3	1	-	-	£30,250

10/18	Donc	6f Cls1 List 2yo gd-sft	£17,013
9/18	Kemp	6f Cls5 2yo std-slw	£3,881
9/18	Hayd	6f Cls4 2yo gd-sft	£6,469

Finished last season on a roll, winning his last three races over 6f including a Listed contest at Doncaster; trainer hopes he'll develop into a Group sprinter and could start in the Pavilion Stakes in May over the Commonwealth Cup course and distance.

Sand Share

3 br f Oasis Dream - Shared Account (Dansili)

Ralph Beckett — K Abdullah

PLACINGS: 134- — RPR **103+**

Starts	1st	2nd	3rd	4th	Win & Pl
3	1	-	1	1	£20,433

8/18	Kemp	7f Cls4 2yo std-slw	£5,822

Ran a fine race on just her second outing when third in the May Hill Stakes at Doncaster, staying on strongly and looking likely to relish middle distances as a three-year-old (dam was Listed-placed up to 1m4f); beaten favourite at Deauville next time.

Sands Of Mali (Fr)

4 b c Panis - Kadiania (Indian Rocket)

Richard Fahey — The Cool Silk Partnership

PLACINGS: 71109/1120051- — RPR **121**

Starts	1st	2nd	3rd	4th	Win & Pl
12	5	1	-	-	£692,207

10/18	Asct	6f Cls1 Gp1 soft	£358,691
5/18	Hayd	6f Cls1 Gp2 3yo good	£51,039
4/18	Chan	6f Gp3 3yo heavy	£35,398
8/17	York	6f Cls1 Gp2 2yo good	£127,598
8/17	Nott	6f Cls5 2yo soft	£3,235

Won last season's Group I Champions Sprint at Ascot, underlining his liking for the course after finishing second in the Commonwealth Cup in the summer; largely disappointing in between but had shown effectiveness on other tracks with Group wins at Chantilly and Haydock in the spring.

Sangarius

3 b c Kingman - Trojan Queen (Empire Maker)

Sir Michael Stoute — K Abdullah

PLACINGS: 114- — RPR **106+**

Starts	1st	2nd	3rd	4th	Win & Pl
3	2	-	-	1	£48,988

9/18	Donc	7f Cls1 List 2yo gd-sft	£17,013
8/18	NmkJ	7f Cls4 2yo gd-fm	£5,175

Won first two starts last season, including a Listed race at Doncaster, but thrown in at the

deep end in the Dewhurst next time and well beaten in fourth; something to prove with previous form amounting to little but it bodes well that his master trainer ran him in such company.

Sea Of Class (Ire)

4 ch f Sea The Stars - Holy Moon (Hernando)

William Haggas — Sunderland Holding

PLACINGS: 211112- — RPR **121**

Starts	1st	2nd	3rd	4th	Win & Pl
6	4	2	-	-	£1,481,736

	Date	Course	Race	Prize
	8/18	York	1m4f Cls1 Gp1 gd-fm	£198,485
	7/18	Curr	1m4f Gp1 3yo gd-fm	£201,770
	6/18	Newb	1m2f Cls1 List 3yo gd-fm	£28,355
	5/18	Newb	1m2f Cls1 List 3yo gd-fm	£39,697

Last season's outstanding three-year-old middle-distance filly, winning the Irish Oaks and Yorkshire Oaks with trademark turn of foot from the rear; arguably given too much to do when just beaten by Enable in the Arc (not helped by bad draw) and is a leading contender for that race again.

Sergei Prokofiev (Can)

3 b/br c Scat Daddy - Orchard Beach (Tapit)

Aidan O'Brien (Ir) — Derrick Smith, Mrs John Magnier & Michael Tabor

PLACINGS: 21135718- — RPR **111+**

Starts	1st	2nd	3rd	4th	Win & Pl
8	3	1	1	-	£109,374

	Date	Course	Race	Prize
	10/18	NmkR	5f Cls1 Gp3 2yo gd-fm	£34,026
	5/18	Naas	5f List 2yo gd-fm	£33,938
	4/18	Navn	5f 2yo yld-sft	£10,903

Hugely talented colt but proved hard to get right last season, boiling over in the Phoenix Stakes and the Middle Park; following those below-par performances he benefited from a breakneck gallop back at 5f when impressively winning the Group 3 Cornwallis Stakes and looks an out-and-out sprinter who needs quick ground.

Settle For Bay (Fr)

5 b g Rio De La Plata - Dissitation (Spectrum)

David Marnane (Ir) — Mcgettigans Management Services & Maurice Case

PLACINGS: 566/1P05111/141-08 — RPR **111**

Starts	1st	2nd	3rd	4th	Win & Pl
15	6	-	-	1	£148,811

	Date	Course	Race	Prize
99	6/18	Asct	1m Cls2 96-108 Hcap gd-fm	£108,938
91	1/18	Dund	1m 71-91 Hcap stand	£13,606
	12/17	Dund	1m App stand	£6,318
	11/17	Dund	1m stand	£6,318
76	11/17	Dund	1m 55-76 3yo Hcap stand	£5,791
69	4/17	Leop	7f 65-89 3yo Hcap gd-yld	£6,581

Remarkably easy winner of last year's Royal Hunt Cup, maintaining sharply progressive form from the all-weather the previous winter; missed the rest of the season after a stone bruise and didn't take to Meydan this winter but trainer had outlined Group 1 ambitions.

Shambolic (Ire)

3 b f Shamardal - Comic (Be My Chief)

John Gosden — Duke of Devonshire & Duke of Roxburghe

PLACINGS: 1147- — RPR **101**

Starts	1st	2nd	3rd	4th	Win & Pl
4	2	-	-	1	£38,702

	Date	Course	Race	Prize
	9/18	Asct	1m Cls4 2yo gd-fm	£6,728
	8/18	NmkJ	7f Cls4 Mdn 2yo gd-sft	£5,175

Narrowly won first two starts at Newmarket and Ascot last season and both subsequent defeats came at Group 1 level; good fourth in the Fillies' Mile, keeping on well having lacked pace of the principals, but below that form when stepped up to 1m2f at Saint-Cloud.

Sharja Bridge

5 b h Oasis Dream - Quetena (Acatenango)

Roger Varian — Sheikh Mohammed Obaid Al Maktoum

PLACINGS: 3212/28471- — RPR **115+**

Starts	1st	2nd	3rd	4th	Win & Pl
9	2	3	1	1	£176,608

	Date	Course	Race	Prize
105	10/18	Asct	1m Cls2 98-110 Hcap soft	£155,625
	8/17	Nott	1m½f Cls5 Mdn gd-sft	£3,235

Took time to live up to market expectations (beaten favourite three times and never bigger than 10-1 last season despite running in big fields every time) but finally delivered with a terrific win in the Balmoral Handicap at Ascot; seems best at a mile having not convinced over further.

Shine So Bright

3 gr c Oasis Dream - Alla Speranza (Sir Percy)

Andrew Balding — King Power Racing

PLACINGS: 15333- — RPR **106**

Starts	1st	2nd	3rd	4th	Win & Pl
5	1	-	3	-	£61,716

	Date	Course	Race	Prize
	6/18	Nott	5f Cls5 Mdn 2yo good	£3,881

Third in three 6f Group 2 races last season, not beaten far in the Richmond and Gimcrack Stakes; favourite for the Mill Reef on the back of those runs but proved much less effective on soft ground; could get further on pedigree (dam won a 1m2f Group 3).

Signora Cabello (Ire)

3 b f Camacho - Journalist (Night Shift)

John Quinn — Phoenix Thoroughbred & Zen Racing

PLACINGS: 4111120- — RPR **113**

Starts	1st	2nd	3rd	4th	Win & Pl
7	4	1	-	1	£232,949

	Date	Course	Race	Prize
	7/18	MsnL	5½f Gp2 2yo good	£65,575
	6/18	Asct	5f Cls1 Gp2 2yo gd-fm	£62,381
	5/18	York	5f Cls1 List 2yo gd-fm	£28,355
	5/18	Bath	5f Cls4 2yo gd-fm	£5,531

Often underrated last season and won the Queen Mary Stakes at Royal Ascot at 25-1 after a 20-1 Listed success at York; continued to progress in France, including a fine second in the

Prix Morny behind Pretty Pollyanna, but flopped in the Cheveley Park on final run.

Sir Dancealot (Ire)

5 b g Sir Prancealot - Majesty's Dancer (Danehill Dancer)

David Elsworth — C Benham, D Whitford, L Quinn & K Quinn

PLACINGS: 056215/231714119550- RPR **119**

Starts	1st	2nd	3rd	4th	Win & Pl
28	8	3	2	1	£481,140

8/18	Newb	7f Cls1 Gp2 good	£85,065
7/18	Gdwd	7f Cls1 Gp2 good	£176,935
6/18	NmkJ	7f Cls1 Gp3 gd-fm	£34,026
6/18	Haml	6f Cls2 good	£16,808
10/17	Donc	7f Cls3 gd-sft	£9,338
10/16	York	6f Cls1 List 2yo good	£28,355
9/16	Kemp	7f Cls4 2yo std-slw	£3,946
8/16	Kemp	7f Cls4 Mdn Auct 2yo std-slw	£3,946

Gained all three wins over 7f last season, including the Lennox Stakes and Hungerford Stakes, with only defeat at the trip coming in a rough Prix de la Foret; tended to get going too late when highly tried over 6f, including when fourth in the July Cup.

Skitter Scatter (USA)

3 b f Scat Daddy - Dane Street (Street Cry)

John Oxx (Ir) — Anthony Rogers & Mrs Sonia Rogers

PLACINGS: 3132111- RPR **112**

Starts	1st	2nd	3rd	4th	Win & Pl
7	4	1	2	-	£293,411

9/18	Curr	7f Gp1 2yo gd-yld	£176,549
8/18	Curr	7f Gp2 2yo yield	£60,044
7/18	Leop	7f Gp3 2yo gd-fm	£31,327
4/18	Dund	5f Mdn 2yo stand	£8,177

Progressed throughout last season and finished by winning Ireland's two biggest juvenile fillies' races, notably the Moyglare Stud Stakes; stayed on strongly that day and should improve again

Sir Dancealot heads to the winner's enclosure at Goodwood after landing the Lennox Stakes

when stepped up in trip; looks a leading 1,000 Guineas contender.

Snazzy Jazzy (Ire)

4 b c Red Jazz - Bulrushes (Byron)

Clive Cox — Mrs Olive Shaw

PLACINGS: 111/8086171- — RPR **110**

Starts	1st	2nd	3rd	4th	Win & Pl
10	5	-	-	-	£207,751

	10/18	MsnL	6f Gp3 v soft	£35,398
95	9/18	Ayr	6f Cls2 86-97 Hcap heavy	£37,350
	9/17	Curr	6½f 2yo sft-hvy	£126,068
	8/17	Wind	6f Cls4 2yo gd-sft	£4,593
	6/17	Gdwd	6f Cls5 2yo good	£3,235

Very smart sprinter in testing conditions, winning all three starts on soft ground or worse including the Silver Cup at Ayr and a Group 3 at Maisons-Laffitte last autumn; yet to run anywhere near that level on quicker ground but type to thrive in autumn again.

So Perfect (USA)

3 b f Scat Daddy - Hopeoverexperience (Songandaprayer)

Aidan O'Brien (Ir) — Derrick Smith, Mrs John Magnier & Michael Tabor

PLACINGS: 1441233- — RPR **110**

Starts	1st	2nd	3rd	4th	Win & Pl
7	2	1	2	2	£192,989

7/18	Curr	6f Gp3 2yo gd-fm	£33,938
4/18	Navn	5f Mdn 2yo yld-sft	£8,995

Proved herself a smart and consistent filly in top juvenile sprints last season, winning twice and beaten less than a length in the Queen Mary, Phoenix and Cheveley Park Stakes; bred to be a sprinter, although running style suggests she may get further than 6f.

Soldier's Call

3 b c Showcasing - Dijarvo (Iceman)

Archie Watson — Clipper Logistics

PLACINGS: 21131136- — RPR **114**

Starts	1st	2nd	3rd	4th	Win & Pl
8	4	1	2	-	£185,369

9/18	Donc	5f Cls1 Gp2 2yo good	£39,697
9/18	Chan	5f Gp3 2yo gd-sft	£35,398
6/18	Asct	5f Cls1 List 2yo gd-fm	£51,039
6/18	Hayd	5f Cls4 2yo gd-fm	£6,469

Last season's leading two-year-old over 5f and even looked unlucky not to beat his elders in the Prix de l'Abbaye, getting nabbed close home after shaking off Battaash up front; had been a brilliant winner of the Flying Childers; undone by a poor start at the Breeders' Cup.

Son Of Rest

5 b h Pivotal - Hightime Heroine (Danetime)

Fozzy Stack (Ir) — B Parker

PLACINGS: 24/181532/52745210- — RPR **113+**

Starts	1st	2nd	3rd	4th	Win & Pl
16	3	4	1	2	£226,978

101	9/18	Ayr	6f Cls2 95-108 Hcap heavy	£80,890
103	6/17	Curr	5f 80-103 3yo Hcap soft	£25,214
	4/17	Cork	5f Mdn heavy	£7,897

Big improver towards the end of last season, running a huge race to finish second in the Flying Five at the Curragh on ground quicker than ideal and taking advantage of a good mark (10lb well

in) to dead-heat in the Ayr Gold Cup; should do well in testing conditions.

Southern France (Ire)

4 b c Galileo - Alta Anna (Anabaa)

Aidan O'Brien (Ir) Derrick Smith, Mrs John Magnier & Michael Tabor

PLACINGS: 2112437- RPR **112**

Starts	1st	2nd	3rd	4th	Win & Pl
7	2	2	1	1	£176,535
5/18	Navn	1m5f List 3yo gd-fm			£39,159
5/18	Leop	1m4f Mdn 3yo good			£7,087

Made rapid strides last season having been unraced until April, soon winning twice and finishing second in the Queen's Vase at Royal Ascot; needed first run back from a subsequent break before a good third in the St Leger and fair seventh in the Cesarewitch; potential Cup horse.

Sparkle Roll (Fr)

3 gr f Kingman - Ysoldina (Kendor)

John Gosden Kin Hung Kei, Qatar Racing & L Dassault

PLACINGS: 51- RPR **82+**

Starts	1st	2nd	3rd	4th	Win & Pl
2	1	-	-	-	£4,787
9/18	Hayd	1m Cls5 2yo gd-sft			£4,787

Half-sister to four winners including 2017 Derby hero Wings Of Eagles; stepped up massively on debut fifth when running away with a novice stakes at Haydock by three and three-quarter lengths; has plenty of scope and should progress again over middle distances.

Speak In Colours

4 gr c Excelebration - Maglietta Fina (Verglas)

Joseph O'Brien (Ir) Mrs CC Regalado-Gonzalez

PLACINGS: 311/230170- RPR **113**

Starts	1st	2nd	3rd	4th	Win & Pl
9	3	1	2	-	£68,033
8/18	Curr	6f Gp3 good			£31,327
10/17	Donc	6f Cls1 List 2yo gd-sft			£17,013
9/17	Asct	6f Cls4 Auct 2yo soft			£6,469

Won a Listed race for Marco Botti as a two-year-old and progressed to a higher level last season following switch to Ireland, winning a Group 3 at the Curragh; slightly disappointing when well beaten in three runs at Group 1 level, twice at Ascot.

Star Terms

3 ch f Sea The Stars - Best Terms (Exceed And Excel)

Richard Hannon R Barnett

PLACINGS: 921123- RPR **108**

Starts	1st	2nd	3rd	4th	Win & Pl
6	2	2	1	-	£74,351
83 8/18	NmkJ	7f Cls2 63-83 2yo Hcap good			£12,938
7/18	Newb	7f Cls4 Mdn 2yo gd-fm			£4,787

Gained biggest win last season in a nursery off 83 but proved herself at a much higher level when placed in the May Hill Stakes and Prix Marcel Boussac (slightly unlucky having been short of room); likely to be aimed at the 1,000 Guineas but could get further.

Son Of Rest (far side) dead-heats with Baron Bolt for the Ayr Gold Cup

Still Standing (Ire)

4 ch c Mastercraftsman - Il Palazzo (Giant's Causeway)

Jessica Harrington (Ir) — Anamoine

PLACINGS: 731/1191- — RPR **100+**

Starts	1st	2nd	3rd	4th	Win & Pl
7	4	-	1	-	£46,800

92	9/18	Fair	1m2f 73-96 Hcap gd-yld	£13,606
84	8/18	Klny	1m3f 66-87 Hcap good	£9,540
81	8/18	Baln	1m2f 73-86 3yo Hcap gd-yld	£13,606
	11/17	Naas	1m Mdn 2yo soft	£8,687

Won three out of four races last season, progressing well in middle-distance handicaps; suffered sole defeat when finishing only ninth on Irish Champions Weekend (sent off favourite) but bounced back to gain biggest success in a valuable handicap at Fairyhouse; should stay further.

Stormy Antarctic

6 ch g Stormy Atlantic - Bea Remembered (Doyen)

Ed Walker — PK Siu

PLACINGS: 76/2523016/12123348- — RPR **117**

Starts	1st	2nd	3rd	4th	Win & Pl
25	6	6	5	1	£521,215

	5/18	Badn	1m Gp2 good	£35,398
	4/18	StCl	1m Gp3 heavy	£35,398
	10/17	Chan	1m List soft	£22,222
	4/16	NmkR	1m Cls1 Gp3 3yo gd-sft	£34,026
	9/15	Newb	1m Cls2 2yo soft	£9,960
	8/15	Sand	7f Cls5 Mdn 2yo gd-sft	£3,881

Has done all his winning abroad since the 2016 Craven Stakes, including Group 2 and Group 3 races last season; ran better than ever in defeat subsequently, finishing second and third at Group 1 level and not beaten far in the Celebration Mile and the QEII.

Stradivarius (Ire)

5 ch h Sea The Stars - Private Life (Bering)

John Gosden — BE Nielsen

PLACINGS: 541/121133/11111- — RPR **121+**

Starts	1st	2nd	3rd	4th	Win & Pl
14	9	1	2	1	£1,613,909

	10/18	Asct	2m Cls1 Gp2 soft	£300,563
	8/18	York	2m½f Cls1 Gp2 gd-fm	£127,598
	7/18	Gdwd	2m Cls1 Gp1 good	£283,550
	6/18	Asct	2m4f Cls1 Gp1 gd-fm	£283,550
	5/18	York	1m6f Cls1 Gp2 gd-fm	£93,572
	8/17	Gdwd	2m Cls1 Gp1 good	£296,593
	6/17	Asct	1m6f Cls1 Gp2 3yo gd-fm	£91,445
78	4/17	Bevl	1m2f Cls4 64-80 3yo Hcap gd-fm	£5,041
	11/16	Newc	1m Cls5 Mdn 2yo stand	£3,235

Last season's outstanding stayer; won all five starts, including the Gold Cup on the way to a £1 million bonus; favoured by quick ground for much of the season but managed to overcome softer conditions than ideal with another win at Ascot in the Long Distance Cup.

Stratum

6 b g Dansili - Lunar Phase (Galileo)

Willie Mullins (Ir) — Tony Bloom

PLACINGS: 8/2223122/31000- — RPR **106+**

Starts	1st	2nd	3rd	4th	Win & Pl
13	2	5	2	-	£80,719

94	7/18	Newb	2m½f Cls2 90-106 Hcap gd-fm	£62,250
	8/16	Wind	1m2f Cls5 Mdn 3-4yo gd-fm	£2,911

Smart dual-purpose performer who proved a handicap snip back on the Flat last season, running away with a new £100,000 contest at Newbury by three lengths; well beaten three times subsequently but looked very unlucky when getting no run in the Ebor.

Stream Of Stars

4 b g Sea The Stars - Precious Gem (Sadler's Wells)

John Gosden — Lady Bamford

PLACINGS: 217- — RPR **91+**

Starts	1st	2nd	3rd	4th	Win & Pl
3	1	1	-	-	£11,628

	5/18	Asct	1m4f Cls3 Mdn 3yo gd-fm	£9,704

Sent off favourite for last season's Queen's Vase at Royal Ascot after winning a 1m4f maiden at Ascot but finished only seventh and missed the rest of the year; clearly held in high regard and should have much more to come in good middle-distance/staying races.

Study Of Man (Ire)

4 b c Deep Impact - Second Happiness (Storm Cat)

Pascal Bary (Fr) — Flaxman Stables

PLACINGS: 1/211359- — RPR **118**

Starts	1st	2nd	3rd	4th	Win & Pl
7	3	1	1	-	£909,060

	6/18	Chan	1m2½f Gp1 3yo soft	£758,496
	5/18	StCl	1m2½f Gp2 3yo good	£65,575
	9/17	StCl	1m 2yo heavy	£11,538

Won last season's Prix du Jockey Club at Chantilly, capping a progressive first half of the year; disappointing when back from a break in the autumn, finishing only fifth in the Irish Champion Stakes and ninth in the Arc; likely to start back in the Prix Ganay.

Stylehunter

4 ch c Raven's Pass - Sunday Bess (Deep Impact)

John Gosden — Princess Haya of Jordan

PLACINGS: 03/221610- RPR **105**

Starts	1st	2nd	3rd	4th	Win & Pl
8	2	2	1	-	£18,189

92	8/18	Gdwd	1m1f Cls3 75-92 Hcap good	£9,704
	5/18	Ling	1m2f Cls5 stand	£3,752

Progressive from 1m-1m2f last season, easing to wide-margin wins at Kempton and Goodwood, either side of eyecatching sixth in the Britannia at Royal Ascot (finished well); unable to overcome lack of experience in the Cambridgeshire.

Suedois (Fr)

8 b/br g Le Havre - Cup Cake (Singspiel)

David O'Meara — George Turner & Clipper Logistics

PLACINGS: 2433/83733114/70324- RPR **117**

Starts	1st	2nd	3rd	4th	Win & Pl
38	8	9	8	4	£1,206,460

10/17	Keen	1m Gd1 firm	£487,805
9/17	Leop	1m Gp2 good	£100,855
8/15	Deau	6f Gp3 v soft	£31,008
4/15	MsnL	6f List good	£20,155
3/15	Chan	6½f stand	£19,380
12/14	Deau	6½f 3yo stand	£12,083
10/14	Chan	7f 3yo stand	£10,000
2/14	Chan	6½f 3yo stand	£10,000

One-time leading sprinter who bounced back to form when stepped up in trip in 2017, winning Group 1 and Group 2 mile races; not quite at that level last season but came within a short head of winning the Group 2 Lennox Stakes and not beaten far in the Summer Mile.

Sydney Opera House

3 ch c Australia - Sitara (Salse)

Aidan O'Brien (Ir) — Mrs John Magnier, Michael Tabor & Derrick Smith

PLACINGS: 4215252- RPR **112**

Starts	1st	2nd	3rd	4th	Win & Pl
7	1	3	-	1	£96,195

9/18	Curr	1m Mdn 2yo gd-yld	£9,540

Busily campaigned in the second half of last season but signed off with a career-best run when second in the Group 1 Criterium de Saint-Cloud over 1m2f; relished that longer trip and should appreciate further, perhaps even the 1m6f of the Queen's Vase and St Leger.

Symbolization (Ire)

4 b c Cape Cross - Yorkshire Lass (Pivotal)

Charlie Appleby — Godolphin

PLACINGS: 21/215452-40 RPR **110**

Starts	1st	2nd	3rd	4th	Win & Pl
10	2	3	-	2	£53,860

100	5/18	NmkR	1m Cls2 85-100 3yo Hcap good	£16,173
	9/17	Kemp	7f Cls4 2yo std-slw	£4,270

Showed huge promise early last season, including when winning a good mile handicap at Newmarket, and highly tried subsequently when fifth in the Irish 2,000 Guineas and fourth in the Jersey Stakes; has plenty of size and should progress with age.

Tabarrak (Ire)

6 b g Acclamation - Bahati (Intikhab)

Richard Hannon — Hamdan Al Maktoum

PLACINGS: 2/21/215921/6134511- RPR **115**

Starts	1st	2nd	3rd	4th	Win & Pl
18	7	5	1	1	£171,238

	10/18	Rdcr	7f Cls1 List good	£28,355
	9/18	Ling	7f Cls3 stand	£9,767
	5/18	Hayd	7f Cls1 List gd-fm	£20,983
	9/17	Newb	7f Cls1 List good	£20,983
	5/17	Asct	1m Cls1 List gd-fm	£20,983
97	5/16	Asct	7f Cls2 89-105 3yo Hcap gd-fm	£18,675
	9/15	Newb	7f Cls4 Mdn 2yo gd-sft	£5,175

Four-time Listed winner, including twice last season at Haydock and Redcar over 7f; didn't run over a mile after below-par reappearance (unsuited by soft ground) but has run well at that trip, coming closest to a Group win when a neck second in the 2017 Sovereign Stakes.

Tabdeed

4 ch c Havana Gold - Puzzled (Peintre Celebre)

Owen Burrows — Hamdan Al Maktoum

PLACINGS: 1/101- RPR **110+**

Starts	1st	2nd	3rd	4th	Win & Pl
4	3	-	-	-	£27,084

96	10/18	Asct	6f Cls2 85-100 3yo Hcap good	£18,675
	5/18	Nott	6f Cls5 gd-fm	£3,881
	8/17	Leic	6f Cls4 2yo good	£4,528

Suffered only defeat last season when well beaten in the Jersey Stakes but got back on track after a break when easily winning a handicap back at Ascot in October; likely to stick to sprinting, starting in handicaps before probably progressing to Group company.

Tarboosh

6 b g Bahamian Bounty - Mullein (Oasis Dream)

Paul Midgley — The Guys & Dolls & Sandfield Racing

PLACINGS: 71715113/7904111221- RPR **113**

Starts	1st	2nd	3rd	4th	Win & Pl
27	9	3	2	1	£101,628

104	10/18	Donc	5f Cls2 83-104 Hcap gd-sft	£28,013
	8/18	Nott	5f Cls3 gd-sft	£9,960
	8/18	Haml	5f Cls3 good	£11,205
	7/18	NmkJ	5f Cls3 gd-fm	£9,704
87	9/17	Ripn	5f Cls3 74-93 Hcap gd-fm	£7,763
84	8/17	Carl	5f Cls4 70-87 Hcap gd-sft	£5,499
77	8/17	Bevl	5f Cls5 60-81 Hcap gd-sft	£3,781
72	6/17	Ripn	5f Cls5 64-76 Hcap good	£3,235
	5/16	Kemp	7f Cls6 Auct Mdn 3-4yo stand	£2,264

Finished last season with a remarkably consistent run of form, winning three small-field conditions races before excelling back in handicap company with a career-best victory at Doncaster; improved throughout the campaign and not far off Group level.

Ten Sovereigns (Ire)

3 b c No Nay Never - Seeking Solace (Exceed And Excel)

Aidan O'Brien (Ir) Derrick Smith, Mrs John Magnier & Michael Tabor

PLACINGS: 111- RPR **120**

Starts	1st	2nd	3rd	4th	Win & Pl
3	3	-	-	-	£198,386

	Date	Course	Race	Prize
	9/18	NmkR	6f Cls1 Gp1 2yo gd-fm	£155,953
	9/18	Curr	6f Gp3 2yo gd-yld	£32,894
	8/18	Curr	6f Mdn 2yo good	£9,540

Big, lengthy colt who made a huge impression when winning by wide margins on first two starts and took a step up in class in his stride when adding the Middle Park Stakes at Newmarket; could be a top-class sprinter but trainer also expects him to stay a mile.

The Tin Man

7 b g Equiano - Persario (Bishop Of Cashel)

James Fanshawe Fred Archer Racing

PLACINGS: 4/18121/51835/14317- RPR **121**

Starts	1st	2nd	3rd	4th	Win & Pl
21	9	1	2	2	£1,180,676

	Date	Course	Race	Prize
	9/18	Hayd	6f Cls1 Gp1 heavy	£184,421
	5/18	Wind	6f Cls1 List gd-fm	£20,983
	6/17	Asct	6f Cls1 Gp1 gd-fm	£340,260
	10/16	Asct	6f Cls1 Gp1 good	£340,260
	7/16	Newb	6f Cls1 Gp3 gd-fm	£34,026
	5/16	Wind	6f Cls1 List good	£20,983
91	10/15	Asct	6f Cls2 84-103 3yo Hcap good	£18,675
79	7/15	Donc	6f Cls4 68-80 3yo Hcap gd-fm	£4,690
	6/15	Donc	6f Cls5 Mdn gd-fm	£2,911

Top-class sprinter who has won Group I races for three years in a row, most recently in last season's Sprint Cup at Haydock; handled heavy ground better than most that day but has also won multiple times on good to firm, including the 2017 Diamond Jubilee Stakes.

Thomas Hobson

9 b g Halling - La Spezia (Danehill Dancer)

Willie Mullins (Ir) Mrs S Ricci

PLACINGS: /3811211/12726/6512- RPR **116**

Starts	1st	2nd	3rd	4th	Win & Pl
17	6	4	1	1	£368,876

	Date	Course	Race	Prize
	9/18	Donc	2m2f Cls1 Gp2 gd-sft	£56,710
100	6/17	Asct	2m4f Cls2 91-100 Hcap gd-fm	£49,800
97	10/13	Donc	1m4f Cls2 86-100 Hcap soft	£12,938
91	10/13	Gdwd	1m4f Cls3 82-91 3yo Hcap soft	£9,704
84	8/13	Newb	1m2f Cls4 69-85 3yo Hcap good	£4,852
75	7/13	Leic	1m2f Cls4 68-78 Hcap soft	£4,852

Smart dual-purpose performer who gained biggest Flat win in last season's Doncaster Cup when beating stablemate Max Dynamite; also pushed Stradivarius close in the Long Distance Cup at Ascot, though probably better suited by the soft ground.

Thundering Blue (USA)

6 rg g Exchange Rate - Relampago Azul (Forestry)

David Menuisier Clive Washbourn

PLACINGS: /30331117/510213120- RPR **119**

Starts	1st	2nd	3rd	4th	Win & Pl
22	6	4	4	-	£459,454

	Date	Course	Race	Prize
	9/18	BroP	1m4f Gp3 good	£72,464
	7/18	York	1m2½f Cls1 Gp2 gd-sft	£68,052
93	5/18	York	1m2½f Cls2 86-99 Hcap gd-fm	£18,675
87	9/17	Sand	1m2f Cls2 87-103 Hcap good	£31,125
83	8/17	NmkJ	1m2f Cls2 80-98 Hcap gd-sft	£12,938
76	7/17	Epsm	1m2f Cls4 72-82 Hcap gd-sft	£5,175

Began last season rated just 93 but progressed into a Group I performer over middle distances, finishing second in the Canadian International and third in the Juddmonte International at York; had gained both wins last season at that track, most notably in the Group 2 York Stakes.

Tip Two Win

4 gr c Dark Angel - Freddie's Girl (More Than Ready)

Roger Teal Mrs Anne Cowley

PLACINGS: 132121/12406- RPR **118**

Starts	1st	2nd	3rd	4th	Win & Pl
11	4	3	1	1	£325,984

	Date	Course	Race	Prize
	2/18	Doh	1m List 3yo good	£105,556
	12/17	Doh	7f 2yo good	£46,341
	9/17	Donc	7f Cls1 List 2yo gd-sft	£17,013
	7/17	Wind	6f Cls5 2yo gd-fm	£2,911

Produced a huge run when second at 50-1 in last season's 2,000 Guineas, building on a big-money double in Doha the previous winter; fair fourth in the St James's Palace Stakes but flopped at Glorious Goodwood and got injured when sixth back in Doha in December.

Too Darn Hot

3 b c Dubawi - Dar Re Mi (Singspiel)

John Gosden Lord Lloyd-Webber

PLACINGS: 1111- RPR **126+**

Starts	1st	2nd	3rd	4th	Win & Pl
4	4	-	-	-	£358,965

	Date	Course	Race	Prize
	10/18	NmkR	7f Cls1 Gp1 2yo gd-fm	£283,550
	9/18	Donc	7f Cls1 Gp2 2yo good	£42,533
	9/18	Sand	7f Cls1 Gp3 2yo good	£28,355
	8/18	Sand	1m Cls5 Mdn 2yo gd-sft	£4,528

Regally bred colt who won all four races last season; ran away with what looked a strong renewal of the Dewhurst Stakes to strengthen position as clear favourite for the 2,000 Guineas;

also has bright prospects of staying further and could go for the Derby after that.

True Mason

3 b c Mayson - Marysienka (Primo Dominie)

Karl Burke — Khalifa Dasmal

PLACINGS: 5313328- RPR **107**

Starts	1st	2nd	3rd	4th	Win & Pl
7	1	1	3	-	£68,450

6/18	Nott	6f Cls5 2yo firm	£3,881

Placed three times at Group 1 or Group 2 level last season and travelled particularly well when second in the Mill Reef Stakes at Newbury before getting outstayed on soft ground by Kessaar; dropped back to 5f in the Cornwallis next time but disappointed in eighth.

True Self (Ire)

6 b m Oscar - Good Thought (Mukaddamah)

Willie Mullins (Ir) — Three Mile House Partnership

PLACINGS: 2111- RPR **111+**

Starts	1st	2nd	3rd	4th	Win & Pl
4	3	1	-	-	£53,683

11/18	NmkR	1m2f Cls1 List soft	£20,983
10/18	Bath	1m6f Cls1 List gd-sft	£22,684
10/18	Cork	1m4f Mdn good	£7,904

Proved herself a smart dual-purpose performer in 2018, flourishing when switched to the Flat in the summer; won a 1m6f Listed race at Bath and showed real versatility when romping home over 1m2f under a penalty at that level at Newmarket; looks a Group horse.

Turgenev

3 b c Dubawi - Tasaday (Nayef)

John Gosden — Princess Haya of Jordan

PLACINGS: 2117- RPR **104**

Starts	1st	2nd	3rd	4th	Win & Pl
4	2	1	-	-	£13,108

10/18	NmkR	1m Cls4 2yo good	£6,469
9/18	Newc	1m Cls5 2yo stand	£3,752

Best of the home team according to the market in the Vertem Futurity Trophy but managed only seventh on sharp step up in class; had won previous two races in impressive fashion and should prove better than Doncaster form; should get 1m2f.

Vazirabad (Fr)

7 b/br g Manduro - Visorama (Linamix)

Alain de Royer-Dupre (Fr) — Aga Khan

PLACINGS: /117121/211112/2112- RPR **119**

Starts	1st	2nd	3rd	4th	Win & Pl
23	15	6	-	-	£2,465,935

5/18	Lonc	1m7f Gp2 gd-sft	£65,575
3/18	Meyd	2m Gp2 good	£444,444
9/17	Chan	2m4½f Gp1 soft	£146,513
9/17	Chan	1m7f Gp3 soft	£34,188
5/17	Chan	1m7f Gp2 good	£63,333
3/17	Meyd	2m Gp2 yield	£487,805
10/16	StCl	1m7½f Gp1 gd-sft	£147,051
9/16	Chan	1m7f Gp3 good	£29,412
5/16	StCl	1m7½f Gp2 gd-sft	£54,485
3/16	Meyd	2m Gp2 good	£408,163
10/15	StCl	1m7½f Gp1 3yo soft	£155,031
10/15	Lonc	1m7f Gp2 3yo good	£88,372
9/15	Lonc	1m7f Gp3 3yo good	£31,008
8/15	Deau	1m5½f 3yo good	£11,240
7/15	Diep	1m7f 3yo v soft	£7,752

Brilliant stayer who has won multiple Group 1

Star stayer Vazirabad (right) will return to action this season

races and remained a force at the top level last season, running Stradivarius close in the Gold Cup on quicker ground than ideal (all previous form on softer); missed the rest of the season.

Veracious

4 b f Frankel - Infallible (Pivotal)

Sir Michael Stoute — Cheveley Park Stud

PLACINGS: 31/3316- — RPR **112+**

Starts	1st	2nd	3rd	4th	Win & Pl
6	2	-	3	-	£173,836

9/18	Sand	1m Cls1 Gp3 good	£39,697
10/17	NmkR	7f Cls4 Mdn 2yo good	£6,469

Lightly raced filly who coped well when thrown in at the deep end last season, finishing third in the Coronation Stakes first time out having won only a maiden at two; also third in the Nassau Stakes and won a Group 3 at Sandown when dropped below Group 1 level for the only time.

Verbal Dexterity (Ire)

4 b c Vocalised - Lonrach (Holy Roman Emperor)

Jim Bolger (Ir) — Mrs JS Bolger

PLACINGS: 1214/476- — RPR **111**

Starts	1st	2nd	3rd	4th	Win & Pl
7	2	1	-	2	£229,759

9/17	Curr	7f Gp1 2yo sft-hvy	£170,513
6/17	Curr	7f Mdn 2yo soft	£9,214

Looked a potential superstar when winning the National Stakes at the Curragh in 2017; yet to build on that win but has had excuses, finishing fourth in that year's Racing Post Trophy after a setback and returning last season only in the autumn after another injury blow.

Vintage Brut

3 b c Dick Turpin - Traditionelle (Indesatchel)

Tim Easterby — King Power Racing

PLACINGS: 119458201- — RPR **111**

Starts	1st	2nd	3rd	4th	Win & Pl
9	3	1	-	1	£66,808

10/18	York	6f Cls1 List 2yo soft	£28,355
5/18	Sand	5f Cls1 List 2yo good	£17,013
4/18	Thsk	5f Cls5 Mdn 2yo soft	£4,787

Did remarkably well to win Listed races as far apart as May and October last season, looking most impressive when signing off with a wide-margin success in the Rockingham Stakes at York on soft ground; largely disappointing on a quicker surface in between.

Wadilsafa

4 b c Frankel - Rumoush (Rahy)

Owen Burrows — Hamdan Al Maktoum

PLACINGS: 2/1911- — RPR **116+**

Starts	1st	2nd	3rd	4th	Win & Pl
5	3	1	-	-	£44,437

	9/18	Sand	1m Cls1 List good	£22,684
100	7/18	York	1m Cls2 81-100 Hcap gd-fm	£15,563
	5/18	NmkR	1m Cls5 3yo gd-fm	£3,881

Won three out of four last season, with only flop coming when stepped up to 1m2f at Royal Ascot (raced too keenly); got back on track with wins at York and Sandown over a mile, staying on strongly; looks ready to return to 1m2f.

Waldgeist

5 ch h Galileo - Waldlerche (Monsun)

Andre Fabre (Fr) — Gestut Ammerland & Newsells Park

PLACINGS: 131/22424/51111455- — RPR **121**

Starts	1st	2nd	3rd	4th	Win & Pl
16	6	3	1	3	£1,288,298

9/18	Lonc	1m4f Gp2 good	£65,575
7/18	StCl	1m4f Gp1 gd-sft	£202,265
6/18	Chan	1m4f Gp2 soft	£65,575
5/18	Lonc	1m4f Gp3 good	£35,398
10/16	StCl	1m2f Gp1 2yo soft	£105,037
9/16	Chan	1m 2yo good	£9,926

Had become disappointing in 2017 after a near miss in the Prix du Jockey Club but confirmed himself a top-class middle-distance performer last season, claiming a second Group 1 win in the Grand Prix de Saint-Cloud; good fourth in the Arc but below that level when travelling abroad.

Waldlied

4 ch f New Approach - Waldlerche (Monsun)

Andre Fabre (Fr) — Newsells Park & Gestut Ammerland

PLACINGS: 7/121- — RPR **112+**

Starts	1st	2nd	3rd	4th	Win & Pl
4	2	1	-	-	£93,008

7/18	StCl	1m4f Gp2 3yo gd-sft	£65,575
5/18	StCl	1m4f 3yo soft	£13,274

Progressive in just four runs, including a comfortable two-and-a-half-length Group 2 win at Saint-Cloud last July on quickest ground ever encountered (good to soft); missed the rest of the season but set to return with Group 1 middle-distance races on agenda.

Waldstern

3 ch c Sea The Stars - Waldlerche (Monsun)

John Gosden — Gestut Ammerland

PLACINGS: 124- RPR **101**

Starts	1st	2nd	3rd	4th	Win & Pl
3	1	1	-	1	£9,244
8/18	NmkJ	1m Cls4 2yo gd-sft			£5,175

Ran a fine race when finishing second to a high-class prospect in Kadar last September but didn't quite go on as expected when managing only fourth in the Zetland Stakes, appearing uncomfortable on quick ground; half-brother to Waldgeist who should flourish over middle distances.

Watan

3 ch c Toronado - Shotgun Gulch (Thunder Gulch)

Richard Hannon — Al Shaqab Racing

PLACINGS: 1251- RPR **105**

Starts	1st	2nd	3rd	4th	Win & Pl
4	2	1	-	-	£45,066
10/18	Leic	6f Cls4 2yo gd-sft			£6,469
7/18	Gdwd	6f Cls2 Mdn 2yo good			£15,753

Showed he possesses a big engine last season, winning both starts over 6f and finishing second in the Acomb Stakes (sent off favourite) despite never learning to settle; should get a mile if more tractable and trainer still considering a 2,000 Guineas bid.

Weekender

5 b g Frankel - Very Good News (Empire Maker)

John Gosden — K Abdullah

PLACINGS: 4/13121d/132237- RPR **116** RPR

Starts	1st	2nd	3rd	4th	Win & Pl
12	3	4	3	1	£189,420
5/18	Chmt	1m6f Cls2 stand			£16,173
87 6/17	NmkJ	1m2f Cls4 66-87 3yo Hcap gd-fm			£5,175
4/17	Chmt	1m2f Cls5 Mdn 3yo stand			£5,175

Ran a huge race when finishing second under a big weight in last season's Ebor at York; otherwise slightly disappointing having looked a potentially top-class stayer when following up a progressive 2017 campaign with a winning reappearance at Chelmsford; has since been gelded and could well have more to give.

MY FIVE TO WATCH
Maddy Playle
•Beringer •Dancing Vega •Dash Of Spice •Mubariz •Persian King

Well Done Fox

3 b c Acclamation - Excelette (Exceed And Excel)

Richard Hannon — King Power Racing

PLACINGS: 5218171220- RPR **107**

Starts	1st	2nd	3rd	4th	Win & Pl
10	3	3	-	-	£91,291
8/18	York	5f Cls1 List 2yo gd-fm			£39,697
7/18	Sand	5f Cls1 List 2yo gd-fm			£17,013
5/18	Sals	5f Cls4 2yo gd-sft			£5,111

Won two 5f Listed races last season and went close at a higher level subsequently, finishing second behind Soldier's Call in the Flying Childers Stakes and Sergei Prokofiev in the Cornwallis; has plenty of scope and could be a high-class sprinter.

Wells Farhh Go (Ire)

4 b c Farhh - Mowazana (Galileo)

Tim Easterby — SA Heley & Partner

PLACINGS: 11/6614- RPR **114**

Starts	1st	2nd	3rd	4th	Win & Pl
6	3	-	-	1	£158,243
7/18	NmkJ	1m5f Cls1 Gp3 3yo gd-fm			£85,065
8/17	York	7f Cls1 Gp3 2yo gd-sft			£51,039
7/17	York	7f Cls3 Auct 2yo gd-sft			£7,763

Strong stayer who produced by far his best performance last season when stepped up in trip to win the Bahrain Trophy; far from disgraced when fourth over shorter in the Great Voltigeur and a leading contender for the St Leger until ruled out through injury; set to return in mid-June.

Western Australia (Ire)

3 ch c Australia - What A Treasure (Cadeaux Genereux)

Aidan O'Brien (Ir) — Derrick Smith, Mrs John Magnier & Michael Tabor

PLACINGS: 961443- RPR **112**

Starts	1st	2nd	3rd	4th	Win & Pl
6	1	-	1	2	£42,376
9/18	Gowr	7f Mdn 2yo gd-fm			£8,995

Seemed to have had limitations exposed in good company when well beaten behind Madhmoon and Persian King last autumn but ran a stormer when beaten just a length at 50-1 in the Vertem Futurity Trophy; looks a strong stayer and should progress over longer trips.

Who's Steph (Ire)

4 gr f Zoffany - Llew Law (Verglas)

Ger Lyons (Ir) — George Strawbridge

PLACINGS: 91/1172- RPR **109**

Starts	1st	2nd	3rd	4th	Win & Pl
6	3	1	-	-	£108,465
5/18	Leop	1m Gp3 3yo good			£31,327
4/18	Leop	7f Gp3 3yo heavy			£33,938
10/17	Naas	1m Mdn 2yo yield			£8,687

Suffered an interrupted campaign last season but had flourished in the spring, winning a pair of

Group 3 races, and returned with a close second in a Group 2 at Leopardstown in September; coped well with step up to 1m2f last time and could get further.

Wild Illusion

4 b f Dubawi - Rumh (Monsun)

Charlie Appleby — Godolphin

PLACINGS: 131/422112- RPR **116**

	Starts		1st	2nd	3rd	4th	Win & Pl
	9		4	3	1	1	£1,185,181
	10/18	Lonc	1m2f Gp1 good				£252,832
	8/18	Gdwd	1m2f Cls1 Gp1 good				£340,260
	10/17	Chan	1m Gp1 2yo soft				£146,513
	8/17	Yarm	1m Cls5 2yo gd-fm				£3,623

Triple Group 1 winner who found her niche at 1m2f last season, winning the Nassau Stakes and Prix de l'Opera; had previously finished second in the Oaks and Ribblesdale Stakes over 1m4f but unlikely to go back up to 1m4f according to her trainer.

Wissahickon (USA)

4 ch c Tapit - No Matter What (Nureyev)

John Gosden — George Strawbridge

PLACINGS: **12/118111-11** RPR **121**

	Starts		1st	2nd	3rd	4th	Win & Pl
	10		8	1	-	-	£260,630
	2/19	Ling	1m2f Cls1 Gp3 stand				£56,710
	2/19	Ling	1m2f Cls1 List stand				£25,520
	12/18	Ling	1m2f Cls1 List stand				£20,983
107	9/18	NmkR	1m1f Cls2 93-107 Hcap gd-fm				£99,600
101	8/18	Chmt	1m2f Cls2 87-101 3yo Hcap stand				£16,173
94	6/18	York	1m2½f Cls2 89-95 3yo Hcap gd-fm				£31,125
	5/18	Ling	1m2f Cls5 stand				£3,752
	10/17	Wolv	1m½f Cls5 2yo stand				£3,881

Different class on the all-weather circuit this winter, easily completing a hat-trick in the Winter Derby to maintain progress made on turf last season when running away with the Cambridgeshire; should be a force in top 1m2f races.

With You

4 b f Dansili - In Clover (Inchinor)

Freddy Head (Fr) — George Strawbridge

PLACINGS: 11/25134- RPR **115**

	Starts		1st	2nd	3rd	4th	Win & Pl
	7		3	1	1	1	£380,770
	7/18	Deau	1m Gp1 gd-sft				£132,743
	10/17	Deau	1m Gp3 2yo v soft				£34,188
	9/17	StCl	1m 2yo heavy				£11,538

Raced exclusively at Group 1 level last season and won the Prix Rothschild before a fine third against the boys in the Prix Jacques le Marois; yet to win beyond a mile but ran Laurens to a short-head in the Prix Saint-Alary; comeback pencilled in for the Prix d'Ispahan.

Withhold

6 b g Champs Elysees - Coming Back (Fantastic Light)

Roger Charlton — Tony Bloom

PLACINGS: 42272121/31/18- RPR **111+aw**

	Starts		1st	2nd	3rd	4th	Win & Pl
	12		4	4	1	1	£265,588
99	6/18	Newc	2m½f Cls2 97-108 Hcap std-slw				£92,385
87	10/17	NmkR	2m2f Cls2 85-103 Hcap good				£155,625
80	10/16	Hayd	2m Cls4 72-84 Hcap good				£4,690
	8/16	Bath	1m5f Cls5 Mdn firm				£3,068

Lightly raced stayer who has easily won big handicaps in each of the last two seasons, adding last year's Northumberland Plate to the 2017 Cesarewitch; ruled out of the Melbourne Cup after breaking a blood vessel when down the field in his prep run.

Without Parole

4 b c Frankel - Without You Babe (Lemon Drop Kid)

John Gosden — John Gunther & Tanya Gunther

PLACINGS: **1/111766-** RPR **120**

	Starts		1st	2nd	3rd	4th	Win & Pl
	7		4	-	-	-	£357,930
	6/18	Asct	1m Cls1 Gp1 3yo gd-fm				£305,525
	5/18	Sand	1m Cls1 List 3yo good				£22,684
	4/18	Yarm	1m Cls5 3yo gd-fm				£3,752
	12/17	Newc	1m Cls5 2yo stand				£4,528

Won first three races last season to take unbeaten record to four, including victory in the St James's Palace Stakes at Royal Ascot; form of that race proved questionable, though, and something to prove after three subsequent defeats, including when stepped up to 1m2f.

Wonderment (Ire)

3 b f Camelot - Wiwilia (Konigstiger)

Nicolas Clement (Fr) — Mme Stella Thayer

PLACINGS: 131- RPR **108**

	Starts		1st	2nd	3rd	4th	Win & Pl
	3		2	-	1	-	£143,230
	10/18	StCl	1m2f Gp1 2yo good				£126,416
	8/18	Evre	1m1f 2yo good				£6,195

Became first filly for 14 years to win the Group 1 Criterium de Saint-Cloud when coming from well off the pace to win last season's big end-of-season prize; relished step up to 1m2f and should prove a force in good fillies' middle-distance/staying races.

Worth Waiting

4 b f Bated Breath - Salutare (Sadler's Wells)

David Lanigan — Saif Ali

PLACINGS: 2/211114- — RPR **108+**

Starts	1st	2nd	3rd	4th	Win & Pl
7	4	2	-	1	£100,897

	8/18	Deau	1m4½f Gp3 3yo gd-sft	£35,398
	7/18	NmkJ	1m4f Cls1 List gd-fm	£22,684
85	6/18	Wind	1m2f Cls4 76-85 3yo Hcap gd-fm	£5,531
	5/18	Rdcr	1m2f Cls5 Auct Mdn 3-5yo gd-fm	£4,464

Progressive last season and completed a four-timer when running away with a Group 3 at Longchamp in August by three lengths; just came up short when stepped up to the top level, finishing fourth in the Prix Vermeille.

Wusool (USA)

4 b c Speightstown - Torrestrella (Orpen)

Francois Rohaut (Fr) — Hamdan Al Maktoum

PLACINGS: 112114- — RPR **112+**

Starts	1st	2nd	3rd	4th	Win & Pl
6	4	1	-	1	£99,106

6/18	Chan	1m Gp3 3yo gd-sft	£35,398
5/18	StCl	1m 3yo gd-sft	£15,487
2/18	Cagn	1m 3yo stand	£11,504
1/18	Cagn	1m 3yo stand	£10,619

Missed the second half of last season after managing only fourth when favourite for the Prix Jean Prat but had previously looked a miler going places; won twice on the all-weather early in 2018 and added two more victories on turf, including a Group 3 by three and a half lengths.

Yafta

4 gr c Dark Angel - Swiss Dream (Oasis Dream)

Richard Hannon — Hamdan Al Maktoum

PLACINGS: 42211/212217- — RPR **114**

Starts	1st	2nd	3rd	4th	Win & Pl
11	4	5	-	1	£108,310

	7/18	Newb	6f Cls1 Gp3 gd-fm	£34,026
93	5/18	NmkR	6f Cls2 76-93 3yo Hcap gd-fm	£31,125
82	9/17	Chmt	6f Cls4 75-84 2yo Hcap stand	£7,116
	8/17	Bath	5½f Cls5 2yo good	£3,235

Progressive and consistent last season, running huge races in three competitive Newmarket handicaps before finishing second in the Chipchase Stakes and winning the Hackwood; only disappointing run when seventh on final start in the Hungerford.

Young Rascal (Fr)

4 b c Intello - Rock My Soul (Clodovil)

William Haggas — Bernard Kantor

PLACINGS: 2/11711- — RPR **120**

Starts	1st	2nd	3rd	4th	Win & Pl
6	4	1	-	-	£124,865

10/18	Newb	1m4f Cls1 Gp3 gd-sft	£23,463
9/18	Newb	1m3f Cls1 Gp3 soft	£34,026
5/18	Ches	1m4½f Cls1 Gp3 3yo good	£56,710
4/18	Newb	1m3f Cls3 Mdn 3yo gd-sft	£9,704

Won four out of five races last season, with sole defeat coming when only seventh in the Derby; won the Chester Vase on good ground but improved on much softer going when back from a break in the autumn, winning twice (including dead heat) at Newbury.

Zabeel Prince (Ire)

6 ch g Lope De Vega - Princess Serena (Unbridled's Song)

Roger Varian — Sheikh Mohammed Obaid Al Maktoum

PLACINGS: 2/1110/102- — RPR **113**

Starts	1st	2nd	3rd	4th	Win & Pl
8	4	2	-	-	£70,529

	3/18	Donc	1m Cls1 List soft	£20,983
96	10/17	York	1m Cls2 82-96 Hcap good	£18,675
86	9/17	Yarm	1m Cls4 78-86 Hcap soft	£5,175
	6/17	Nott	1m½f Cls5 Mdn soft	£3,235

Lightly raced and progressive miler who earned a step up to Group 1 level with an easy win in the Listed Doncaster Mile first time out last season but picked up an injury in the Lockinge; good second to Mustashry in the Joel Stakes on ground quicker than ideal.

Zagitova (Ire)

3 ch f Galileo - Penchant (Kyllachy)

Aidan O'Brien (Ir) — Michael Tabor, Derrick Smith & Mrs John Magnier

PLACINGS: 21345- — RPR **103**

Starts	1st	2nd	3rd	4th	Win & Pl
5	1	1	1	1	£46,303

8/18	Cork	1m Mdn 2yo good	£8,995

Didn't quite build on maiden win last season, finishing no better than third in three runs at Pattern level when well fancied every time (favourite when third in the Debutante); may well prove capable of better but trip hard to work out (sprinting pedigree on dam's side).

Zakouski

3 b c Shamardal - O'Giselle (Octagonal)

Charlie Appleby — Godolphin

PLACINGS: 1- — RPR **90+aw**

Starts	1st	2nd	3rd	4th	Win & Pl
1	1	-	-	-	£3,881

11/18	Kemp	7f Cls5 2yo std-slw	£3,881

Claimed a notable scalp in Headman when making a winning debut at Kempton in November, with the pair pulling well clear; out of an unraced half-sister to multiple Australian Group 1 winners Lonhro (7f-1m2f) and Niello (1m2f) so likely to prove best at around a mile.

Form figures for the 250 key horses are correct up to and including February 26, 2018

KEY HORSES LISTED BY TRAINER

Charlie Appleby
Auxerre
Beyond Reason
Blue Point
Brundtland
Cross Counter
D'Bai
Ghaiyyath
Ghostwatch
Glorious Journey
La Pelosa
Line Of Duty
Loxley
Masar
Oasis Charm
Old Persian
Quorto
Symbolization
Wild Illusion
Zakouski

Bruno Audouin
Holdthasigreen

Andrew Balding
Beat The Bank
Donjuan Triumphant
Fox Tal
Maid Up
Morando
Shine So Bright

Pascal Bary
Study Of Man

Ralph Beckett
Antonia De Vega
Dancing Vega
Feliciana De Vega
Manuela De Vega
Mitchum Swagger
Rock Eagle
Sand Share

Michael Bell
Fabricate
Pretty Pollyanna

Jim Bolger
Guaranteed
Verbal Dexterity

Karl Burke
Kadar
Laurens
True Mason

Owen Burrows
Elwazir
Laraaib
Tabdeed
Wadilsafa

Henry Candy
Limato

Mick Channon
Chairmanoftheboard

Fabrice Chappet
Rocques

Roger Charlton
Herculean
Projection
Red Impression
Withhold

Nicolas Clement
Wonderment

Ken Condon
Romanised

Clive Cox
Snazzy Jazzy

Simon Crisford
Century Dream
Jash
Ostilio

Tom Dascombe
Arthur Kitt
Great Scot
Kachy

Alain de Royer-Dupre
Vazirabad

Michael Dods
Mabs Cross

Harry Dunlop
Jackfinbar
Knight To Behold

Tim Easterby
Vintage Brut
Wells Farhh Go

David Elsworth
Dandhu
Dash Of Spice
Desert Skyline
Sir Dancealot

Andre Fabre
Le Brivido
Persian King
Plumatic
Waldgeist
Waldlied

Richard Fahey
Forest Ranger
Mr Lupton
Sands Of Mali

James Fanshawe
The Tin Man

Charlie Fellowes
King Ottokar
Prince Of Arran

John Gosden
Angel's Hideaway
Beatboxer
Ben Vrackie
Calyx
Coronet
Dreamfield
Dubai Warrior
Emblazoned
Enable
First Eleven
Highgarden
Kick On
Lah Ti Dar
Royal Line
Shambolic
Sparkle Roll
Stradivarius
Stream Of Stars
Stylehunter
Too Darn Hot
Turgenev
Waldstern
Weekender
Wissahickon
Without Parole

William Haggas
Addeybb
One Master
Pretty Baby
Rainbow Heart
Sea Of Class
Young Rascal

Richard Hannon
Billesdon Brook
Boitron
Danehill Kodiac
Raymond Tusk
Star Terms
Tabarrak
Watan
Well Done Fox
Yafta

Jessica Harrington
Still Standing

Freddy Head
Anodor
Call The Wind
Lily's Candle
Polydream
With You

Charlie Hills
Battaash
Equilateral
Khaadem
Phoenix Of Spain

Eve Johnson Houghton
Accidental Agent

Dean Ivory
Flaming Spear
Librisa Breeze

Mark Johnston
Arctic Sound
Baghdad
Communique
Dark Vision
Dee Ex Bee
Elarqam
Main Edition
Marie's Diamond
Mildenberger
Natalie's Joy

Sylvester Kirk
Salouen

Carlos Laffon-Parias
Matematica

David Lanigan
Worth Waiting

Sheila Lavery
Lady Kaya

Ger Lyons
Psychedelic Funk
Who's Steph

David Marnane
Settle For Bay

Martyn Meade
Advertise

Brian Meehan
Bacchus

David Menuisier
Thundering Blue

Paul Midgley
Tarboosh

Hughie Morrison
Marmelo

Willie Mullins
Low Sun
Stratum
Thomas Hobson
True Self

Aidan O'Brien
Amedeo Modigliani
Anthony Van Dyck
Broome
Cape Of Good Hope
Capri
Chablis
Circus Maximus
Constantinople
Fairyland
Flag Of Honour
Fleeting
Frosty
Goddess
Hermosa
I Can Fly
Idaho
Japan
Just Wonderful
Kew Gardens
Magic Wand
Magical
Magna Grecia
Mohawk
Mount Everest
Norway
Old Glory
Peach Tree
Pink Dogwood
Sergei Prokofiev
So Perfect
Southern France
Sydney Opera House
Ten Sovereigns
Western Australia
Zagitova

Joseph O'Brien
Iridessa
Latrobe
Speak In Colours

David O'Meara
Lord Glitters
Suedois

Hugo Palmer
Gifted Master

Kevin Prendergast
Madhmoon

Patrick Prendergast
Skitter Scatter

John Quinn
El Astronaute
Signora Cabello

Francois Rohaut
Wusool

Jean-Claude Rouget
Olmedo

Kevin Ryan
Brando
East
Emaraaty Ana
Hello Youmzain

David Simcock
Desert Encounter
Raakib Alhawa

Bryan Smart
Alpha Delphini

Richard Spencer
Rumble Inthejungle

Fozzy Stack
Son Of Rest

Sir Michael Stoute
Crystal Ocean
Eqtidaar
Mekong
Mirage Dancer
Mustashry
Regal Reality
Sangarius
Veracious

Saeed Bin Suroor
Benbatl
Best Solution
Dream Castle
Royal Marine
Royal Meeting

James Tate
Hey Gaman
Invincible Army

Roger Teal
Tip Two Win

Marcus Tregoning
Mohaather

Roger Varian
Cape Byron
Defoe
Mot Juste
Pilaster
Prince Eiji
San Donato
Sharja Bridge
Zabeel Prince

Ed Walker
Royal Intervention
Stormy Antarctic

Archie Watson
Soldier's Call

Stephane Wattel
City Light

Dermot Weld
Hazapour
Imaging
Rakan

Ian Williams
Magic Circle

RACING POST RATINGS: LAST SEASON'S LEADING TWO-YEAR-OLDS

KEY: Horse name, best RPR figure, finishing position when earning figure, (details of race where figure was earned)

Too Darn Hot 126[1] (7f, Newm, GF, Oct 13)
Quorto (IRE) 121[1] (7f, Curr, Yld, Sep 16)
Ten Sovereigns (IRE) 120[1] (6f, Newm, GF, Sep 29)
Jash (IRE) 119[2] (6f, Newm, GF, Sep 29)
Advertise 118[2] (7f, Newm, GF, Oct 13)
Anthony Van Dyck (IRE) 118[2] (7f, Curr, Yld, Sep 16)
Calyx 116[1] (6f, Asco, GF, Jun 19)
Persian King (IRE) 115[1] (1m, Newm, GF, Oct 13)
Pretty Pollyanna 115[1] (6f, Newj, GF, Jul 13)
Iridessa (IRE) 114[1] (1m, Newm, GF, Oct 12)
Kessaar (IRE) 114[1] (6f, Newb, Sft, Sep 22)
Madhmoon (IRE) 114[1] (1m, Leop, GF, Sep 15)
Magna Grecia (IRE) 114[1] (1m, Donc, GS, Oct 27)
Phoenix Of Spain (IRE) 114[2] (1m, Donc, GS, Oct 27)
Soldier's Call 114[1] (5f 3y, Donc, Gd, Sep 14)
Circus Maximus (IRE) 112[4] (1m, Donc, GS, Oct 27)
Fairyland (IRE) 112[1] (6f, Newm, GF, Sep 29)
Mohawk (IRE) 112[1] (1m, Newm, GF, Sep 29)
Skitter Scatter (USA) 112[1] (7f, Curr, Yld, Sep 16)
Western Australia (IRE) 112[3] (1m, Donc, GS, Oct 27)
Great Scot 111[5] (1m, Donc, GS, Oct 27)
Hermosa (IRE) 111[2] (1m, Newm, GF, Oct 12)
Sergei Prokofiev (CAN) 111[1] (5f, Newm, GF, Oct 12)
The Mackem Bullet (IRE) 111[2] (6f, Newm, GF, Sep 29)
Vintage Brut 111[1] (6f, York, Sft, Oct 13)
Christmas (IRE) 110[2] (7f, Curr, Yld, Aug 26)
Dark Vision (IRE) 110[1] (7f, Good, Gd, Jul 31)
Emaraaty Ana 110[1] (6f, York, GF, Aug 24)
Just Wonderful (USA) 110[1] (7f, Newm, GF, Sep 28)
Land Force (IRE) 110[1] (6f, Good, Gd, Aug 2)
So Perfect (USA) 110[3] (6f, Newm, GF, Sep 29)
Japan 109[1] (1m, Naas, Gd, Sep 30)
Legends Of War (USA) 109[2] (6f, York, GF, Aug 24)
Mount Everest (IRE) 109[2] (1m, Naas, Gd, Sep 30)
Rumble Inthejungle (IRE) 109[1] (5f, Good, Gd, Aug 1)
Sydney Opera House 109[2] (1m, Newm, GF, Sep 29)
The Irish Rover (IRE) 109[3] (6f, Curr, Gd, Aug 12)
Arctic Sound 108[1] (7f, Newm, Gd, Sep 27)
Arthur Kitt 108[2] (7f, Sand, Gd, Sep 1)
Broome (IRE) 108[2] (1m, Leop, GF, Sep 15)
Vange 108[4] (6f, Asco, GF, Jun 19)
Boitron (FR) 107[1] (7f, Newb, Gd, Aug 18)
Fleeting (IRE) 107[1] (1m, Donc, Gd, Sep 13)
Kick On 107[6] (1m, Donc, GS, Oct 27)
Lady Kaya (IRE) 107[2] (7f, Curr, Yld, Sep 16)
Main Edition (IRE) 107[1] (7f, Newj, GS, Aug 11)
Marie's Diamond (IRE) 107[4] (6f, Newm, GF, Sep 29)
Mohaather 107[1] (7f, Newb, GS, Oct 27)
Queen Of Bermuda (IRE) 107[1] (6f, Ayr, Hvy, Sep 22)
Well Done Fox 107[2] (5f, Newm, GF, Oct 12)
Dunkerron 106[2] (7f, Good, Gd, Jul 31)
Konchek 106[2] (6f, Newj, GF, Jul 12)
La Pelosa (IRE) 106[2] (6f, Asco, GF, Jun 22)
Pocket Dynamo (USA) 106[2] (5f, Asco, GF, Jun 21)
Sangarius 106[1] (7f 6y, Donc, GS, Sep 14)
Shine So Bright 106[3] (6f, York, GF, Aug 24)
True Mason 106[2] (6f, Newb, Sft, Sep 22)
Angel's Hideaway (IRE) 105[2] (7f, Newm, GF, Oct 12)
Bye Bye Hong Kong (USA) 105[2] (7f, Newm, Gd, Sep 27)
Cape Of Good Hope (IRE) 105[3] (1m, Newm, GF, Sep 29)
Cardini (USA) 105[3] (7f 6y, Donc, Gd, Sep 15)
Charming Kid 105[3] (6f, Newj, GF, Jul 12)
Dandhu 105[2] (7f, Newm, GF, Sep 28)
Gossamer Wings (USA) 105[5] (6f, Newm, GF, Sep 29)
Guaranteed (IRE) 105[1] (1m 1f, Leop, Gd, Oct 27)
Masaff (IRE) 105[3] (1m, Leop, GF, Sep 15)
Norway (IRE) 105[1] (1m 2f, Newm, GF, Oct 13)
Van Beethoven (CAN) 105[4] (7f 6y, Donc, Gd, Sep 15)
Watan 105[2] (7f, York, GF, Aug 22)
Bandiuc Eile (IRE) 104[2] (7f, Curr, Yld, Aug 26)
Foxtrot Liv 104[2] (7f, Naas, Gd, Sep 30)
Indigo Balance (IRE) 104[1] (5f, Curr, Gd, Aug 25)
Mot Juste (USA) 104[1] (7f, Newm, GF, Oct 12)
Neverland Rock 104[3] (7f, Newj, GF, Jul 14)
Peach Tree (IRE) 104[2] (1m, Curr, Yld, Sep 1)
Sabre 104[5] (6f, Good, Gd, Aug 2)
Star Terms 104[2] (1m, Donc, Gd, Sep 13)
Turgenev 104[7] (1m, Donc, GS, Oct 27)
Azano 103[2] (7f, Newb, GS, Oct 27)
Confiding 103[3] (7f, Good, Gd, Jul 31)
Could Be King 103[4] (7f, Curr, Yld, Aug 26)
Khaadem (IRE) 103[1] (6f 2y, Donc, GS, Sep 12)
Kuwait Currency (USA) 103[5] (7f, Newm, GF, Oct 13)
Nate The Great 103[3] (1m 2f, Newm, GF, Oct 13)
Sand Share 103[3] (1m, Donc, Gd, Sep 13)
Shang Shang Shang (USA) 103[1] (5f, Asco, GF, Jun 21)
Shumookhi (IRE) 103[1] (5f 34y, Newb, Gd, Aug 17)
Victory Command (IRE) 103[4] (1m, Newm, GF, Sep 29)
Zagitova (IRE) 103[4] (7f, Curr, Yld, Sep 16)
Coral Beach (IRE) 102[1] (7f, Leop, Yld, Oct 20)
Magnetic Charm 102[4] (1m, Donc, Gd, Sep 13)
Old Glory (IRE) 102[3] (7f, Leop, Yld, Oct 20)
Persian Moon (IRE) 102[1] (1m 113y, Epso, Gd, Sep 30)
Power Of Now (IRE) 102[3] (1m, Naas, Gd, Sep 30)
Prince Eiji 102[3] (7f, Newm, Gd, Sep 27)
San Donato (IRE) 102[1] (6f 2y, Donc, GS, Oct 27)
Viadera 102[2] (6f 63y, Curr, Gd, Jul 21)
Yourtimeisnow 102[1] (6f, Sali, GF, Sep 6)
Chaleur 101[1] (7f, Newm, GF, Sep 29)
I'll Have Another (IRE) 101[2] (1m 2f, Newm, GF, Oct 13)
Lady Aria 101[2] (6f, Sali, GF, Sep 6)
No Needs Never (IRE) 101[1] (7f, Dunw, SD, Oct 5)
Royal Intervention (IRE) 101[1] (6f, Newj, GF, Jun 30)
Shambolic (IRE) 101[4] (1m, Newm, GF, Oct 12)
Sovereign (IRE) 101[3] (1m 1f, Leop, Gd, Oct 27)
Sporting Chance 101[1] (6f, Ripo, GS, Aug 27)
Sunday Star 101[3] (7f, Newm, GF, Oct 12)
Waldstern 101[4] (1m 2f, Newm, GF, Oct 13)
All The King's Men (IRE) 100[1] (5f 164y, Nava, Yld, Oct 14)
Antonia De Vega (IRE) 100[1] (7f, Good, Gd, Aug 25)
Barbill (IRE) 100[2] (6f 2y, Donc, GS, Oct 27)
Bruce Wayne (IRE) 100[2] (6f, Curr, Yld, Sep 1)
Cava (IRE) 100[3] (6f, Curr, GF, Jul 1)
Certain Lad 100[3] (6f, Curr, GF, Jun 30)
Comedy (IRE) 100[9] (6f, Newm, GF, Sep 29)
Concierge (IRE) 100[1] (6f, Ncsw, SD, Oct 23)
Dashing Willoughby 100[8] (1m, Donc, GS, Oct 27)
Dave Dexter 100[1] (5f, Ayr, Hvy, Sep 21)
Dubai Dominion 100[2] (7f 6y, Donc, GS, Sep 14)
Firelight (FR) 100[4] (6f, York, GF, Aug 23)
Life Of Riley 100[2] (5f, Good, Gd, Aug 1)
Queen Jo Jo 100[3] (6f, York, GF, Aug 23)
Sparkle'n'joy (IRE) 100[1] (7f, Leop, GF, Sep 15)
Walkinthesand (IRE) 100[1] (7f, Sand, Gd, Sep 19)
Beat Le Bon (FR) 99[2] (7f 6y, Donc, GS, Oct 27)
Chuck Willis (IRE) 99[2] (6f, Newb, GF, Jul 20)
Floating Artist 99[2] (1m 37y, Hayd, Hvy, Sep 8)
Getchagetchagetcha 99[4] (7f, Good, Gd, Jul 31)
Junius Brutus (FR) 99[2] (6f, Kemw, SS, Sep 8)
Mackqeez (IRE) 99[5] (1m, Naas, Gd, Sep 30)
Moravia 99[2] (7f 20y, Leop, GF, Jul 26)
Natalie's Joy 99[1] (6f, Newb, GF, Jul 20)
Showout 99[5] (6f, York, GF, Aug 24)
Signora Cabello (IRE) 99[1] (5f, Asco, GF, Jun 20)
Zander 99[2] (1m, List, Hvy, Sep 10)
Boerhan 98[5] (1m, Newm, GF, Oct 13)
Dark Jedi (IRE) 98[2] (1m, Sali, Gd, Aug 24)
Dom Carlos (IRE) 98[3] (5f, Asco, GF, Jun 23)
Gee Rex (IRE) 98[4] (6f, Curr, GF, May 26)
Highland Fortune (USA) 98[2] (7f 100y, Tipp, Gd, Aug 10)
Iconic Choice 98[1] (7f, Newb, GS, Oct 27)
Inverleigh (IRE) 98[2] (6f, Fair, Yld, Sep 24)
Lethal Promise (IRE) 98[1] (6f, Fair, Yld, Sep 24)
Light My Fire (IRE) 98[3] (6f, Ayr, Hvy, Sep 22)
More Than This 98[1] (7f, Good, Gd, Aug 2)
Pythion (FR) 98[6] (1m, Naas, Gd, Sep 30)
Quiet Endeavour (IRE) 98[1] (6f, Kemw, SS, Aug 15)
Servalan (IRE) 98[1] (6f, Naas, GF, May 20)

Shades Of Blue (IRE) 98[3] (5f, Asco, GF, Jun 20)
Space Traveller 98[8] (6f, Newm, GF, Sep 29)
Swissterious 98[2] (6f 2y, Donc, GS, Sep 12)
The Cruising Lord 98[4] (5f, Newm, GF, Oct 12)
Accordance 97[2] (7f, Good, Gd, Aug 25)
Cosmic Law (IRE) 97[6] (7f, Good, Gd, Jul 31)
King Ottokar (FR) 97[9] (1m, Donc, GS, Oct 27)
Look Around 97[1] (7f, Sand, GF, Jul 26)
Pogo (IRE) 97[3] (7f 6y, Donc, GS, Sep 14)
Spanish Mission (USA) 97[1] (1m 2f, Chmf, SD, Nov 10)
Sunsprite (IRE) 97[3] (6f, Ripo, GS, Aug 27)
Angelic Light (IRE) 96[1] (6f, Newm, Sft, Nov 2)
Chynna 96[2] (6f, Newm, Sft, Nov 2)
Cruciatus (IRE) 96[4] (6f 63y, Curr, Gd, Jul 21)
Deputise 96[1] (6f 20y, Wolw, SD, Dec 8)
Drogon (IRE) 96[1] (6f 212y, Hayd, GF, Jul 5)
Federal Law (CAN) 96[7] (7f, Good, Gd, Jul 31)
Fox Power (IRE) 96[2] (1m, Donc, GS, Oct 26)
Goddess (USA) 96[1] (7f, Leop, GF, Jul 12)
Good Fortune 96[1] (7f, Ling, GF, Jul 21)
Manuela De Vega (IRE) 96[1] (1m 6y, Pont, GS, Oct 22)
Model Guest 96[4] (7f, Newm, GF, Sep 28)
Moyassar 96[2] (5f 8y, Nott, GF, Oct 31)
Ninetythreetwenty (IRE) 96[6] (6f, Asco, GF, Jun 19)
Rainbow Heart (IRE) 96[1] (7f, Newm, Gd, Oct 24)
Red Balloons 96[1] (6f, York, GF, Aug 23)
Secret Thoughts (USA) 96[3] (7f 20y, Leop, GF, Jul 26)
Summer Daydream (IRE) 96[5] (6f, Ayr, Hvy, Sep 22)
Tarnawa (IRE) 96[2] (1m, Nava, Yld, Oct 14)
You Never Can Tell (IRE) 96[4] (7f 6y, Donc, GS, Sep 14)
Aim Power (IRE) 95[3] (6f, Good, Gd, Sep 4)
Beatboxer (USA) 95[1] (7f 212y, Hayd, GF, Aug 10)
Blown By Wind 95[7] (6f, Asco, GF, Jun 19)
Blue Gardenia (IRE) 95[1] (1m, Newm, Sft, Nov 3)
Byron Bay (FR) 95[6] (6f, Asco, GF, Jun 22)
Come On Leicester (IRE) 95[5] (5f, Asco, GF, Jun 20)
Constantinople (IRE) 95[1] (1m, Thur, GF, Oct 25)
Credenza (IRE) 95[3] (1m, Nava, Yld, Oct 14)
Dirty Rascal (IRE) 95[2] (6f 111y, Donc, Gd, Sep 13)
Duke Of Hazzard (FR) 95[3] (7f, Asco, GF, Jun 23)
Dutch Treat 95[5] (1m, Donc, Gd, Sep 13)
Fox Tal 95[4] (1m, Sali, Gd, Aug 24)
Fuente 95[3] (6f, Kemw, SS, Sep 8)
Glorious Lover (IRE) 95[2] (7f, Asco, GF, Jul 28)
Gypsy Spirit 95[3] (6f, Newm, Sft, Nov 2)
Happy Power (IRE) 95[1] (7f 6y, Donc, GS, Oct 27)
Jonah Jones (IRE) 95[5] (7f 6y, Donc, GS, Sep 14)
Little Kim 95[5] (6f, York, GF, Aug 23)
Mordred (IRE) 95[2] (1m, Newm, Gd, Sep 27)
Nayef Road (IRE) 95[3] (1m 2f, Newm, Gd, Oct 24)
North Wind (IRE) 95[5] (6f, Curr, GF, Jun 30)
Raakib Alhawa (IRE) 95[1] (1m, Newb, GS, Sep 21)
Rockin Roy (IRE) 95[1] (5f, Beve, GS, Aug 26)
Shining Armor 95[2] (6f 20y, Wolw, SD, Dec 8)
Third Of March (IRE) 95[1] (5f 164y, Nava, Yld, Oct 14)
Three Comets (GER) 95[2] (1m 6y, Pont, GS, Oct 22)
Western Frontier (USA) 95[1] (5f, Nava, Gd, Oct 24)
Zuenoon (IRE) 95[1] (1m 30y, Kill, Gd, Aug 23)
Ajrar 94[5] (7f, Good, Gd, Aug 25)
Blonde Warrior (IRE) 94[2] (7f, Chmf, SD, Sep 1)
Bold Approach (IRE) 94[2] (7f 20y, Leop, GF, Jul 26)
Broken Spear 94[1] (5f, York, Gd, Oct 12)
Canton Queen (IRE) 94[5] (7f, Newm, GF, Sep 28)
Catan (GER) 94[1] (7f 211y, Brig, GF, Oct 9)
Chairmanoftheboard (IRE) 94[1] (6f, Good, Sft, Oct 14)
Chapelli 94[4] (6f, Asco, GF, Jul 28)
Chicas Amigas (IRE) 94[2] (6f, Naas, GF, May 20)
Eagle Song (IRE) 94[1] (7f, Dunw, SD, Oct 19)
Forever In Dreams (IRE) 94[7] (5f, Asco, GF, Jun 20)
Glass Slippers 94[6] (6f, Ayr, Hvy, Sep 22)
He'zanarab (IRE) 94[1] (6f, York, GS, Jul 28)
Hello Youmzain (FR) 94[2] (6f, Hayd, GS, Sep 6)
Leroy Leroy 94[1] (1m, Donc, Gd, Sep 15)
Recon Mission (IRE) 94[2] (5f 164y, Nava, Yld, Oct 14)
Royal Marine (IRE) 94[1] (7f 6y, Donc, GS, Sep 14)
Semoum (USA) 94[6] (6f, York, GF, Aug 24)
Street Parade 94[1] (5f 16y, Chep, GF, Jul 13)
Tin Hat (IRE) 94[5] (5f, Asco, GF, Jun 23)
Trethias 94[4] (7f, Leop, GF, Sep 15)
Vivid Diamond (IRE) 94[2] (1m, Newm, Sft, Nov 3)
Wargrave (IRE) 94[7] (7f, Curr, Yld, Sep 16)
Al Hilalee 93[1] (7f, Newj, GF, Jul 13)
Athmad (IRE) 93[6] (7f 6y, Donc, GS, Sep 14)
Chocolate Music (IRE) 93[7] (7f, Curr, Yld, Aug 26)
Deia Glory 93[2] (5f, York, GF, Aug 25)
Don Armado (IRE) 93[1] (6f, Good, GF, Aug 3)
Dubai Legacy (USA) 93 (6f, Asco, GF, Jun 19)
Eclipse Storm 93[3] (5f 164y, Nava, Yld, Oct 14)
Elleanthus (IRE) 93[4] (1m 1f, Leop, Gd, Oct 27)
Even Keel (IRE) 93[2] (7f 192y, York, Sft, Oct 13)
Fanaar (IRE) 93[2] (7f 6y, Donc, GS, Sep 12)
Flashcard (IRE) 93[2] (6f 63y, Curr, Yld, Sep 16)
Garrus (IRE) 93[1] (6f, Ncsw, SD, Aug 31)
Good Luck Fox (IRE) 93[1] (5f 10y, Sand, GS, Aug 9)
Headman 93[1] (1m 5y, Ncsw, SD, Nov 1)
Hot Team (IRE) 93[3] (6f 63y, Curr, Yld, Sep 16)
Implicit (IRE) 93[1] (5f, Chmf, SD, Aug 10)
Kinks 93[6] (5f, Asco, GF, Jun 21)
Massam 93[1] (1m 3y, Yarm, GF, Sep 18)
Master Brewer (FR) 93[4] (7f, Asco, GF, Jul 28)
Never No More (IRE) 93[1] (5f, Dunw, SD, Oct 5)
Second Generation 93[1] (5f, Catt, GF, May 24)

TOPSPEED: LAST SEASON'S LEADING TWO-YEAR-OLDS

Ten Sovereigns (IRE) 109[1] (6f, Newm, GF, Sep 29)
Persian King (IRE) 108[1] (1m, Newm, GF, Oct 13)
Fairyland (IRE) 107[1] (6f, Newm, GF, Sep 29)
Jash (IRE) 107[2] (6f, Newm, GF, Sep 29)
Magna Grecia (IRE) 107[2] (1m, Newm, GF, Oct 13)
Quorto (IRE) 107[1] (7f, Curr, Yld, Sep 16)
The Mackem Bullet (IRE) 106[2] (6f, Newm, GF, Sep 29)
Too Darn Hot 106[1] (7f, Newm, GF, Oct 13)
Mohawk (IRE) 104[1] (1m, Newm, GF, Sep 29)
So Perfect (USA) 104[3] (6f, Newm, GF, Sep 29)
Anthony Van Dyck (IRE) 103[2] (7f, Curr, Yld, Sep 16)
Pretty Pollyanna 103[1] (6f, Newj, GF, Jul 13)
Soldier's Call 103[1] (5f 3y, Donc, Gd, Sep 14)
Phoenix Of Spain (IRE) 101[2] (1m, Donc, GS, Oct 27)
Sergei Prokofiev (CAN) 101[1] (5f, Newm, GF, Oct 12)
Advertise 100[1] (6f, Newj, GF, Jul 12)
Sydney Opera House 100[2] (1m, Newm, GF, Sep 29)
Western Australia (IRE) 99[3] (1m, Donc, GS, Oct 27)
Christmas (IRE) 98[2] (7f, Curr, Yld, Aug 26)
Circus Maximus (IRE) 98[4] (1m, Donc, GS, Oct 27)
Gossamer Wings (USA) 98[5] (6f, Newm, GF, Sep 29)
Iridessa (IRE) 98[1] (1m, Newm, GF, Oct 12)
Rumble inthejungle (IRE) 98[1] (5f, Good, Gd, Aug 1)
Great Scot 97[5] (1m, Donc, GS, Oct 27)
Japan 97[1] (1m, Naas, Gd, Sep 30)
Lady Kaya (IRE) 97[6] (6f, Newm, GF, Sep 29)
Mount Everest (IRE) 96[2] (1m, Naas, Gd, Sep 30)
Queen Of Bermuda (IRE) 96[7] (6f, Newm, GF, Sep 29)
Well Done Fox 96[2] (5f, Newm, GF, Oct 12)
Cape Of Good Hope (IRE) 95[3] (1m, Newm, GF, Sep 29)
Main Edition (IRE) 95[1] (7f, Newj, GS, Aug 11)
Arctic Sound 94[1] (7f, Newm, Gd, Sep 27)
Arthur Kitt 94[2] (7f, Sand, Gd, Sep 1)
Kessaar (IRE) 94[1] (6f, Newb, Sft, Sep 22)
Nayef Road (IRE) 94[3] (1m 2f, Newm, Gd, Oct 24)
Angel's Hideaway (IRE) 93[8] (6f, Newm, GF, Sep 29)
Broken Spear 93[1] (5f, York, Gd, Oct 12)
Chairmanoftheboard (IRE) 93[1] (6f, Good, Sft, Oct 14)
Dark Vision (IRE) 93[1] (7f, Good, Gd, Jul 31)
Hermosa (IRE) 93[2] (1m, Newm, GF, Oct 12)
Turgenev 93[1] (1m, Newm, Gd, Oct 6)
Vintage Brut 93[1] (6f, York, Sft, Oct 13)
Boitron (FR) 92[1] (7f, Newb, Gd, Aug 18)
Calyx 92[1] (6f, Asco, GF, Jun 19)
Comedy (IRE) 92[9] (6f, Newm, GF, Sep 29)
Coral Beach (IRE) 92[1] (7f, Leop, Yld, Oct 20)
Fleeting (IRE) 92[1] (1m, Donc, Gd, Sep 13)
Guaranteed (IRE) 92[2] (7f, Leop, Yld, Oct 20)

Konchek 92 [2] (6f, Newj, GF, Jul 12)
Marie's Diamond (IRE) 92 [1] (6f 63y, Curr, Gd, Jul 21)
Skitter Scatter (USA) 92 [1] (7f, Curr, Yld, Sep 16)
Victory Command (IRE) 92 [4] (1m, Newm, GF, Sep 29)
Bye Bye Hong Kong (USA) 91 [2] (7f, Newm, Gd, Sep 27)
Charming Kid 91 [3] (6f, Newj, GF, Jul 12)
Dubai Beauty (IRE) 91 [1] (7f, Newj, GF, Aug 4)
Kick On 91 [6] (1m, Donc, GS, Oct 27)
Legends Of War (USA) 91 [4] (5f 3y, Donc, Gd, Sep 14)
Old Glory (IRE) 91 [3] (7f, Leop, Yld, Oct 20)
Quiet Endeavour (IRE) 91 [1] (6f, Kemw, SS, Aug 15)
Azano 90 [1] (7f 3y, Yarm, GS, Oct 15)
Could Be King 90 [4] (7f, Leop, Yld, Oct 20)
Emaraaty Ana 90 [1] (6f, York, GF, Aug 24)
Fox Coach (IRE) 90 [1] (7f, Chmf, SD, Aug 14)
Garrus (IRE) 90 [1] (6f, Newj, GF, Aug 3)
Mohaather 90 [1] (7f, Newb, GS, Oct 27)
Moyassar 90 [3] (6f, York, GF, Aug 22)
Natalie's Joy 90 [1] (6f, Good, Gd, May 26)
Peach Tree (IRE) 90 [1] (1m, Nava, Yld, Oct 14)
San Donato (IRE) 90 [1] (6f 2y, Donc, GS, Oct 27)
Signora Cabello (IRE) 90 [1] (5f, Asco, GF, Jun 20)
Van Beethoven (CAN) 90 [1] (6f, Curr, GF, Jun 30)
Ginger Nut (IRE) 89 [1] (6f, York, GF, Aug 22)
Just Wonderful (USA) 89 [1] (1m, Curr, Yld, Sep 1)
Luxor 89 [1] (6f, Newb, GS, Oct 27)
Barys 88 [1] (1m 1y, Linw, SD, Nov 17)
Burj 88 [1] (6f 20y, Wolw, SD, Jun 6)
Cap Francais 88 [1] (1m 37y, Hayd, GS, Sep 29)
Cava (IRE) 88 [3] (6f, Curr, GF, Jul 1)
Cosmic Law (IRE) 88 [1] (6f 3y, Epso, Sft, Jun 1)
Dunkerron 88 [2] (7f, Good, Gd, Jul 31)
Even Keel (IRE) 88 [2] (7f 192y, York, Sft, Oct 13)
Fognini (IRE) 88 [2] (6f 17y, Ches, GS, Sep 29)
Indigo Balance (IRE) 88 [1] (6f, Curr, Gd, May 27)
Jonah Jones (IRE) 88 [1] (6f, York, Sft, Oct 13)
La Pelosa (IRE) 88 [2] (7f, Newj, GS, Aug 11)
Life Of Riley 88 [2] (5f, Good, Gd, Aug 1)
Marhaba Milliar (IRE) 88 [2] (6f, Chmf, SD, Sep 1)
Sabre 88 [2] (5f, Asco, GF, Jun 23)
Shades Of Blue (IRE) 88 [3] (5f, Asco, GF, Jun 20)
Barbill (IRE) 87 [2] (6f 2y, Donc, GS, Oct 27)
Bruce Wayne (IRE) 87 [2] (6f, Curr, Yld, Sep 1)
Chuck Willis (IRE) 87 [2] (6f, Newb, GF, Jul 20)
Dashing Willoughby 87 [2] (1m, Newb, GS, Sep 21)
Dave Dexter 87 [1] (5f 15y, Ches, Sft, Sep 15)
Don Armado (IRE) 87 [1] (6f, Good, GF, Aug 3)
Fox Power (IRE) 87 [2] (1m, Donc, GS, Oct 26)
Kinks 87 [4] (6f 17y, Ches, GS, Sep 29)
Land Force (IRE) 87 [1] (6f, Good, Gd, Aug 2)
Leroy Leroy 87 [1] (1m, Donc, Gd, Sep 15)
Lincoln Park 87 [1] (7f 37y, Hayd, Hvy, Oct 19)
Power Of Now (IRE) 87 [3] (1m, Naas, Gd, Sep 30)
Prince Eiji 87 [3] (7f, Newm, Gd, Sep 27)
Star Terms 87 [2] (1m, Donc, Gd, Sep 13)
Sunday Star 87 [1] (7f, Newm, GF, Sep 29)
The Irish Rover (IRE) 87 [1] (6f, Newb, GF, May 19)
Viadera 87 [2] (6f 63y, Curr, Gd, Jul 21)
Al Hilalee 86 [1] (7f, Newj, GF, Jul 13)
Barristan The Bold 86 [1] (7f 1y, Ches, GS, Sep 29)
Dubai Blue (USA) 86 [1] (1m 1y, Linw, SD, Sep 15)
Feliciana De Vega 86 [1] (7f, Newm, Sft, Nov 3)
Kuwait Currency (USA) 86 [1] (1m, Sali, Gd, Aug 24)
Line Of Duty (IRE) 86 [1] (1m, Good, Gd, Sep 4)
No Lippy (IRE) 86 [1] (5f 1y, Muss, Gd, Jun 2)
Posted 86 [2] (7f, Newj, GF, Aug 4)
Princes Des Sables 86 [1] (6f 17y, Ches, GS, Sep 29)
Red Impression 86 [1] (6f 1y, Linw, SD, Nov 24)
Shumookhi (IRE) 86 [1] (5f 34y, Newb, Gd, Aug 17)
The Cruising Lord 86 [4] (5f, Newm, GF, Oct 12)
All The King's Men (IRE) 85 [1] (5f 164y, Nava, Yld, Oct 14)
Boerhan 85 [5] (1m, Newm, GF, Oct 13)
Concierge (IRE) 85 [2] (5f, Hayd, GS, Sep 28)
Critical Data (IRE) 85 [1] (7f 36y, Wolw, SD, Aug 17)
Decrypt 85 [1] (6f, Curr, GF, Jun 9)
Deep Intrigue 85 [1] (6f, Chmf, SD, Dec 6)
Dirty Rascal (IRE) 85 [1] (7f, Newb, GS, Sep 21)
Dutch Treat 85 [1] (7f 3y, Yarm, GF, Aug 8)
Frederickbarbarosa (IRE) 85 [2] (7f, Kemw, SS, Nov 23)
Invincible Karma (IRE) 85 [1] (7f 92y, Rosc, Sft, Aug 20)
Junius Brutus (FR) 85 [1] (6f, Ripo, Gd, Aug 18)
Mount Tabora (USA) 85 [2] (7f, Curr, Gd, Jul 21)
Mubakker (USA) 85 [1] (6f 20y, Wolw, SD, Nov 1)
Nate The Great 85 [2] (7f, Asco, GF, Jun 23)
Raakib Alhawa (IRE) 85 [1] (1m, Newb, GS, Sep 21)

Poet's Word beats Cracksman in the Prince of Wales's Stakes at Royal Ascot. The pair make the top three in the RPR list of horses aged three and older

RACING POST RATINGS: LAST SEASON'S TOP PERFORMERS 3YO+

Cracksman 131[1] (1m 1f 212y, Asco, Sft, Oct 20)
Battaash (IRE) 129[1] (5f, Good, GF, Aug 3)
Poet's Word (IRE) 128[1] (1m 3f 211y, Asco, GF, Jul 28)
Crystal Ocean 127[2] (1m 3f 219y, Kemw, SS, Sep 8)
Harry Angel (IRE) 127[1] (6f, York, GF, May 16)
Roaring Lion (USA) 127[1] (1m 2f 56y, York, GF, Aug 22)
Enable 126[1] (1m 3f 219y, Kemw, SS, Sep 8)
Alpha Centauri (IRE) 124[1] (1m, Newj, GF, Jul 13)
Blue Point (IRE) 123[1] (5f, Asco, GF, Jun 19)
Lightning Spear 122[1] (1m, Good, Gd, Aug 1)
Masar (IRE) 122[1] (1m 4f 6y, Epso, Gd, Jun 2)
Merchant Navy (AUS) 122[1] (6f, Asco, GF, Jun 23)
Saxon Warrior (JPN) 122[2] (1m 1f 209y, Sand, GF, Jul 7)
U S Navy Flag (USA) 122[1] (6f, Newj, GF, Jul 14)
Addeybb (IRE) 121[1] (1m, Sand, GS, Apr 27)
City Light (FR) 121[2] (6f, Asco, GF, Jun 23)
Kew Gardens (IRE) 121[1] (1m 6f 115y, Donc, Gd, Sep 15)
Monarchs Glen 121[1] (1m 1f 212y, Asco, GF, Jun 19)
Romanised (IRE) 121[1] (1m, Curr, GF, May 26)
Sands Of Mali (FR) 121[1] (6f, Asco, Sft, Oct 20)
Stradivarius (IRE) 121[1] (2m, Good, Gd, Jul 31)
The Tin Man 121[1] (6f, Hayd, Hvy, Sep 8)
Wissahickon (USA) 121[1] (1m 1f, Newm, GF, Sep 29)
Beat The Bank 120[1] (7f 213y, Asco, GF, Jul 14)
Expert Eye 120[1] (7f, Asco, GF, Jun 20)
Gifted Master (IRE) 120[1] (6f, Good, GF, Aug 4)
Sea Of Class (IRE) 120[1] (1m 3f 188y, York, GF, Aug 23)
Without Parole 120[1] (7f 213y, Asco, GF, Jun 19)
Young Rascal (FR) 120[1] (1m 3f, Newb, Sft, Sep 22)
Bound For Nowhere (USA) 119[3] (6f, Asco, GF, Jun 23)
Brando 119[2] (6f, Hayd, Hvy, Sep 8)
Century Dream (IRE) 119[3] (1m, Asco, Sft, Oct 20)
Dee Ex Bee 119[2] (1m 4f 6y, Epso, Gd, Jun 2)
Gustav Klimt (IRE) 119[2] (7f 213y, Asco, GF, Jun 19)
Lancaster Bomber (USA) 119[1] (1m 2f 110y, Curr, GF, May 27)
Mirage Dancer 119[2] (1m 3f, Newb, Sft, Sep 22)
Order Of St George (IRE) 119[1] (1m 6f, Nava, Sft, Apr 22)
Rhododendron (IRE) 119[1] (1m, Newb, GF, May 19)
Sir Dancealot (IRE) 119[1] (7f, Newb, Gd, Aug 18)
Thundering Blue (USA) 119[3] (1m 2f 56y, York, GF, Aug 22)
Torcedor (IRE) 119[2] (2m, Good, Gd, Jul 31)
Vazirabad (FR) 119[2] (2m 3f 210y, Asco, GF, Jun 21)
Accidental Agent 118[1] (1m, Asco, GF, Jun 19)
Caspian Prince (IRE) 118[2] (5f, Curr, GF, Jun 30)
Cross Counter 118[1] (1m 3f 218y, Good, GF, Aug 4)
Limato (IRE) 118[1] (6f, York, GS, Sep 9)
Lord Glitters (FR) 118[2] (7f 213y, Asco, GF, Jul 14)
Magic Circle (IRE) 118[1] (2m 50y, Sand, Gd, May 24)
Magical (IRE) 118[1] (1m 3f 211y, Asco, Sft, Oct 20)
Muntahaa (IRE) 118[1] (1m 5f 188y, York, GF, Aug 25)
Old Persian 118[1] (1m 3f 188y, York, GF, Aug 22)
Salouen (IRE) 118[2] (1m 4f 6y, Epso, Sft, Jun 1)
Tip Two Win 118[2] (1m, Newm, Gd, May 5)
Wuheida 118[1] (1m 1f, Newm, GF, May 6)
Alpha Delphini 117[1] (5f, York, GF, Aug 24)
Cliffs Of Moher (IRE) 117[3] (1m 1f 209y, Sand, GF, Jul 7)
Defoe (IRE) 117[1] (1m 4f, Newb, GS, Apr 21)
Forever Together (IRE) 117[1] (1m 4f 6y, Epso, Sft, Jun 1)
I Can Fly 117[2] (1m, Asco, Sft, Oct 20)
Kachy 117[1] (6f 20y, Wolw, SD, Dec 26)
Lah Ti Dar 117[1] (1m 3f 188y, York, GF, Aug 23)
Laurens (FR) 117[1] (1m, Newm, Gd, Oct 6)
Mustashry 117[1] (1m, Newm, GF, Sep 28)
Recoletos (FR) 117[5] (1m, Asco, Sft, Oct 20)
Stormy Antarctic 117[4] (1m, Asco, Sft, Oct 20)
Suedois (FR) 117[3] (7f 213y, Asco, GF, Jul 14)
Aljazzi 116[1] (1m, Asco, GF, Jun 20)
Best Solution (IRE) 116[1] (1m 4f, Newj, GF, Jul 12)
Capri (IRE) 116[1] (1m 2f, Naas, Hvy, Apr 13)
Coronet 116[2] (1m 3f 211y, Asco, Sft, Oct 20)
Desert Encounter (IRE) 116[1] (1m 3f 99y, Wind, Gd, Aug 25)
Desert Skyline (IRE) 116[2] (1m 5f 188y, York, GF, May 18)
Elarqam 116[4] (1m, Newm, Gd, May 5)
Emaraaty 116[2] (7f, Good, Gd, May 26)
Flag Of Honour (IRE) 116[1] (1m 6f, Curr, Gd, Sep 16)
Flaming Spear (IRE) 116[1] (7f, Good, Gd, Aug 25)
Forest Ranger (IRE) 116[1] (1m 2f 70y, Ches, Gd, May 11)
Happily (IRE) 116[2] (1m, Newm, Gd, Oct 6)
Here Comes When (IRE) 116[1] (1m 37y, Hayd, Hvy, Sep 8)
Hunting Horn (IRE) 116[1] (1m 1f 212y, Asco, GF, Jun 21)
Idaho (IRE) 116[1] (1m 5f 84y, Ches, Gd, May 10)
Latrobe (IRE) 116[1] (1m 4f, Curr, GF, Jun 30)
Morando (FR) 116[1] (1m 4f, Newb, GS, Oct 27)
Oh This Is Us (IRE) 116[3] (7f 6y, Donc, Gd, Sep 15)
Plumatic 116[1] (1m, Sali, GS, Aug 16)
Red Verdon (USA) 116[2] (1m 3f 211y, Asco, GF, Jun 23)
Subway Dancer (IRE) 116[3] (1m 1f 212y, Asco, Sft, Oct 20)
Thomas Hobson 116[2] (1m 7f 209y, Asco, Sft, Oct 20)
Wadilsafa 116[1] (1m, Sand, Gd, Sep 19)
Weekender 116[2] (1m 5f 188y, York, GF, Aug 25)
Wild Illusion 116[1] (1m 1f 197y, Good, Gd, Aug 2)
Air Pilot 115[2] (1m 2f, Newm, Sft, Nov 3)
Ardhoomey (IRE) 115[2] (6f 63y, Curr, Gd, Jul 21)
Barsanti (IRE) 115[1] (1m 3f 211y, Asco, GF, May 12)
Benbatl 115[5] (1m 2f 56y, York, GF, Aug 22)
Billesdon Brook 115[1] (1m, Newm, GF, May 6)
Breton Rock (IRE) 115[3] (7f, Good, Gd, Jul 31)
D'bai (IRE) 115[2] (7f 6y, Donc, Gd, Sep 15)
Deauville (IRE) 115[3] (1m 2f, Leop, GF, Sep 15)
Donjuan Triumphant (IRE) 115[4] (7f, Good, Gd, Jul 31)
Emmaus (IRE) 115[1] (7f, Leic, Hvy, Apr 28)
Emotionless (IRE) 115[1] (1m 2f, Newb, GF, Jul 21)
Eqtidaar (IRE) 115[1] (6f, Asco, GF, Jun 22)
Fabricate 115[2] (1m 1f 209y, Sand, GS, Apr 27)
Havana Grey 115[1] (5f, Curr, Yld, Sep 16)
Hawkbill (USA) 115[4] (1m 1f 209y, Sand, GF, Jul 7)
Mendelssohn (USA) 115[1] (1m, Dunw, SD, Mar 9)
Mjjack (IRE) 115[3] (1m, Asco, Sft, Oct 20)
Mr Lupton (IRE) 115[1] (5f 34y, Newb, Sft, Sep 22)
Projection 115[5] (6f, Asco, GF, Jun 23)
Rostropovich (IRE) 115[2] (1m 4f, Curr, GF, Jun 30)
Royal Line 115[1] (1m 3f 197y, Donc, Sft, Nov 10)
Sharja Bridge 115[1] (1m, Asco, Sft, Oct 20)
Sioux Nation (USA) 115[1] (6f, Naas, GF, May 20)
So Beloved 115[2] (7f, York, Gd, May 26)
Tabarrak (IRE) 115[1] (7f 1y, Linw, SD, Sep 15)
Urban Fox 115[1] (1m 2f, Curr, GF, Jul 1)
Washington Dc (IRE) 115[2] (5f, Hayd, Gd, May 26)
Yoshida (JPN) 115[5] (1m, Asco, GF, Jun 19)
Above The Rest (IRE) 114[1] (6f, Ncsw, SS, Jun 30)
Arod (IRE) 114[1] (1m 31y, Wind, Gd, May 14)
Astronomer (IRE) 114[2] (1m 4f, Newm, GF, Oct 12)
Bacchus 114[1] (6f, Asco, GF, Jun 23)
Chain Of Daisies 114[1] (1m 1f 201y, Sali, Gd, Aug 15)
Corinthia Knight (IRE) 114[1] (5f 6y, Linw, SD, Dec 4)
Dal Harraild 114[1] (2m, Chmf, SD, Mar 10)
Danehill Kodiac (IRE) 114[2] (1m 5f 84y, Ches, Gd, May 10)
Duretto 114[3] (1m 4f, Newj, GF, Jul 12)
Dutch Connection 114[4] (1m, Newb, GF, May 19)
Fleet Review (USA) 114[3] (6f, Newj, GF, Jul 14)
Invincible Army (IRE) 114[2] (6f, Hayd, Gd, May 26)
Lancelot Du Lac (ITY) 114[1] (6f 20y, Wolw, SD, Mar 10)
Laraaib (IRE) 114[1] (1m 3f 211y, Asco, Sft, Oct 6)
Larchmont Lad (IRE) 114[2] (7f 37y, Hayd, GF, Jun 9)
Mabs Cross 114[2] (5f, York, GF, Aug 24)
Magic Wand (IRE) 114[1] (1m 3f 211y, Asco, GF, Jun 21)
Max Dynamite (FR) 114[2] (2m 1f 197y, Donc, GS, Sep 14)
Nelson (IRE) 114[1] (1m 2f, Leop, Hvy, Apr 14)
Prince Of Arran 114[2] (2m 56y, Ncsw, SS, Jun 30)
Riven Light (IRE) 114[1] (1m 123y, Galw, Sft, Jul 31)
Second Step (IRE) 114[1] (1m 4f, Newj, GF, Jun 30)
Sir Erec (IRE) 114[3] (1m 7f 209y, Asco, Sft, Oct 20)
Teodoro (IRE) 114[1] (1m 2f 100y, Hayd, GF, Aug 11)
Wells Farhh Go (IRE) 114[1] (1m 5f, Newj, GF, Jul 12)
Whisky Baron (AUS) 114[2] (1m, Donc, Gd, Sep 15)
Yafta 114[1] (6f, Newb, GF, Jul 21)
Altyn Orda (IRE) 113[2] (1m, Newj, GF, Jul 13)
Cardsharp 113[4] (7f, Newj, GF, Jul 14)
Cenotaph (USA) 113[1] (7f, Chmf, SD, Sep 1)
Circus Couture (IRE) 113[2] (1m 37y, Hayd, Hvy, Sep 8)
Communique (IRE) 113[2] (1m 3f 211y, Asco, Sft, Oct 6)
Count Octave 113[2] (2m 56y, York, GF, Aug 24)

Cypress Creek (IRE) 113[6] (1m 7f 209y, Asco, Sft, Oct 20)
Dolphin Vista (IRE) 113[1] (1m 2f, Ayr, Sft, Sep 20)
Dream Of Dreams (IRE) 113[2] (6f, Asco, Sft, Oct 6)
Dreamfield 113[6] (6f, Newj, GF, Jul 14)
Dylan Mouth (IRE) 113[1] (1m 5f 188y, York, GF, Jul 14)
Encore D'or 113[2] (5f 6y, Linw, SD, Mar 24)
Euginio (IRE) 113[2] (1m 1f 212y, Asco, GF, Jun 19)
First Contact (IRE) 113[1] (1m, Newj, GF, Jul 14)
Gordon Lord Byron (IRE) 113[2] (7f, York, GF, Aug 25)
Hamada 113[1] (1m 5f 61y, Newb, Gd, Aug 18)
Intisaab 113[1] (6f 63y, Curr, Gd, Jul 21)
Judicial (IRE) 113[1] (5f 10y, Sand, GF, Jul 7)
Kimberella 113[1] (7f, Thir, GS, Apr 21)
Leshlaa (USA) 113[6] (1m 1f 212y, Asco, GF, Jun 19)
Mankib 113[1] (7f, Newb, GS, Sep 21)
Marmelo 113[1] (1m 5f 188y, York, GF, Jun 16)
Mitchum Swagger 113[1] (1m, Newm, Sft, Nov 3)
Perfect Pasture 113[1] (6f 2y, Donc, Sft, Mar 24)
Psychedelic Funk 113[1] (7f, Naas, Hvy, Apr 13)
Renneti (FR) 113[2] (2m 5f 143y, Asco, GF, Jun 23)
Son Of Rest 113[2] (5f, Curr, Yld, Sep 16)
Speak In Colours 113[1] (6f, Curr, Gd, Aug 12)
Spirit Of Valor (USA) 113[2] (6f, Curr, GF, May 26)
Tarboosh 113[1] (5f 3y, Donc, GS, Oct 27)
Top Score 113[2] (6f, Newj, GF, Aug 25)
War Decree (USA) 113[2] (1m 2f 70y, Ches, Gd, May 11)
Zaaki 113[2] (1m 2f, Newj, GF, Jul 13)
Zabeel Prince (IRE) 113[2] (1m, Newm, GF, Sep 28)
Zhui Feng (IRE) 113[2] (7f, Asco, GF, May 12)
Ajman King (IRE) 112[1] (1m 2f 17y, Epso, Sft, Jun 1)
Big Country (IRE) 112[2] (1m 2f, Linw, SD, Dec 22)
Call To Mind 112[3] (1m 5f 188y, York, GF, May 18)
Doctor Sardonicus 112[1] (5f 21y, Wolw, SD, Dec 21)
Eziyra (IRE) 112[3] (1m 3f 188y, York, GF, Aug 23)
First Eleven 112[1] (1m 3f 211y, Asco, GF, Sep 8)
Game Starter (IRE) 112[2] (1m 3f 99y, Wind, Gd, Aug 25)
Hazapour (IRE) 112[1] (1m 2f, Leop, Gd, May 13)
Hey Jonesy (IRE) 112[2] (6f 2y, Donc, Sft, Nov 10)
Hit The Bid 112[1] (5f, Dunw, SD, Oct 19)
Kenya (IRE) 112[1] (1m, Curr, Yld, Sep 1)
Muntadab (IRE) 112[1] (7f 6y, Donc, GS, Oct 27)
Muthmir (IRE) 112[3] (5f, York, GF, Jul 14)
Primo Uomo (IRE) 112[1] (5f, Nava, Sft, Apr 23)
Southern France (IRE) 112[3] (1m 6f 115y, Donc, Gd, Sep 15)
Spark Plug (IRE) 112[2] (1m 1f 209y, Sand, GF, Jul 6)
Straight Right (FR) 112[1] (7f, Chmf, SD, Sep 29)
Take Cover 112[2] (5f 34y, Newb, Sft, Sep 22)
Unforgetable Filly 112[1] (1m 37y, Hayd, GF, Aug 11)
Veracious 112[3] (1m 1f 197y, Good, Gd, Aug 2)
Windstoss (GER) 112[3] (1m 4f 6y, Epso, Sft, Jun 1)
Wootton (FR) 112[3] (7f 213y, Asco, GF, Jun 19)
Almodovar (IRE) 111[4] (1m 1f 209y, Sand, GS, Apr 27)
Baron Bolt 111[1] (6f, Ayr, Hvy, Sep 22)
Cannonball (IRE) 111[2] (1m 2f, Naas, Hvy, Apr 13)
Clemmie (IRE) 111[3] (1m, Leop, GF, Sep 15)
Crazy Horse 111[2] (1m, Asco, Sft, May 2)
Crowned Eagle 111[2] (1m 3f 175y, Hayd, GF, Jul 7)
Delano Roosevelt (IRE) 111[4] (1m 4f, Curr, GF, Jun 30)
Downforce (IRE) 111[3] (7f, Leic, Hvy, Apr 28)
El Astronaute (IRE) 111[1] (5f 89y, York, GF, Aug 22)
Equilateral 111[1] (5f, Leic, GF, Sep 11)
First Sitting 111[1] (1m 1f 197y, Good, Gd, May 26)
Flavius (USA) 111[1] (1m 2f, Leop, Yld, Oct 20)
Frontiersman 111[3] (2m 120y, Wolw, SD, Jan 15)
George Bowen (IRE) 111[1] (6f 6y, Hami, GF, Jul 20)
Hathal (USA) 111[2] (1m, Sand, Gd, Sep 19)
Horseplay 111[4] (1m 3f 188y, York, GF, Aug 23)
Ice Age (IRE) 111[1] (6f 12y, Wind, GF, Jul 2)
James Garfield (IRE) 111[7] (1m, Newm, Gd, May 5)
Laugh A Minute 111[1] (6f 2y, Donc, GF, Aug 4)
Lost Treasure (IRE) 111[3] (5f, Dunw, SD, Oct 19)
Loxley (IRE) 111[2] (1m 5f, Newj, GF, Jul 12)
Magical Memory (IRE) 111[4] (6f, Newm, Gd, Apr 19)
Major Jumbo 111[1] (6f, York, Sft, Oct 13)
Mary Tudor (IRE) 111[3] (1m 4f, Curr, GF, Jul 21)
Master The World (IRE) 111[2] (1m 2f, Linw, SD, Feb 24)
Mazzini 111[1] (6f, Kemw, SS, Oct 10)
Mr Owen (USA) 111[1] (1m 2f, Linw, SD, Feb 24)
Nakeeta 111[5] (2m 110y, Newb, GF, Jul 21)
Nearly Caught (IRE) 111[1] (2m, Newm, Gd, Sep 27)
Opal Tiara (IRE) 111[1] (1m, Curr, GF, May 26)
Ostilio 111[1] (1m, Donc, Gd, Sep 15)
Proschema (IRE) 111[2] (1m 5f 188y, York, Gd, Oct 12)
Regal Reality 111[3] (1m 37y, Hayd, Hvy, Sep 8)
Scotland (GER) 111[3] (1m 5f 188y, York, GF, Jul 14)
Settle For Bay (FR) 111[1] (1m, Asco, GF, Jun 20)
Spring Loaded (IRE) 111[1] (5f, Asco, GF, Jul 14)
Stars Over The Sea (USA) 111[1] (2m 2f, Newm, Gd, Sep 22)
Threading (IRE) 111[1] (7f 192y, York, GF, May 18)
Time To Study (FR) 111[2] (1m 7f 209y, Asco, Sft, May 2)
Tropics (USA) 111[1] (5f, Chmf, SD, Jun 13)
True Self (IRE) 111[1] (1m 2f, Newm, Sft, Nov 3)
Verbal Dexterity (IRE) 111[6] (1m 1f 212y, Asco, Sft, Oct 20)
Vintager 111[1] (1m, Newj, GF, Jul 21)
Watersmeet 111[1] (2m 120y, Wolw, SD, Jan 15)
What About Carlo (FR) 111[3] (1m 4f, Newb, GS, Apr 21)
Withhold 111[1] (2m 56y, Ncsw, SS, Jun 30)
Zaman 111[2] (1m 1f 197y, Good, Gd, Aug 2)
Zonderland 111[2] (7f, Newm, GF, Oct 12)
Afaak 110[2] (1m, Asco, GF, Jun 20)
Anna Nerium 110[1] (7f, Good, Sft, Aug 26)
Athena (IRE) 110[4] (1m 2f, Leop, GF, Sep 15)
Autocratic 110[4] (1m 1f 212y, Asco, GF, Jun 19)
Cape Byron 110[2] (7f, Asco, GF, Sep 8)
Could It Be Love (USA) 110[2] (1m, Curr, Gd, May 27)
Court House (IRE) 110[2] (1m 2f 17y, Epso, GS, Jun 2)
Danceteria (FR) 110[5] (1m 2f, Curr, Gd, Sep 16)
Desert Diamond 110[1] (1m 2f 56y, York, GS, Jul 27)
Emblazoned (IRE) 110[3] (6f, Asco, GF, Jun 22)
Encrypted 110[1] (6f 1y, Linw, SD, Nov 17)
Euchen Glen 110[1] (1m 2f 56y, York, GF, Jul 14)
Funny Kid (USA) 110[2] (2m 120y, Wolw, SD, Jan 15)
Grey Britain 110[1] (1m 4f 51y, Wolw, SD, Dec 8)
Gulliver 110[5] (6f 1y, Linw, SD, Feb 3)
Hydrangea (IRE) 110[2] (1m, Curr, GF, May 26)
Justanotherbottle (IRE) 110[2] (6f, Good, GF, Aug 4)
Khafoo Shememi (IRE) 110[3] (1m 31y, Wind, Gd, May 14)
Kyllang Rock (IRE) 110[1] (5f 1y, Muss, Hvy, Mar 31)
Love Dreams (IRE) 110[1] (7f, Good, GF, May 24)
Making Light (IRE) 110[1] (1m, Cork, Gd, Aug 11)
Mootasadir 110[1] (1m 2f 150y, Dunw, SD, Sep 28)
Mubtasim (IRE) 110[2] (7f 37y, Hayd, GF, May 12)
Oasis Charm 110[1] (1m 1f, Newm, Gd, May 5)
Pincheck (IRE) 110[1] (1m, Leop, Gd, Aug 16)
Pivoine (IRE) 110[1] (1m 2f 56y, York, GF, Aug 25)
Prize Money 110[3] (1m 3f 99y, Wind, Gd, Aug 25)
Saltonstall 110[1] (1m, Curr, Gd, May 27)
Second Thought (IRE) 110[1] (7f 36y, Wolw, SD, Mar 10)
Smash Williams (IRE) 110[2] (7f 100y, Tipp, Sft, Oct 7)
Soliloquy 110[1] (7f, Newm, Gd, Apr 18)
Study Of Man (IRE) 110[5] (1m 2f, Leop, GF, Sep 15)
Symbolization (IRE) 110[1] (1m, Newm, Gd, May 5)
Tabdeed 110[1] (6f, Asco, Gd, Oct 5)
The Pentagon (IRE) 110[5] (1m 4f, Curr, GF, Jun 30)
Threeandfourpence (USA) 110[4] (1m, Curr, GF, May 26)
Top Tug (IRE) 110[2] (1m 6f, Good, Gd, May 26)
True Valour (IRE) 110[1] (7f 30y, Leop, GF, Jun 14)
Victory Wave (USA) 110[1] (7f, Chmf, SD, Sep 15)
A Momentofmadness 109[1] (5f 143y, Donc, Gd, Sep 15)
Aeolus 109[1] (6f, Newm, GS, Apr 18)
Allegio (IRE) 109[2] (1m, Curr, GF, Jun 30)
Another Batt (IRE) 109[1] (7f 127y, Ches, Gd, May 10)
Aquarium 109[1] (1m 2f 56y, York, Sft, Oct 13)
Arcanada (IRE) 109[1] (1m 142y, Wolw, SD, Feb 5)
Argentello (IRE) 109[1] (1m, Kemw, SS, Oct 16)
Aspetar (FR) 109[3] (1m 2f, Ayr, Sft, Sep 20)
Bear Slam (USA) 109[1] (7f, Newm, GS, Apr 17)
Ben Vrackie 109[3] (1m 4f, Newm, GF, Oct 12)
Blakeney Point 109[1] (1m 4f 63y, Ches, Sft, Sep 15)
Burnt Sugar (IRE) 109[6] (7f, Leop, GF, Sep 15)
Connect 109[1] (1m 2f 17y, Epso, GS, Jun 2)
Dash Of Spice 109[1] (1m 3f 211y, Asco, GF, Jun 22)
Dubai Horizon (IRE) 109[1] (1m 1f 209y, Sand, GS, Sep 1)
Elegiac 109[2] (1m 6f, Chmf, SD, Nov 10)
Elidor 109[3] (1m 5f 84y, Ches, Gd, May 10)
Elwazir 109[1] (1m 1f 212y, Asco, GF, Jul 14)
Eminent (IRE) 109[6] (7f 213y, Asco, GF, Jul 14)
Escobar (IRE) 109[2] (1m, Asco, Sft, Oct 20)
Fajjaj (IRE) 109[3] (1m 2f, Newb, GF, Jul 21)
Final Venture 109[2] (5f 89y, York, GF, Aug 22)

Flight Risk (IRE) 109 [2] (1m 2f, Leop, Yld, Oct 20)
Gabrial (IRE) 109 [3] (1m 31y, Wind, GF, Jun 30)
Ghostwatch (IRE) 109 [1] (1m 6f 34y, Asco, Gd, Oct 5)
Global Applause 109 [1] (5f 10y, Sand, GS, Sep 1)
Gunmetal (IRE) 109 [1] (6f, Ripo, Gd, Aug 18)
Happy Family 109 [1] (7f 1y, Linw, SD, Mar 3)
Higher Power 109 [2] (1m 7f 218y, Kemw, SS, Nov 21)
Highgarden 109 [1] (1m 4f, Newm, GF, Sep 28)
Huge Future 109 [1] (1m 3f 140y, Hayd, GS, Sep 6)
Intelligence Cross (USA) 109 [2] (6f, Curr, GF, Jun 30)
Kasperenko 109 [1] (1m 3f 219y, Kemw, SS, Nov 5)
Key Victory (IRE) 109 [1] (1m 2f, Newm, Gd, May 5)
Kitesurf 109 [4] (1m 3f 211y, Asco, Sft, Oct 20)
Marnie James 109 [1] (5f, Chmf, SD, Sep 22)
Mount Moriah 109 [1] (1m 6f, Nott, GS, Apr 21)
Mustajeer 109 [4] (1m 5f 188y, York, GF, Aug 25)
Nyaleti (IRE) 109 [5] (1m, Good, Gd, Aug 25)
On The Go Again (IRE) 109 [1] (1m, Leop, Hvy, Apr 16)
Pilaster 109 [3] (1m 6f 115y, Donc, Gd, Sep 13)
Raising Sand 109 [1] (7f, Asco, Sft, Oct 6)
Raymond Tusk (IRE) 109 [2] (1m 5f 61y, Newb, Gd, Aug 18)
Red Mist 109 [1] (1m, Ripo, Gd, Aug 28)
Robin Of Navan (FR) 109 [4] (1m, Sand, GS, Apr 27)
Salateen 109 [3] (7f, Chmf, SD, Sep 1)
Scarlet Dragon 109 [3] (1m 4f, Newb, GS, Oct 27)
Scottish Jig (USA) 109 [1] (1m 2f, Newm, GF, Oct 12)
Sevenna Star (IRE) 109 [1] (1m 1f 209y, Sand, GS, Apr 27)
St Michel 109 [5] (2m, Good, Gd, Jul 31)
Stone Of Destiny 109 [4] (6f, Asco, GF, Jun 22)
Stormbringer 109 [2] (6f, Newj, GF, Jul 12)
Tasleet 109 [3] (6f, Curr, GF, May 26)
Tis Marvellous 109 [1] (5f, Asco, Gd, Aug 11)
Trais Fluors 109 [5] (7f 213y, Asco, GF, Jul 14)
Very Talented (IRE) 109 [1] (1m, Chmf, SD, Sep 20)
Victory Bond 109 [1] (1m 2f, Linw, SD, Mar 30)
Walton Street 109 [3] (1m 5f 61y, Newb, Gd, Aug 18)
Who's Steph (IRE) 109 [2] (1m 2f, Curr, Gd, Sep 16)
Actress (IRE) 108 [1] (6f, Curr, GF, Jun 8)
Alfarris (FR) 108 [2] (1m 2f 56y, York, GF, Aug 25)
Arbalet (IRE) 108 [3] (7f, York, GF, Aug 25)
Atty Persse (IRE) 108 [2] (1m 3f 211y, Asco, GF, Jul 27)
Battle Of Marathon (USA) 108 [3] (1m 2f, Linw, SD, Feb 24)
Brorocco 108 [2] (1m 2f 100y, Hayd, GF, Aug 11)
Byron Flyer 108 [1] (1m 3f 179y, Leic, Gd, Oct 9)
Dark Red (IRE) 108 [2] (1m 5y, Ncsw, SD, Jun 28)
Declarationofpeace (USA) 108 [4] (5f, Curr, GF, Jul 22)
Double Up 108 [2] (6f, Chmf, SD, Apr 26)
Escalator 108 [1] (1m 53y, Leic, GS, Oct 29)
Gabr 108 [1] (1m 1f 197y, Good, GS, Sep 26)
Giuseppe Garibaldi (IRE) 108 [2] (1m 4f, Leop, GF, Sep 15)
Global Giant 108 [2] (1m 2f, Wind, Gd, Aug 25)
God Given 108 [1] (1m 6f 115y, Donc, Gd, Sep 13)
Gold Chest (USA) 108 [1] (1m, Newj, GF, Jul 12)
Goring (GER) 108 [4] (1m 2f, Linw, SD, Dec 22)
Hey Gaman 108 [3] (7f, Newb, GS, Apr 21)
Hochfeld (IRE) 108 [2] (1m 3f 179y, Leic, GS, Oct 29)
I'm So Fancy (IRE) 108 [3] (1m 2f, Curr, Gd, Sep 16)
Ispolini 108 [2] (1m 1f 209y, Sand, GS, Apr 27)
Jallota 108 [1] (7f, Kemw, SD, May 1)
Karar 108 [8] (7f, Good, Gd, Jul 31)
King Of Hearts (IRE) 108 [2] (7f, Asco, GF, Jun 20)
Kings Shield (USA) 108 [5] (7f 213y, Asco, GF, Jun 19)
Knight To Behold (IRE) 108 [1] (1m 3f 133y, Ling, GF, May 12)
Lord George (IRE) 108 [3] (1m 4f, Linw, SD, Dec 22)
Low Sun 108 [1] (2m 2f, Newm, GF, Oct 13)
Lucymai 108 [1] (7f, Chmf, SD, Aug 11)
Major Partnership (IRE) 108 [1] (6f 20y, Wolw, SD, Oct 6)
Mekong 108 [2] (1m 6f 34y, Asco, Gd, Oct 5)
Mildenberger 108 [2] (1m 2f 56y, York, GF, May 17)
Mount Tahan (IRE) 108 [1] (1m 4f 51y, Wolw, SD, Mar 5)
Mountain Hunter (USA) 108 [5] (1m 2f 43y, Donc, Gd, Sep 13)
Move Swiftly 108 [2] (1m, Newm, GS, Oct 6)
Mrs Sippy (USA) 108 [2] (1m 4f, Newm, GF, Sep 28)
On To Victory 108 [2] (1m 6f, Nott, GS, Apr 21)
Platinum Warrior (IRE) 108 [1] (1m 2f, Curr, GF, May 27)
Platitude 108 [1] (1m 6f, Good, Gd, May 26)
Raid (IRE) 108 [8] (1m, Newm, Gd, May 5)
Raven's Lady 108 [4] (6f, Asco, Sft, Oct 6)
Sheikha Reika (FR) 108 [1] (1m 2f 23y, Yarm, GF, Sep 19)
Silent Attack 108 [1] (7f 1y, Linw, SD, Apr 14)
South Seas (IRE) 108 [4] (7f 127y, Ches, Gd, May 26)
Sovereign Debt (IRE) 108 [1] (7f 192y, York, GF, Jun 15)
Success Days (IRE) 108 [2] (1m 2f, Naas, Yld, May 7)
Tandem 108 [3] (1m 4f, Cork, GF, Jun 17)
Titus 108 [4] (1m 6f 115y, Donc, GS, Sep 14)
Tomily (IRE) 108 [1] (6f, Kemw, SD, Mar 31)
Tomyris 108 [4] (7f, Newb, Gd, Aug 18)
Tricorn (IRE) 108 [2] (1m, Chmf, SD, Sep 10)
Wilamina (IRE) 108 [5] (1m 1f 197y, Good, Gd, Aug 2)
Yucatan (IRE) 108 [3] (1m 4f, Leop, GF, Aug 9)
Absolutely So (IRE) 107 [1] (7f, Sand, Gd, Sep 14)
Appeared 107 [4] (1m 3f 211y, Asco, GF, Jun 22)
Atletico (IRE) 107 [2] (5f 6y, Linw, SD, Mar 3)
Austrian School (IRE) 107 [2] (1m 6f 115y, Donc, GS, Sep 14)
Banditry (IRE) 107 [2] (1m 2f, Chmf, SD, Sep 29)
Bandua (USA) 107 [8] (1m 4f, Curr, GF, Jun 30)
Born To Be Alive (IRE) 107 [2] (1m, Donc, Sft, Mar 24)
Clear Skies 107 [1] (1m 2f 150y, Dunw, SD, Jan 26)
Convey 107 [4] (1m 2f, Linw, SD, Feb 24)
Crimson Rosette (IRE) 107 [3] (1m 4f, Newm, GF, Sep 28)
Crossed Baton 107 [2] (1m 1f 212y, Asco, GF, Jun 21)
Dancing Star 107 [1] (7f 6y, Donc, Gd, Sep 14)
Firmament 107 [2] (1m, Chmf, SD, Sep 20)
Gidu (IRE) 107 [6] (6f, Asco, GF, Jun 22)
Glencadam Glory 107 [5] (1m 3f 211y, Asco, GF, May 12)
Gracious John (IRE) 107 [2] (5f 6y, Linw, SD, Dec 4)
Il Primo Sole 107 [5] (1m, Asco, GF, Jun 21)
Intense Romance (IRE) 107 [1] (5f, Asco, Sft, Oct 6)
Le Brivido (FR) 107 [6] (6f, Newm, Gd, Apr 19)
Lucius Tiberius (IRE) 107 [1] (1m 2f, Leop, GF, Jul 12)
Lucky Team (FR) 107 [1] (1m 1y, Linw, SD, Mar 30)
Maid Up 107 [2] (1m 6f, Good, Gd, Aug 2)
Makzeem 107 [5] (7f, Newj, GF, Jul 14)
Marshall Jennings (IRE) 107 [1] (1m, Naas, Yld, May 7)
Massif Central (IRE) 107 [1] (1m 2f 150y, Dunw, SD, Nov 16)
Mirza 107 [3] (5f 10y, Sand, GF, Jul 7)
Murillo (USA) 107 [9] (1m, Newm, Gd, May 5)
My Lord And Master (IRE) 107 [2] (1m 2f 56y, York, Sft, Oct 13)
Mythmaker 107 [1] (6f, Hayd, GF, Jul 7)
One Master 107 [1] (7f 100y, Tipp, Yld, Aug 30)
Pallasator 107 [1] (2m 5f 143y, Asco, GF, Jun 23)
Raa Atoll 107 [4] (1m 3f 211y, Asco, GF, Jun 22)
Rainbow Rebel (IRE) 107 [1] (1m 3f 75y, Ches, Gd, Jul 13)
Rastrelli (FR) 107 [1] (1m 2f, Newb, GS, Apr 20)
Rebel Streak 107 [3] (5f 34y, Newb, Sft, Sep 22)
Rufus King 107 [2] (7f, Chmf, SD, Sep 15)
Safe Voyage (IRE) 107 [1] (7f, Galw, Yld, Aug 5)
Saunter (FR) 107 [1] (1m 4f, Newj, Gd, Aug 18)
Savalas (IRE) 107 [2] (6f, York, GF, Jun 16)
Seniority 107 [1] (1m, Good, GF, Aug 3)
Sheikhzayedroad 107 [3] (2m 1f 197y, Donc, GS, Sep 14)
Silent Echo 107 [2] (6f 12y, Wind, GF, Aug 20)
Sir Chauvelin 107 [1] (1m 6f, Good, GF, Aug 4)
Smart Call (SAF) 107 [3] (1m 2f 56y, York, GF, May 17)
Snazzy Jazzy (IRE) 107 [1] (6f, Ayr, Hvy, Sep 22)
The King (IRE) 107 [3] (1m 4f, Leop, GF, Sep 15)
Tigre Du Terre (FR) 107 [1] (1m, Sand, GF, Jul 7)
Tribute Act 107 [2] (1m, Asco, GF, Jun 20)
Twilight Payment (IRE) 107 [3] (1m 4f 110y, Lime, Hvy, Oct 13)
Udontdodou 107 [2] (6f, Kemw, SD, Mar 31)
Utmost (USA) 107 [1] (1m 2f, Linw, SD, Feb 3)
Yulong Gold Fairy 107 [1] (7f 100y, Tipp, Sft, Oct 7)
Abe Lincoln (USA) 106 [3] (1m 2f, Linw, SD, Mar 30)
African Ride 106 [2] (7f, Chmf, SD, Sep 29)
Algometer 106 [4] (2m 1f 197y, Donc, GS, Sep 14)
Amazour (IRE) 106 [1] (7f 14y, Ncsw, SD, Jun 28)
Another Touch 106 [3] (7f 192y, York, GF, Jun 15)
Archetype (FR) 106 [1] (1m 2f, Chmf, SD, Oct 11)
Auxerre (IRE) 106 [1] (1m, Kemw, SS, Oct 10)
Awesometank 106 [2] (1m, Sand, Gd, Sep 1)
Beautiful Morning 106 [1] (1m 2f, Curr, Yld, Aug 26)
Blue Uluru (IRE) 106 [1] (5f, Curr, GF, Jun 8)
Breathless Times 106 [1] (6f, Chmf, SD, Sep 15)
Broadway (IRE) 106 [1] (1m 1f 100y, Gowr, Hvy, Sep 22)
Brother Bear (IRE) 106 [1] (7f, Naas, GF, May 20)
Bucchero (USA) 106 [5] (5f, Asco, GF, Jun 19)
Bye Bye Baby (IRE) 106 [1] (1m 2f, Curr, Hvy, May 12)
Classical Times 106 [2] (6f, Newm, GF, Oct 13)
Copper Knight (IRE) 106 [1] (5f, Ncsw, SS, Jun 29)
Curbyourenthusiasm (IRE) 106 [2] (1m 7f 218y, Kemw, SD, Apr 7)

Curly (IRE) 106[4] (1m 2f, Curr, Gd, Sep 16)
Dali (USA) 106[1] (5f, Naas, GF, Jun 18)
Dan's Dream 106[2] (7f 100y, Tipp, Yld, Aug 30)
Di Fede (IRE) 106[1] (7f, Asco, Sft, Oct 6)
Duke Of Bronte 106[4] (1m 3f 218y, Good, Gd, May 26)
Emirates Flyer 106[2] (1m 2f, Chmf, SD, May 24)
Fas (IRE) 106[3] (7f, Curr, Gd, Jul 21)
Fighting Irish (IRE) 106[8] (6f, Asco, GF, Jun 22)
Finsbury Square (IRE) 106[4] (5f, Asco, GF, Jun 19)
Flying Pursuit 106[2] (6f, York, Sft, Oct 13)
Foxtrot Lady 106[1] (6f, Sali, GF, Sep 14)
Fun Mac (GER) 106[2] (2m 2f 140y, Ches, Gd, May 11)
Hors De Combat 106[6] (1m, Asco, GF, Jun 20)
Imaging 106[2] (7f, Leop, Gd, Oct 27)
King's Field (IRE) 106[1] (1m, Dunw, SD, Dec 7)
Kynren (IRE) 106[2] (7f 192y, York, GF, Aug 23)
Lake Volta (IRE) 106[1] (7f 3y, Epso, Sft, Jun 1)
Leader's Legacy (USA) 106[1] (1m 1f 104y, Wolw, SD, May 2)
Lincoln Rocks 106[2] (7f, Ling, GF, May 12)
Mr Scaramanga 106[2] (1m 1y, Linw, SD, Feb 24)
My Reward 106[1] (1m 4f 5y, Pont, GF, Jun 11)
Never Back Down (IRE) 106[1] (6f, Newb, GF, May 19)
Original Choice (IRE) 106[1] (1m 142y, Wolw, SD, Dec 1)
Orvar (IRE) 106[1] (5f, Beve, GS, Sep 25)
Pacify 106[1] (1m 3f 188y, York, GF, Jul 13)
Pactolus (IRE) 106[2] (1m 142y, Wolw, SD, Mar 10)
Poet's Society 106[1] (7f 192y, York, GF, Aug 23)
Redicean 106[1] (1m 4f, Linw, SD, Dec 22)
Repercussion 106[1] (1m 75y, Nott, Sft, May 30)
Restorer 106[1] (1m 2f 70y, Ches, Gd, May 11)
Rock On Baileys 106[1] (6f 17y, Ches, Gd, Jul 14)
Sacred Act 106[3] (1m 1y, Linw, SD, Jan 13)
Saigon City 106[3] (1m 6f, Hayd, GS, Sep 29)
Sea The Lion (IRE) 106[3] (1m 5f 188y, York, GF, Aug 25)
Shady Mccoy (USA) 106[3] (7f 6y, Donc, Sft, Nov 10)
Silver Quartz 106[1] (1m, Asco, Gd, Sep 7)
Solar Flair 106[1] (6f, Ncsw, SS, Jun 30)
St Patrick's Day (USA) 106[3] (1m, Curr, GF, Jun 30)
Star Rock 106[3] (1m 6f, Good, Gd, Aug 2)
Staxton 106[2] (6f, Ripo, Gd, Sep 29)
Stellar Mass (IRE) 106[2] (1m 2f, Curr, GF, Jul 1)
Stratum 106[1] (2m 110y, Newb, GF, Jul 21)
Sunny Speed 106[2] (7f 192y, York, GF, Aug 24)
Temple Church (IRE) 106[1] (1m 4f, Newb, Sft, Sep 22)
The Broghie Man 106[1] (5f 164y, Nava, Sft, Apr 22)
Toast Of New York (USA) 106[3] (1m 2f, Linw, SD, Dec 5)
Urban Beat (IRE) 106[1] (6f, Curr, Yld, Sep 1)
Ventura Knight (IRE) 106[1] (1m, Ayr, GF, Jul 8)
Via Via (IRE) 106[2] (1m, Newj, GS, Aug 17)
Winter Lightning (IRE) 106[3] (1m, Sand, Gd, Sep 1)
Zabriskie (IRE) 106[3] (1m 2f 56y, York, GF, May 17)
Zorion 106[4] (1m, Leop, GF, Sep 15)
Abareeq 105[2] (1m 2f, Chmf, SD, Apr 12)
Across Dubai 105[1] (1m 2f, Chmf, SD, Sep 29)
Across The Stars (IRE) 105[2] (1m 3f 188y, York, Gd, May 26)
Amazing Red (IRE) 105[1] (1m 6f, Newj, GF, Jun 9)
Ambassadorial (USA) 105[2] (7f, Dunw, SD, Apr 6)
Castle Hill Cassie (IRE) 105[1] (7f 36y, Wolw, SD, Nov 16)
Charity Go (IRE) 105[2] (1m 1f, Newm, GS, Apr 17)
Chief Ironside 105[3] (1m 177y, York, GF, Aug 25)
Collide 105[1] (1m 2f 50y, Nott, Sft, Oct 17)
Commander Cole 105[1] (1m 2f 43y, Donc, GF, Aug 4)
Crossing The Line 105[1] (7f, Chmf, SD, Dec 6)
Danzeno 105[4] (6f, Chmf, SD, Apr 26)
Dubawi Fifty 105[2] (2m 3f 210y, Asco, GF, Jun 19)
Early Morning (IRE) 105[2] (7f 1y, Linw, SD, Jan 12)
Enjazaat 105[5] (6f, Newb, GF, Jul 21)
Epic 105[4] (1m 2f 56y, York, GF, May 17)
Foolaad 105[1] (5f 3y, Pont, GS, Apr 23)
Glendevon (USA) 105[2] (1m 2f, Chmf, SD, Nov 8)
Great Hall 105[1] (1m 4f 10y, Ripo, GS, Apr 28)
Great Prospector (IRE) 105[3] (7f, Redc, Gd, Oct 6)
Here And Now 105[1] (2m 56y, York, GF, Aug 22)
Humbert (IRE) 105[1] (1m 5y, Ncsw, SD, Jun 28)
Indian Blessing 105[3] (7f, Good, GF, Aug 3)
Ka Ying Star 105[1] (7f 192y, York, GF, Aug 24)
Khalidi 105[7] (1m 2f, Linw, SD, Feb 24)
Koditime (IRE) 105[2] (5f 21y, Wind, Gd, May 28)
Lord Yeats 105[2] (1m 6f, Nava, Sft, Apr 22)
Making Miracles 105[3] (1m 3f 218y, Good, Gd, Aug 1)
Medahim (IRE) 105[1] (7f, Good, Gd, Aug 1)
Melting Dew 105[2] (1m 6f, Good, GF, Aug 4)
Mountain Bell 105[3] (1m 6f, Chmf, SD, Jun 20)
Not So Sleepy 105[2] (1m 3f 197y, Donc, Sft, Nov 10)
Orbaan 105[8] (1m, Good, Gd, Aug 1)
Panstarr 105[1] (1m 1f, List, Sft, Sep 10)
Petite Jack 105[5] (1m 2f, Linw, SD, Feb 24)
Plutonian (IRE) 105[2] (1m 1f 197y, Good, GS, Sep 26)
Precioussship (IRE) 105[2] (7f, Naas, GF, May 20)
Pretty Baby (IRE) 105[1] (6f 18y, Nott, GF, May 12)
Primero (FR) 105[1] (1m 2f, Chmf, SD, Nov 8)
Princess Yaiza (IRE) 105[2] (1m 4f, Galw, Sft, Aug 3)
Raheen House (IRE) 105[4] (1m 4f, Newb, GS, Oct 27)
Raucous 105[2] (6f 3y, Yarm, GF, Jul 18)
Raydiance 105[2] (7f, Thir, GS, Aug 3)
Reckless Endeavour (IRE) 105[2] (7f 1y, Linw, SD, Mar 30)
Royal Birth 105[2] (6f, Kemw, SD, Jan 10)
Sizzling (IRE) 105[1] (1m 4f, Cork, Gd, Aug 11)
Sofia's Rock (FR) 105[2] (1m 3f 99y, Wind, GF, Jun 30)
Stylehunter 105[1] (1m 1f 11y, Good, Gd, Aug 25)
Summerghand (IRE) 105[1] (6f, Newj, Sft, Aug 10)
Sun Maiden 105[3] (1m 3f 211y, Asco, GF, Jun 21)
Taqdeer (IRE) 105[1] (1m, Newb, GS, Apr 21)
The Grand Visir 105[1] (1m 6f 115y, Donc, GS, Oct 26)
Vale Of Kent (IRE) 105[4] (7f, Good, Gd, Aug 25)
Waarif (IRE) 105[2] (7f 192y, York, Gd, Oct 12)
Whiskey Sour (IRE) 105[5] (2m 3f 210y, Asco, GF, Jun 19)
Wicklow Brave 105[1] (2m 1f, Kill, Gd, Aug 23)
Battle Of Jericho (USA) 104[1] (5f 164y, Nava, Gd, Sep 8)
Beshaayir 104[1] (1m, Newm, GF, Sep 28)
Bloomfield (IRE) 104[1] (1m 6f, Gowr, Hvy, May 9)
Brendan Brackan (IRE) 104[3] (1m, Leop, Hvy, Apr 16)
Brian The Snail (IRE) 104[1] (6f 2y, Donc, GF, Jun 17)
Buzz (FR) 104[2] (1m 2f 219y, Kemw, SS, Nov 19)
Calling Out (FR) 104[3] (1m 2f, Linw, SD, Jan 24)
Charles Molson 104[2] (7f, Chmf, SD, Sep 22)
Chatez (IRE) 104[2] (1m 2f, Newb, GS, Oct 27)
Chilean 104[4] (1m 1f 209y, Sand, GS, Apr 27)
Cleonte (IRE) 104[3] (2m 2f, Newm, GF, Oct 13)
Clon Coulis (IRE) 104[1] (7f 213y, Asco, GF, Jul 27)
Cosmelli (ITY) 104[1] (2m 56y, Ncsw, SS, Jun 30)
Culturati 104[4] (5f 89y, York, GF, Aug 22)
Dakota Gold 104[1] (5f, Hayd, GS, Sep 29)
Duke Of Firenze 104[6] (5f, Epso, Gd, Jun 2)
Dynamic 104[2] (1m 2f, Newm, GS, Oct 6)
Ekhtiyaar 104[3] (6f, Ncsw, SS, Jun 30)
Elgin 104[1] (1m 4f 13y, Catt, Gd, Jun 1)
Falcon Eight (IRE) 104[3] (2m, Naas, Gd, Sep 30)
Finniston Farm 104[1] (1m 3f 175y, Hayd, GS, Sep 29)
First Nation 104[4] (1m 2f, Newb, Sft, Sep 22)
Flattering (IRE) 104[1] (1m 4f, Cork, GF, Jun 17)
G Force (IRE) 104[3] (5f 164y, Nava, Sft, Apr 23)
Get Knotted (IRE) 104[1] (7f, York, Sft, Jul 28)
Gilgamesh 104[1] (7f, York, Gd, May 26)
Glorious Journey 104[4] (1m, Good, GF, Aug 3)
Golden Apollo 104[2] (6f, York, Sft, Jul 28)
Gorane (IRE) 104[5] (5f, Curr, GF, Jul 22)
Greatest Journey 104[1] (1m 1f 104y, Wolw, SD, Nov 28)
Gronkowski (USA) 104[1] (1m 5y, Ncsw, SD, Mar 30)
Growl 104[3] (5f 110y, Ches, Gd, Sep 1)
Heartache 104[7] (6f, Asco, GF, Jun 22)
Intern (IRE) 104[5] (1m 2f, Linw, SD, Feb 3)
Jukebox Jive (FR) 104[3] (2m 50y, Sand, GF, Jul 7)
Laws Of Spin (IRE) 104[2] (2m, Curr, GF, Jun 30)
Mafaaheem (IRE) 104[1] (1m 2f, Ayr, Hvy, Sep 22)
Masaarr (USA) 104[3] (1m, Newj, GF, Jul 12)
Maths Prize 104[1] (1m 2f, Curr, GF, Jul 1)
Mizaah (IRE) 104[1] (7f, Chmf, SD, Sep 25)
Mordin (IRE) 104[2] (1m, Sand, Gd, Sep 14)
Mrs Gallagher 104[1] (5f 110y, Naas, Yld, May 7)
Nordic Lights 104[5] (1m 2f 56y, York, GF, May 17)
Normandy Barriere (IRE) 104[2] (6f 111y, Donc, GS, Sep 14)
Now Children (IRE) 104[1] (1m 3f 218y, Good, Sft, Oct 14)
Onenightidreamed (IRE) 104[5] (1m, Naas, Hvy, Mar 25)
Perfection 104[1] (6f, Newm, GF, Oct 13)
Precious Ramotswe 104[3] (1m 3f 175y, Hayd, GF, Jul 7)
Rasima 104[1] (1m 1y, Linw, SD, Nov 1)
Reach High 104[2] (7f 6y, Donc, GF, Jul 19)
Red Starlight 104[1] (1m 1y, Linw, SD, Sep 1)
Ripp Orf (IRE) 104[2] (7f, Asco, Sft, Oct 6)

Roussel (IRE) 104[3] (5f, York, GF, May 17)
Sabador (FR) 104[2] (1m, Kemw, SS, Oct 16)
Seahenge (USA) 104[3] (1m, Dunw, SD, Mar 9)
Ship Of Dreams (IRE) 104[2] (1m 1f, List, Sft, Sep 10)
Silver Line (IRE) 104[3] (1m, Sand, GF, Jun 16)
Sir Thomas Gresham (IRE) 104[3] (7f 1y, Linw, SD, Nov 24)
Soldier In Action (FR) 104[4] (1m 4f 51y, Wolw, SD, Mar 5)
Stargazer (IRE) 104[1] (2m 56y, Ncsw, SD, Dec 15)
Turret Rocks (IRE) 104[1] (1m 1f, Leop, GF, Jul 19)
Uae Prince (IRE) 104[2] (1m 4f, Newm, GF, May 6)
Uradel (GER) 104[2] (2m 2f, Newm, GF, Oct 13)
Vibrant Chords 104[1] (5f 10y, Sand, GF, Jul 6)
Wahash (IRE) 104[2] (1m, Sali, GF, Jun 27)
What's The Story 104[4] (1m, Asco, GF, Jun 20)
Wolf Country 104[2] (1m 3f 218y, Good, Sft, Oct 14)
Zwayyan 104[2] (1m, Asco, Gd, Sep 7)
Al Qahwa (IRE) 103[2] (6f, Ripo, GS, Apr 28)
Alemaratalyoum (IRE) 103[1] (1m 37y, Hayd, Hvy, Oct 19)
Almoghared (IRE) 103 (2m 110y, Newb, GF, Jul 21)
Alwaysandforever (IRE) 103[2] (1m 4f, Newj, GF, Aug 4)
Bella Estrella (IRE) 103[1] (1m 25y, Kill, Gd, Jul 15)
Bengali Boys (IRE) 103[2] (6f, Ncsw, SD, Mar 20)
Betty F 103[3] (7f, York, GF, Aug 23)
Blue De Vega (GER) 103[1] (5f, Asco, GF, Jul 27)
Blue Mist 103[1] (1m, Asco, Gd, Oct 5)
Calder Prince (IRE) 103[1] (6f 20y, Wolw, SD, Apr 5)
Captain Colby (USA) 103[2] (5f, Catt, Sft, Oct 20)
Carolinae 103[1] (7f, Chmf, SD, Jun 20)
Clever Cookie 103[3] (1m 6f, Nott, GS, Apr 21)
Clongowes (IRE) 103[3] (1m 4f, Leop, Gd, May 13)
Company Asset (IRE) 103[1] (1m 2f 43y, Donc, Sft, Nov 10)
Corelli (USA) 103[1] (1m 4f 14y, Souw, SD, Nov 30)
Curiosity (IRE) 103[2] (1m, Newj, GF, Jul 14)
Danzan (IRE) 103[3] (6f, Kemw, SS, Dec 5)
Downdraft (IRE) 103[1] (1m 2f, Naas, Yld, Oct 21)
Dragon Mall (USA) 103[3] (7f 14y, Ncsw, SD, Jan 2)
Dramatic Queen (USA) 103[1] (1m 3f 219y, Kemw, SS, Oct 31)
Dubhe 103[1] (1m 1f 209y, Sand, GS, Apr 27)
Eirene 103[2] (7f 6y, Donc, Gd, Sep 14)
Elector 103[7] (1m 3f 211y, Asco, GF, Jun 22)
Family Tree 103[6] (1m 6f, Naas, Yld, Nov 4)
Fire Brigade 103[2] (1m 37y, Hayd, Sft, Apr 28)
Four White Socks 103[3] (1m 1f 197y, Good, Gd, Aug 1)
Golden Spell 103[1] (5f 164y, Nava, Sft, Apr 22)
Gulf Of Poets 103[1] (1m 37y, Hayd, Sft, Apr 28)
Hakam (USA) 103[1] (1m 1y, Linw, SD, Nov 17)
High Jinx (IRE) 103[4] (2m, Ripo, GS, Apr 28)
Highbrow 103[3] (1m 3f 197y, Donc, Gd, Sep 15)
Island Brave (IRE) 103[2] (1m 4f 98y, Ncsw, SD, Mar 30)
Kaanoon 103[2] (1m 2f, Newj, GS, Jul 28)
Keyser Soze (IRE) 103[1] (7f 1y, Linw, SD, Dec 12)
Kyllachy Gala 103[1] (1m 1f 219y, Kemw, SD, Mar 7)
Lethal Steps 103[4] (1m, Newj, GF, Jul 12)
Lightening Quick 103[6] (1m, Curr, Gd, May 27)
Limini (IRE) 103[1] (1m 4f 180y, Leop, GF, Sep 15)
Line Of Reason (IRE) 103[4] (5f, Beve, GF, Sep 1)
Lualiwa 103[1] (7f 33y, Muss, Sft, Mar 31)
Magical Dreamer (IRE) 103[1] (6f, Chmf, SD, Aug 25)
Masham Star (IRE) 103[4] (1m, Chmf, SD, Sep 10)
Medicine Jack 103[1] (5f 164y, Nava, Yld, Oct 14)
Montaly 103[8] (1m 5f 188y, York, GF, Aug 25)
Mutaaqeb 103[2] (7f, Newm, GF, May 19)
North Face (IRE) 103[5] (1m 2f, Linw, SD, Dec 5)
Now You're Talking (IRE) 103[4] (6f, Naas, GF, May 20)
Ocean Of Love 103[1] (1m 5f 219y, Wolw, SD, Apr 14)
Pipers Note 103[1] (6f, Ripo, Gd, Aug 6)
Poetic Charm 103[1] (7f, Newj, GF, Jul 14)
Polybius 103[1] (6f, Kemw, SS, Oct 27)

TOPSPEED: LAST SEASON'S TOP PERFORMERS 3YO+

Poet's Word (IRE) 120[1] (1m 3f 211y, Asco, GF, Jul 28)
Crystal Ocean 119[2] (1m 3f 211y, Asco, GF, Jul 28)
Alpha Centauri (IRE) 118[1] (7f 213y, Asco, GF, Jun 22)
Battaash (IRE) 118[1] (5f, Good, GF, Aug 3)
Masar (IRE) 118[1] (1m 4f 6y, Epso, Gd, Jun 2)
Blue Point (IRE) 117[1] (5f, Asco, GF, Jun 19)
Dee Ex Bee 115[2] (1m 4f 6y, Epso, Gd, Jun 2)
Sands Of Mali (FR) 115[1] (6f, Asco, Sft, Oct 20)
Roaring Lion (USA) 114[3] (1m 4f 6y, Epso, Gd, Jun 2)
Cracksman 113[1] (1m 4f 6y, Epso, Sft, Jun 1)
Salouen (IRE) 112[2] (1m 4f 6y, Epso, Sft, Jun 1)
Harry Angel (IRE) 111[2] (6f, Asco, Sft, Oct 20)
Emaraaty 110[2] (7f, Good, Gd, May 26)
Old Persian 110[1] (1m 3f 188y, York, GF, Aug 22)
Stradivarius (IRE) 110[1] (2m 56y, York, GF, Aug 24)
Wissahickon (USA) 110[1] (1m 1f, Newm, GF, Sep 29)
Alpha Delphini 109[1] (5f, York, GF, Aug 24)
Merchant Navy (AUS) 109[1] (6f, Asco, GF, Jun 23)
Saxon Warrior (JPN) 109[4] (1m 4f 6y, Epso, Gd, Jun 2)
City Light (FR) 108[2] (6f, Asco, GF, Jun 23)
Expert Eye 108[1] (7f, Asco, GF, Jun 20)
Gifted Master (IRE) 108[1] (6f, Good, GF, Aug 4)
Kew Gardens (IRE) 108[1] (1m 6f 115y, Donc, Gd, Sep 15)
Cross Counter 107[1] (1m 3f 218y, Good, GF, Aug 4)
Forever Together (IRE) 107[1] (1m 4f 6y, Epso, Sft, Jun 1)
Kachy 107[1] (5f 15y, Ches, Gd, May 11)
Tarboosh 107[1] (5f 3y, Donc, GS, Oct 27)
Bacchus 106[1] (6f, Asco, GF, Jun 23)
Donjuan Triumphant (IRE) 106[3] (6f, Asco, Sft, Oct 20)
Mabs Cross 106[3] (5f, Asco, GF, Jun 19)
Magical (IRE) 106[1] (1m 3f 211y, Asco, Sft, Oct 20)
Monarchs Glen 106[1] (1m 1f 212y, Asco, GF, Jun 19)
Washington Dc (IRE) 106[2] (5f, Hayd, Gd, May 26)
Bound For Nowhere (USA) 105[3] (6f, Asco, GF, Jun 23)
Coronet 105[2] (1m 3f 211y, Asco, Sft, Oct 20)
Count Octave 105[2] (2m 56y, York, GF, Aug 24)
Desert Skyline (IRE) 105[2] (1m 5f 188y, York, GF, May 18)
Without Parole 105[1] (7f 213y, Asco, GF, Jun 19)
Another Batt (IRE) 104[1] (7f 127y, Ches, Gd, May 10)
Baron Bolt 104[1] (6f, Ayr, Hvy, Sep 22)
Brando 104[4] (6f, Asco, Sft, Oct 20)
Hazapour (IRE) 104[5] (1m 4f 6y, Epso, Gd, Jun 2)
Hey Jonesy (IRE) 104[2] (6f 2y, Donc, Sft, Nov 10)
Mr Lupton (IRE) 104[1] (5f 34y, Newb, Sft, Sep 22)
Son Of Rest 104[1] (6f, Ayr, Hvy, Sep 22)
Symbolization (IRE) 104[1] (1m, Newm, Gd, May 5)
The Tin Man 104[4] (6f, Asco, GF, Jun 23)
Windstoss (GER) 104[3] (1m 4f 6y, Epso, Sft, Jun 1)
A Momentofmadness 103[1] (5f 143y, Donc, Gd, Sep 15)
Aeolus 103[1] (6f, Newm, GS, Apr 18)
Beat The Bank 103[1] (1m, Good, Gd, Aug 25)
Caspian Prince (IRE) 103[1] (5f 1y, Muss, GF, Jun 9)
Dreamfield 103[2] (6f, Asco, GF, Jun 23)
El Astronaute (IRE) 103[1] (5f 89y, York, GF, Aug 22)
Eqtidaar (IRE) 103[1] (6f, Asco, GF, Jun 22)
Flaming Spear (IRE) 103[1] (7f, Good, Gd, Aug 25)
Gustav Klimt (IRE) 103[2] (7f 213y, Asco, GF, Jun 19)
Hunting Horn (IRE) 103[1] (1m 1f 212y, Asco, GF, Jun 21)
Pilaster 103[1] (1m 6f, Good, Gd, Aug 2)
Sharja Bridge 103[4] (7f 192y, York, GF, Aug 23)
Classical Times 102[2] (6f, Newm, GF, Oct 13)
Court House (IRE) 102[2] (1m 2f 17y, Epso, GS, Jun 2)
Lah Ti Dar 102[3] (1m 3f 211y, Asco, Sft, Oct 20)
Maid Up 102[2] (1m 6f, Good, Gd, Aug 2)
Proschema (IRE) 102[3] (1m 5f 188y, York, GF, Aug 25)
Regal Reality 102[1] (1m, Good, GF, Aug 3)
Renneti (FR) 102[2] (2m 5f 143y, Asco, GF, Jun 23)
Sioux Nation (USA) 102[1] (6f, Naas, GF, May 20)
Sir Dancealot (IRE) 102[5] (6f, Asco, Sft, Oct 20)
Thomas Hobson 102[1] (2m 1f 197y, Donc, GS, Sep 14)
Vintager 102[1] (1m, Newj, GF, Jul 21)
Billesdon Brook 101[1] (1m, Newm, GF, May 6)
Call To Mind 101[3] (1m 5f 188y, York, GF, May 18)
Connect 101[1] (1m 2f 17y, Epso, GS, Jun 2)
Final Venture 101[2] (5f 89y, York, GF, Aug 22)
First Eleven 101[1] (1m 3f 211y, Asco, GF, Sep 8)
King Of Hearts (IRE) 101[1] (7f, Good, Gd, May 26)
Major Jumbo 101[3] (5f, York, GF, May 17)
Max Dynamite (FR) 101[2] (2m 1f 197y, Donc, GS, Sep 14)
Muntahaa (IRE) 101[1] (1m 5f 188y, York, GF, Aug 25)
Projection 101[6] (6f, Asco, Sft, Oct 20)
Seniority 101[1] (1m, Good, GF, Aug 3)

Settle For Bay (FR) 101[1] (1m, Asco, GF, Jun 20)
Star Rock 101[3] (1m 6f, Good, Gd, Aug 2)
Take Cover 101[2] (5f 34y, Newb, Sft, Sep 22)
Tis Marvellous 101[1] (5f, Asco, Gd, Aug 11)
Actress (IRE) 100[1] (6f, Curr, GF, Jun 8)
Circus Couture (IRE) 100[3] (1m, Asco, GF, Jun 20)
D'bai (IRE) 100[2] (6f 12y, Wind, GF, May 21)
Growl 100[3] (5f 110y, Ches, Gd, Sep 1)
Idaho (IRE) 100[3] (2m 56y, York, GF, Aug 24)
Judicial (IRE) 100[2] (5f, Newm, Gd, May 5)
Lucky Team (FR) 100[1] (1m 1y, Linw, SD, Mar 30)
Mustashry 100[1] (1m, Newm, GF, Sep 28)
Muthmir (IRE) 100[1] (5f, Hayd, GF, Jun 9)
Perfection 100[1] (6f, Newm, GF, Oct 13)
Red Verdon (USA) 100[2] (1m 3f 211y, Asco, GF, Jun 23)
Spring Loaded (IRE) 100[1] (5f, Asco, GF, Jul 14)
Stormy Antarctic 100[3] (1m, Good, Gd, Aug 25)
Tabdeed 100[1] (6f, Asco, Gd, Oct 5)
Threading (IRE) 100[2] (7f 213y, Asco, GF, Jun 22)
Victory Wave (USA) 100[1] (7f, Chmf, SD, Sep 15)
Young Rascal (FR) 100[1] (1m 4f 63y, Ches, Gd, May 9)
Zhui Feng (IRE) 100[2] (7f, Asco, GF, May 12)
Austrian School (IRE) 99[2] (1m 6f 115y, Donc, GS, Sep 14)
Dream Of Dreams (IRE) 99[3] (6f, Newb, GF, Jul 21)
Encore D'or 99[2] (5f 6y, Linw, SD, Mar 24)
Encrypted 99[2] (5f 143y, Donc, Gd, Sep 15)
Euginio (IRE) 99[2] (1m 1f 212y, Asco, GF, Jun 19)
Kenya (IRE) 99[1] (1m, Curr, Yld, Sep 1)
Lancelot Du Lac (ITY) 99[1] (6f, Chmf, SD, Apr 26)
Leshlaa (USA) 99[6] (1m 1f 212y, Asco, GF, Jun 19)
Mirage Dancer 99[1] (1m 3f 218y, Good, GF, Aug 3)
Nakeeta 99[5] (2m 110y, Newb, GF, Jul 21)
Savalas (IRE) 99[2] (6f, York, GF, Jun 16)
Smash Williams (IRE) 99[2] (6f, Curr, Yld, Sep 16)
Straight Right (FR) 99[1] (7f 14y, Ncsw, SD, Feb 21)
Titus 99[4] (1m 6f 115y, Donc, GS, Sep 14)
Yafta 99[1] (6f, Newb, GF, Jul 21)
Afaak 98[2] (1m, Asco, GF, Jun 20)
Ajman King (IRE) 98[1] (1m 2f 17y, Epso, Sft, Jun 1)
Astronomer (IRE) 98[2] (1m 4f, Newm, GF, Oct 12)
Captain Colby (USA) 98[2] (5f, Catt, Sft, Oct 20)
Finsbury Square (IRE) 98[4] (5f, Asco, GF, Jun 19)
Ghostwatch (IRE) 98[2] (1m 3f 211y, Asco, GF, Sep 8)
Grey Britain 98[1] (1m 4f 51y, Wolw, SD, Dec 8)
Hochfeld (IRE) 98[4] (2m 56y, York, GF, Aug 22)
Ice Age (IRE) 98[1] (6f, Newb, GF, May 18)
Kasperenko 98[1] (1m 3f 219y, Kemw, SS, Nov 5)
Kynren (IRE) 98[2] (7f 192y, York, GF, Aug 23)
Limini (IRE) 98[1] (1m 4f 180y, Leop, GF, Sep 15)
Mjjack (IRE) 98[1] (7f, Newm, GS, Apr 17)
Poet's Society 98[1] (7f 192y, York, GF, Aug 23)
Riven Light (IRE) 98[1] (1m 123y, Galw, Sft, Jul 31)
Royal Line 98[1] (1m 3f 197y, Donc, Sft, Nov 10)
Rufus King 98[2] (7f, Chmf, SD, Sep 15)
Sheikha Reika (FR) 98[1] (1m 2f 23y, Yarm, GF, Sep 19)
Silent Attack 98[1] (7f 1y, Linw, SD, Apr 14)
Tomily (IRE) 98[1] (6f, Kemw, SD, Mar 31)
Whisky Baron (AUS) 98[2] (1m, Good, Gd, Aug 25)
Wild Illusion 98[2] (1m 4f 6y, Epso, Sft, Jun 1)
Bucchero (USA) 97[5] (5f, Asco, GF, Jun 19)
Cape Byron 97[4] (1m, Good, GF, Aug 3)
Cardsharp 97[4] (7f, Newj, GF, Jul 14)
Cliffs Of Moher (IRE) 97[3] (1m 1f 209y, Sand, GF, Jul 7)
Emblazoned (IRE) 97[3] (6f, Asco, GF, Jun 22)
Firmament 97[3] (7f 192y, York, GF, Aug 23)
George Bowen (IRE) 97[1] (6f 6y, Hami, GF, Jul 20)
Goring (GER) 97[1] (1m 1y, Linw, SD, Feb 24)
Gunmetal (IRE) 97[1] (6f, Ripo, Gd, Aug 18)
Havana Grey 97[5] (5f, York, GF, Aug 24)
Justanotherbottle (IRE) 97[2] (6f, Good, GF, Aug 4)
Ka Ying Star 97[1] (7f 192y, York, GF, Aug 24)
Kimberella 97[1] (7f, Thir, GS, Apr 21)
Laurens (FR) 97[1] (1m, Newm, Gd, Oct 6)
Marnie James 97[2] (5f, Good, Gd, Aug 2)
Mr Scaramanga 97[2] (1m 1y, Linw, SD, Feb 24)
Original Choice (IRE) 97[3] (1m, Good, GF, Aug 3)
Ostilio 97[2] (1m, Good, GF, Aug 3)
Primo Uomo (IRE) 97[1] (5f, Nava, Sft, Apr 23)
Speak In Colours 97[1] (6f, Curr, Gd, Aug 12)
Spirit Of Valor (USA) 97[2] (6f, Curr, GF, May 26)
Sunny Speed 97[2] (7f 192y, York, GF, Aug 24)
Tip Two Win 97[2] (1m, Newm, Gd, May 5)
Udontdodou 97[2] (6f, Kemw, SD, Mar 31)
Visionary (IRE) 97[2] (6f, Chmf, SD, Apr 26)
Weekender 97[2] (1m 5f 188y, York, GF, Aug 25)
Wells Farhh Go (IRE) 97[4] (1m 3f 188y, York, GF, Aug 22)
Autocratic 96[4] (1m 1f 212y, Asco, GF, Jun 19)
Breathless Times 96[1] (6f, Chmf, SD, Sep 15)
Cenotaph (USA) 96[1] (7f, Chmf, SD, Sep 1)
Chief Ironside 96[3] (1m, Good, GF, Aug 3)
Copper Knight (IRE) 96[4] (5f, Catt, Sft, Oct 20)
Di Fede (IRE) 96[1] (7f, Asco, Sft, Oct 6)
Double Up 96[2] (6f, Chmf, SD, Apr 26)
Dubai Horizon (IRE) 96[1] (1m 1f 209y, Sand, GS, Sep 1)
Euchen Glen 96[1] (1m 5f 26y, Ayr, Gd, Jun 23)
Examiner (IRE) 96[1] (1m, Newm, GS, Apr 17)
Foolaad 96[1] (5f, Catt, Sft, Oct 20)
Happily (IRE) 96[2] (1m, Newm, Gd, Oct 6)
Hit The Bid 96[2] (5f, Tipp, Yld, Aug 30)
Kitesurf 96[4] (1m 3f 211y, Asco, Sft, Oct 20)
Limato (IRE) 96[1] (7f, Newm, GF, Oct 12)
Morando (FR) 96[1] (1m 4f, Newb, GS, Oct 27)
Mordin (IRE) 96[2] (1m, Sand, Gd, Sep 14)
Move Swiftly 96[2] (1m, Newm, GS, Oct 6)
Mrs Gallagher 96[1] (5f 110y, Naas, Yld, May 7)
Nordic Lights 96[1] (1m 2f, Newm, Gd, Apr 19)
Pallasator 96[1] (2m 5f 143y, Asco, GF, Jun 23)
Pivoine (IRE) 96[4] (1m 1f 209y, Sand, GF, Jul 6)
Second Thought (IRE) 96[2] (1m 1y, Linw, SD, Mar 30)
Sir Chauvelin 96[6] (2m 56y, York, GF, Aug 24)
Stone Of Destiny 96[4] (6f, Asco, GF, Jun 22)
Thundering Blue (USA) 96[1] (1m 2f 56y, York, GS, Jul 28)
Addeybb (IRE) 95[1] (1m, Donc, Sft, Mar 24)
Air Pilot 95[2] (1m 2f, Newm, Sft, Nov 3)
Barsanti (IRE) 95[4] (1m 3f 211y, Asco, GF, Jun 23)
Berkshire Blue (IRE) 95[5] (1m 5f 188y, York, GF, Aug 25)
Brorocco 95[2] (1m 2f 56y, York, GS, Jul 28)
Corgi 95[6] (1m 5f 188y, York, GF, Aug 25)
Culturati 95[4] (5f 89y, York, GF, Aug 22)
Dali (USA) 95[3] (5f, Nava, Gd, Sep 8)
Delano Roosevelt (IRE) 95[6] (1m 4f 6y, Epso, Gd, Jun 2)
Elegiac 95[2] (1m 6f 17y, Yarm, GF, Sep 20)
G Force (IRE) 95[1] (6f, Naas, Hvy, Apr 13)
Gorane (IRE) 95[2] (6f, Curr, GF, Jun 8)
Gracious John (IRE) 95[2] (5f, Asco, Gd, Aug 11)
Haddaf (IRE) 95[1] (5f 10y, Sand, Gd, Apr 27)
Hawkbill (USA) 95[3] (1m 1f 212y, Asco, GF, Jun 20)
Here And Now 95[1] (2m 56y, York, GF, Aug 22)
Hors De Combat 95[6] (1m, Good, GF, Aug 3)
Intisaab 95[4] (6f 1y, Linw, SD, Feb 3)
Jumira Bridge 95[2] (5f, Kemw, SD, Apr 7)
Just In Time 95[1] (1m 6f 115y, Donc, GS, Sep 14)
Koditime (IRE) 95[2] (5f 21y, Wind, Gd, May 28)
Lord Glitters (FR) 95[2] (1m, Donc, Sft, Mar 24)
Magic Circle (IRE) 95[1] (2m 50y, Sand, Gd, May 24)
Rebel Streak 95[3] (5f 34y, Newb, Sft, Sep 22)
Red Starlight 95[1] (1m 1y, Linw, SD, Sep 1)
Silver Quartz 95[1] (1m, Asco, Gd, Sep 7)
The Broghie Man 95[1] (5f 164y, Nava, Sft, Apr 22)
The Pentagon (IRE) 95[5] (1m 3f 188y, York, GF, Aug 22)
Urban Fox 95[1] (1m, Asco, GF, May 12)
Veracious 95[3] (7f 213y, Asco, GF, Jun 22)
Waarif (IRE) 95[1] (1m, Ripo, Gd, Aug 18)
Zabeel Prince (IRE) 95[2] (1m, Newm, GF, Sep 28)
Zonderland 95[4] (1m, Good, Gd, Aug 25)
Ardhoomey (IRE) 94[2] (6f 63y, Curr, Gd, Jul 21)
Baghdad (FR) 94[1] (1m 3f 211y, Asco, GF, Jun 21)
Big Country (IRE) 94[1] (1m 2f 1y, Redc, GF, May 28)
Blue Uluru (IRE) 94[1] (5f, Tipp, Yld, Aug 30)
Borderforce (FR) 94[1] (1m, Ripo, GS, Aug 27)
Century Dream (IRE) 94[3] (1m, Asco, Sft, Oct 20)
Crossed Baton 94[2] (1m 1f 212y, Asco, GF, Jun 21)
Curly (IRE) 94[1] (1m 4f, Naas, Yld, Oct 21)
Elarqam 94[4] (1m, Newm, Gd, May 5)
Equilateral 94[4] (5f 34y, Newb, Sft, Sep 22)
First Contact (IRE) 94[1] (1m, Newj, GF, Jul 14)
Fleet Review (USA) 94[2] (6f, Naas, GF, May 20)
Frontiersman 94[3] (2m 120y, Wolw, SD, Jan 15)
Glorious Journey 94[4] (1m, Good, GF, Aug 3)
Gordon Lord Byron (IRE) 94[2] (6f, Curr, Gd, Aug 12)

I Can Fly 94[2] (1m, Asco, Sft, Oct 20)
Invincible Army (IRE) 94[1] (6f, Asco, Sft, May 2)
King's Field (IRE) 94[1] (1m, Dunw, SD, Dec 7)
Laugh A Minute 94[4] (6f 2y, Donc, Sft, Nov 10)
Low Sun 94[1] (2m 2f, Newm, GF, Oct 13)
Magic Wand (IRE) 94[1] (1m 3f 211y, Asco, GF, Jun 21)
Magical Dreamer (IRE) 94[1] (6f, Chmf, SD, Aug 25)
Making Miracles 94[3] (1m 3f 218y, Good, Gd, Aug 1)
Melting Dew 94[1] (1m 1f 209y, Sand, GF, Jul 6)
Oasis Charm 94[1] (1m 1f, Newm, Gd, May 5)
One Master 94[3] (6f, Curr, GF, Jun 8)
Orvar (IRE) 94[1] (5f 3y, Donc, GF, Aug 18)
Rostropovich (IRE) 94[1] (1m 4f, Leop, GF, Sep 15)
Sandra's Secret (IRE) 94[1] (6f, York, GF, Jun 15)
Sea Of Class (IRE) 94[1] (1m 3f 188y, York, GF, Aug 23)
Sheikhzayedroad 94[3] (2m 1f 197y, Donc, GS, Sep 14)
Solar Flair 94[1] (6f, Ncsw, SS, Jun 30)
Southern France (IRE) 94[3] (1m 6f 115y, Donc, Gd, Sep 15)
Staxton 94[4] (6f, York, GF, Jun 16)
Wahash (IRE) 94[2] (1m, Sali, GF, Jun 27)
Watchable 94[1] (5f 3y, Pont, GF, Jul 20)
Watersmeet 94[1] (2m 120y, Wolw, SD, Jan 15)
Adamant (GER) 93[1] (1m 2f, Chmf, SD, Aug 17)
Alfarris (FR) 93[2] (1m 1f 209y, Sand, GF, Jul 6)
Algometer 93[4] (2m 1f 197y, Donc, GS, Sep 14)
Aljady (FR) 93[2] (6f, Asco, Gd, Oct 5)
Alsvinder 93[1] (5f, Kemw, SS, Oct 15)
Arod (IRE) 93[1] (1m 31y, Wind, Gd, May 14)
Boom The Groom (IRE) 93[4] (5f, Epso, Gd, Apr 25)
Burnt Sugar (IRE) 93[1] (7f, Newj, GF, Jul 14)
Daira Prince (IRE) 93[1] (1m, Bath, Fm, Sep 15)
Danzeno 93[4] (6f, Chmf, SD, Apr 26)
Duke Of Firenze 93[6] (5f, Epso, Gd, Jun 2)
Emmaus (IRE) 93[1] (7f, Leic, Hvy, Apr 28)
Equimou 93[4] (5f, Newm, Gd, May 5)
Espere (IRE) 93[1] (1m 123y, Galw, Sft, Aug 1)
Forest Ranger (IRE) 93[2] (1m 1f, Newm, GF, Oct 13)
Funny Kid (USA) 93[2] (2m 120y, Wolw, SD, Jan 15)
Gidu (IRE) 93[6] (6f, Asco, GF, Jun 22)
Giuseppe Garibaldi (IRE) 93[2] (1m 4f, Leop, GF, Sep 15)
God Given 93[4] (1m 6f, Good, Gd, Aug 2)
Gulliver 93[5] (6f 1y, Linw, SD, Feb 3)
Gurkha Friend 93[2] (1m, Ripo, GS, Aug 27)
Hamada 93[1] (1m 5f 61y, Newb, Gd, Aug 18)
Intelligence Cross (USA) 93[2] (6f, Curr, GF, Jun 30)
James Garfield (IRE) 93[1] (7f, Newb, GS, Apr 21)
King Malpic (FR) 93[4] (1m 1y, Linw, SD, Mar 30)
Kyllang Rock (IRE) 93[1] (5f 1y, Muss, Hvy, Mar 31)
Lucymai 93[1] (7f, Chmf, SD, May 10)
Masham Star (IRE) 93[1] (7f 219y, Redc, GF, Aug 11)
Miracle Of Medinah 93[3] (6f, Asco, GF, Jul 13)
Mustajeer 93[1] (1m 3f 190y, Naas, Yld, Nov 4)
Rainbow Rebel (IRE) 93[1] (1m 3f 75y, Ches, Gd, Jul 13)
Reputation (IRE) 93[2] (5f 110y, Ches, Gd, Sep 1)
Roundhay Park 93[1] (5f, Ripo, Gd, Jun 20)
Silent Echo 93[1] (6f 12y, Wind, Gd, May 14)
Speedo Boy (FR) 93[5] (1m 6f 115y, Donc, GS, Sep 14)
Still Standing (IRE) 93[1] (1m 2f, Fair, Yld, Sep 24)
Stratum 93[1] (2m 110y, Newb, GF, Jul 21)
Suedois (FR) 93[2] (7f, Good, Gd, Jul 31)
Summer Icon 93[2] (7f, Good, GS, May 5)
Teodoro (IRE) 93[1] (1m 2f 100y, Hayd, GF, Aug 11)
U S Navy Flag (USA) 93[1] (6f, Newj, GF, Jul 14)
Unfortunately (IRE) 93[1] (6f, Naas, Gd, Sep 30)
Ventura Knight (IRE) 93[1] (7f 213y, Donc, GF, May 19)
Wootton (FR) 93[3] (7f 213y, Asco, GF, Jun 19)
Zaaki 93[3] (1m 1f 212y, Asco, GF, Jun 21)
Zwayyan 93[2] (1m, Asco, Gd, Sep 7)
Above The Rest (IRE) 92[1] (6f, Ncsw, SS, Jun 30)
Ben Vrackie 92[3] (1m 4f, Newm, GF, Oct 12)
Beringer 92[2] (1m 2f 56y, York, GF, Jun 30)
Blue De Vega (GER) 92[5] (5f, Epso, Sft, Aug 27)
Breton Rock (IRE) 92[3] (7f, Good, Gd, Jul 31)
Calder Prince (IRE) 92[1] (6f 20y, Wolw, SD, Apr 5)
Completion (IRE) 92[2] (1m 37y, Hayd, Gd, May 26)
Dakota Gold 92[1] (5f, Hayd, GS, Sep 29)
Eastern Impact (IRE) 92[2] (6f, Newj, GF, Jun 9)
Everything For You (IRE) 92[2] (1m 1f, Newm, GF, Sep 28)
Intense Romance (IRE) 92[1] (5f, Asco, Sft, Oct 6)
Ispolini 92[4] (1m 4f 63y, Ches, Gd, May 9)
Kick On Kick On 92[4] (5f, Leic, Gd, Sep 24)
Lady Aurelia (USA) 92[7] (5f, Asco, GF, Jun 19)
Makzeem 92[5] (7f, Newj, GF, Jul 14)
Marshall Jennings (IRE) 92[1] (1m, Naas, Yld, May 7)
Mekong 92[4] (1m 5f 188y, York, GF, Aug 25)
Mitchum Swagger 92[3] (1m, Donc, Sft, Mar 24)
My Target (IRE) 92[2] (1m 1y, Linw, SD, Mar 24)
Mythical Madness 92[5] (1m, Good, GF, Aug 3)
Nyaleti (IRE) 92[5] (1m, Good, Gd, Aug 25)
Oh This Is Us (IRE) 92[2] (1m 31y, Wind, Gd, May 14)
Perfect Pasture 92[1] (6f 2y, Donc, Sft, Mar 24)
Pettochside 92[2] (5f, Epso, Gd, Jun 2)
Raymond Tusk (IRE) 92[1] (1m 3f 15y, Hami, GF, Jul 20)
Restorer 92[2] (1m 4f 51y, Wolw, SD, Dec 8)
Silverkode (IRE) 92[3] (7f, Gowr, GF, Jun 24)
Sofia's Rock (FR) 92[2] (1m 3f 99y, Wind, GF, Jun 30)
South Seas (IRE) 92[2] (1m, Good, GS, Sep 26)
Spark Plug (IRE) 92[7] (1m 1f 212y, Asco, GF, Jun 19)
Spoof 92[5] (5f 89y, York, GF, Aug 22)
Tasleet 92[3] (6f, Curr, GF, May 26)
The King (IRE) 92[3] (1m 4f, Leop, GF, Sep 15)
Under The Covers 92[1] (5f, Good, Gd, Jul 31)
Urban Beat (IRE) 92[1] (6f, Curr, Yld, Sep 1)
Walton Street 92[8] (1m 6f 115y, Donc, GS, Sep 14)
Wentworth Falls 92[3] (5f 143y, Donc, Gd, Sep 15)
Accidental Agent 91[1] (1m, Asco, GF, Jun 19)
Alternative Fact 91[5] (1m 1f 209y, Sand, GF, Jul 6)
Atletico (IRE) 91[2] (6f 20y, Wolw, SD, Feb 26)
Beshaayir 91[1] (1m, Asco, GF, Jul 14)
Bravery (IRE) 91[2] (7f 219y, Redc, GF, Aug 11)
Bye Bye Baby (IRE) 91[3] (1m 4f 6y, Epso, Sft, Jun 1)
Clear Skies 91[1] (1m 2f 150y, Dunw, SD, Jan 26)
Company Asset (IRE) 91[1] (1m 2f 43y, Donc, Sft, Nov 10)
Curiosity (IRE) 91[2] (1m, Newm, Gd, May 5)
Dan's Dream 91[1] (7f, Newb, GS, Apr 21)
Dark Red (IRE) 91[3] (1m 2f 17y, Epso, Sft, Jun 1)
Dash Of Spice 91[1] (1m 4f 6y, Epso, Gd, Jun 2)
Dragons Tail (IRE) 91[3] (7f 212y, Hayd, GF, Jun 13)
Edward Lewis 91[5] (5f, York, GF, May 17)
Eirene 91[3] (6f 2y, Donc, Sft, Nov 10)
Ekhtiyaar 91[3] (6f, Ncsw, SS, Jun 30)
Eljaddaaf (IRE) 91[1] (7f 1y, Linw, SD, Feb 23)
Elnadim Star (IRE) 91[1] (5f, Ayr, Gd, Jun 23)
Epic 91[1] (1m, Sand, GS, Apr 27)
Escobar (IRE) 91[8] (1m, Good, GF, Aug 3)
Eye Of The Storm (IRE) 91[3] (1m 5f 26y, Ayr, Gd, Jun 23)
Fabricate 91[2] (1m 1f 209y, Sand, GS, Apr 27)
Fighting Irish (IRE) 91[8] (6f, Asco, GF, Jun 22)
Flag Of Honour (IRE) 91[5] (1m 4f 63y, Ches, Gd, May 9)
Golden Spell 91[2] (5f 110y, Naas, Yld, May 7)
Great Hall 91[1] (1m 4f 10y, Ripo, GS, Apr 28)
Green Power 91[7] (6f, York, GF, Jun 16)
Hajjam 91[1] (7f 50y, Ayr, Hvy, Sep 22)
Jallota 91[1] (7f, Kemw, SD, May 1)
Knight To Behold (IRE) 91[1] (1m 3f 133y, Ling, GF, May 12)
Lake Volta (IRE) 91[1] (7f 3y, Epso, Sft, Jun 1)
Line Of Reason (IRE) 91[1] (5f, Ayr, GF, Jul 9)
Lord Riddiford (IRE) 91[3] (5f 3y, Donc, GS, Oct 27)
Lost Treasure (IRE) 91[3] (5f, Dunw, SD, Oct 19)
Love Dreams (IRE) 91[1] (7f, Chmf, SD, Apr 26)
Masaarr (USA) 91[1] (1m, Donc, Gd, May 5)
Merhoob (IRE) 91[1] (6f, Chmf, SD, Sep 10)
Moqarrar (USA) 91[2] (1m, Chmf, SD, May 31)
Nine Below Zero 91[2] (5f, Kemw, SS, Oct 15)
Ower Fly 91[2] (6f, Newm, GS, Apr 18)
Polybius 91[1] (6f, Kemw, SS, Oct 27)
Rasima 91[1] (1m 1y, Linw, SD, Nov 1)
Raucous 91[2] (6f, Ncsw, SS, Jun 30)
Recoletos (FR) 91[5] (1m, Asco, Sft, Oct 20)
Roussel (IRE) 91[3] (5f, York, GF, May 17)
Salateen 91[3] (7f, Chmf, SD, Sep 1)
Saunter (FR) 91[5] (2m 1f 197y, Donc, GS, Sep 14)
Shady Mccoy (USA) 91[4] (1m, Asco, Gd, Sep 7)
St Patrick's Day (USA) 91[2] (6f, Naas, Gd, Sep 30)
The Grand Visir 91[1] (1m 6f 115y, Donc, GS, Oct 26)
True Self (IRE) 91[1] (1m 2f, Newm, Sft, Nov 3)
Vibrant Chords 91[1] (5f 10y, Sand, GF, Jul 6)
What A Welcome 91[1] (1m 5f 61y, Newb, Gd, Aug 17)
What's The Story 91[4] (1m, Asco, GF, Jun 20)
Altyn Orda (IRE) 90[5] (1m, Newm, GF, May 6)

Another Touch 90 [3] (1m 2f 17y, Epso, Gd, Apr 25)
Benbatl 90 [5] (1m 2f 56y, York, GF, Aug 22)
Captain Joy (IRE) 90 [6] (1m 1y, Linw, SD, Mar 30)
Chevallier 90 [3] (1m 1y, Linw, SD, Mar 3)
Cleonte (IRE) 90 [3] (2m 2f, Newm, GF, Oct 13)
Corrosive (USA) 90 [1] (1m, Asco, GF, May 11)
Could It Be Love (USA) 90 [3] (7f, Asco, GF, Jun 20)
Dark Shot 90 [2] (5f, York, GF, May 17)
Different League (FR) 90 [6] (5f, Asco, GF, Jun 19)
Emotionless (IRE) 90 [1] (1m 2f, Newb, GF, Jul 21)
Finniston Farm 90 [5] (1m 37y, Hayd, Gd, May 26)
Gabrial (IRE) 90 [4] (1m, Donc, Sft, Mar 24)
Global Giant 90 [5] (1m 1f 212y, Asco, GF, Jun 21)
Hey Gaman 90 [3] (7f, Newb, GS, Apr 21)
Isabel De Urbina (IRE) 90 [5] (1m 6f, Good, Gd, Aug 2)
Lynwood Gold (IRE) 90 [3] (1m 6f 115y, Donc, Sft, Jun 2)
Mildenberger 90 [1] (1m 1f, Newm, GS, Apr 17)
Mubtasim (IRE) 90 [3] (6f, Chmf, SD, Apr 26)
Mystic Flight (IRE) 90 [3] (7f 192y, York, GF, Aug 24)
Now You're Talking (IRE) 90 [3] (5f 110y, Naas, Yld, May 7)
Pretty Baby (IRE) 90 [1] (5f 217y, Redc, GF, May 3)
Red Tea 90 [2] (1m, Newm, GS, Apr 17)
Right Direction (IRE) 90 [1] (7f, Newm, Gd, Sep 27)
Second Step (IRE) 90 [3] (1m 3f 218y, Good, GF, Aug 3)
Secret Art (IRE) 90 [2] (1m 2f, Chmf, SD, Aug 17)
Sir Thomas Gresham (IRE) 90 [1] (6f, Newm, Sft, Nov 2)
Stormbringer 90 [2] (6f, Newj, GF, Jul 12)
Supernova 90 [2] (1m 5f 188y, York, GF, Aug 25)
Tabarrak (IRE) 90 [1] (7f, Redc, Gd, Oct 6)
Taurean Star (IRE) 90 [1] (7f, Good, GS, May 5)
Thammin 90 [1] (6f, Chmf, SD, Aug 4)
Uber Cool (IRE) 90 [1] (1m 6f 17y, Yarm, GF, Sep 20)
Uradel (GER) 90 [2] (2m 2f, Newm, GF, Oct 13)
Volatile 90 [1] (7f 14y, Souw, SD, Mar 14)
Wadilsafa 90 [1] (7f 192y, York, GF, Jul 14)
Wafy (IRE) 90 [3] (1m, Donc, GF, Jun 1)
Agrotera (IRE) 89 [1] (1m, Asco, GF, Jun 22)
Arbalet (IRE) 89 [5] (7f, Asco, GF, Jun 20)
Architecture (IRE) 89 [2] (1m 3f 219y, Kemw, SS, Nov 5)
Awesometank 89 [1] (1m, Chmf, SD, May 31)
Book Of Dreams (IRE) 89 [1] (1m 2y, Muss, Hvy, Mar 31)
Constantino (IRE) 89 [1] (1m 1y, Linw, SD, Mar 3)
Corinthia Knight (IRE) 89 [1] (5f 6y, Linw, SD, Dec 4)
Cote D'azur 89 [5] (1m, Ripo, GS, Aug 27)
Deja (FR) 89 [1] (1m 2f 5y, Pont, GS, Oct 22)
Desert Frost (IRE) 89 [2] (6f, Ayr, Gd, Jul 30)
Dream Today (IRE) 89 [4] (7f 192y, York, GF, Aug 24)
Drombeg Dream (IRE) 89 [1] (1m, Lime, Hvy, Apr 21)
Dynabee (USA) 89 [2] (1m 4f, Naas, Yld, Oct 21)
Evergate 89 [2] (5f, Ncsw, SS, Jun 29)
Exec Chef (IRE) 89 [1] (1m 2f, Newb, GS, Sep 21)
Fire Brigade 89 [3] (1m, Asco, Gd, Sep 7)
Flavius (USA) 89 [2] (1m 1f, Tipp, Yld, Aug 30)
Gilgamesh 89 [7] (6f, Asco, GF, Jun 23)
Heartache 89 [7] (6f, Asco, GF, Jun 22)
Holiday Magic (IRE) 89 [2] (7f 14y, Souw, SD, Mar 14)
Humbert (IRE) 89 [2] (1m, Donc, Sft, Mar 24)
Imaging 89 [2] (7f, Leop, Hvy, Apr 14)
Kerosin (GER) 89 [5] (1m, Gowr, GF, May 30)
Key Victory (IRE) 89 [6] (1m 1f 212y, Asco, GF, Jun 21)
Light Pillar (IRE) 89 [4] (2m 5f 143y, Asco, GF, Jun 23)
Lil Rockerfeller (USA) 89 [1] (2m 4f 134y, Good, Gd, Aug 1)
M C Muldoon (IRE) 89 [4] (1m 6y, Pont, GS, Oct 8)
Majboor (IRE) 89 [1] (1m, Sand, Gd, Sep 14)
Medieval (IRE) 89 [2] (1m 2f, Newb, GS, Sep 21)
Mendelssohn (USA) 89 [1] (1m, Dunw, SD, Mar 9)
Midnight Malibu (IRE) 89 [1] (5f, Ripo, GF, Jul 16)
Mikmak 89 [2] (1m, Ripo, Gd, Aug 18)
Naadirr (IRE) 89 [1] (6f 2y, Donc, Sft, Mar 25)
Never Back Down (IRE) 89 [1] (6f, Newb, GF, May 19)
On The Go Again (IRE) 89 [1] (1m, Naas, Hvy, Mar 25)
Oneoveryou (IRE) 89 [2] (5f, Nava, GF, May 19)
Open Wide (USA) 89 [1] (5f, Sali, GF, Jun 17)
Perfect Clarity 89 [1] (1m 3f 133y, Ling, GF, May 12)
Pincheck (IRE) 89 [1] (1m, Leop, Gd, Aug 16)
Poet's Prince 89 [4] (1m 2f 17y, Epso, GS, Jun 2)
Raising Sand 89 [7] (1m, Asco, GF, Jun 20)
Repercussion 89 [1] (1m 75y, Nott, Sft, May 30)
Rock On Baileys 89 [4] (6f, Newm, GF, Oct 6)
Saracen Knight (IRE) 89 [6] (1m 4f 180y, Leop, GF, Sep 15)
Snazzy Jazzy (IRE) 89 [1] (6f, Ayr, Hvy, Sep 22)
Soliloquy 89 [6] (1m, Newm, GF, May 6)
Sparkalot 89 [1] (6f, Kemw, SD, Mar 21)
Third Time Lucky (IRE) 89 [3] (1m, Ayr, Gd, Jun 23)
Ultimate Avenue (IRE) 89 [4] (6f, Newj, GF, Jun 9)
Vale Of Kent (IRE) 89 [4] (7f, Good, Gd, Aug 25)
Via Via (IRE) 89 [3] (1m 1f, Newm, GF, Sep 29)
Zap 89 [1] (7f, Newj, GF, Jul 13)
Abel Handy (IRE) 88 [6] (5f 143y, Donc, Gd, Sep 15)
Across The Stars (IRE) 88 [3] (1m 4f 6y, Epso, Gd, Jun 2)
Bella Ragazza 88 [1] (1m, Newm, GS, Oct 6)
Bengali Boys (IRE) 88 (6f, York, GF, Jun 16)
Camacho Chief (IRE) 88 [1] (5f, Leic, Gd, Sep 24)
Capton 88 [4] (1m 1f, Newm, GF, Sep 28)
Castle Hill Cassie (IRE) 88 [1] (7f 36y, Wolw, SD, Nov 16)
Charity Go (IRE) 88 [2] (1m 1f, Newm, GS, Apr 17)
Dancer Cross 88 [3] (1m 2f, Chmf, SD, Sep 1)
Donncha (IRE) 88 [3] (7f, Good, GS, May 5)
Eminent (IRE) 88 [5] (1m 1f 212y, Asco, GF, Jun 20)
Enable 88 [1] (1m 3f 219y, Kemw, SS, Sep 8)
Enjazaat 88 [5] (6f, Newb, GF, Jul 21)
Existential (IRE) 88 [1] (1m 75y, Nott, Gd, Aug 17)
Eziyra (IRE) 88 [3] (1m 3f 188y, York, GF, Aug 23)
Foxtrot Lady 88 [5] (6f, York, GF, Jun 16)
Francis Xavier (IRE) 88 [1] (1m 2f 5y, Pont, Gd, Sep 27)
Gronkowski (USA) 88 [1] (1m 5y, Ncsw, SD, Mar 30)
Handsome Dude 88 [1] (6f 16y, Souw, SD, Jan 18)
Harome (IRE) 88 [1] (5f, York, GF, Jul 13)
Hateya (IRE) 88 [2] (1m, Good, Gd, Jul 31)
Island Brave (IRE) 88 [1] (1m 6f, Nott, Gd, Aug 17)
Jazeel (IRE) 88 [1] (1m 1f, Newm, GF, Sep 28)
Just Hiss 88 [3] (1m, Ripo, Gd, Aug 18)
Kings Shield (USA) 88 [5] (7f 213y, Asco, GF, Jun 19)
Law Girl (FR) 88 [2] (1m 4f 180y, Leop, GF, Sep 15)
Leo Minor (USA) 88 [2] (5f, Leic, Gd, Sep 24)
Lightning Spear 88 [3] (1m, Asco, GF, Jun 19)
Lord Yeats 88 [7] (2m 1f 197y, Donc, GS, Sep 14)
Main Desire (IRE) 88 [1] (5f, York, GF, May 17)
Majeed 88 [1] (1m 3f 99y, Wind, GF, Jun 30)
Master The World (IRE) 88 (1m, Good, GF, Aug 3)
Medahim (IRE) 88 [4] (7f, Good, GS, May 5)
Mutamaded (IRE) 88 [1] (1m 1f 170y, Ripo, Sft, Apr 19)
Mutawathea 88 [4] (1m 1y, Linw, SD, Feb 24)
Mythmaker 88 [2] (5f, Beve, GF, Sep 1)
Nelson (IRE) 88 [6] (1m 3f 188y, York, GF, Aug 22)
Raid (IRE) 88 [4] (7f, Newb, GS, Apr 21)
Raselasad (IRE) 88 [1] (7f 6y, Catt, GF, Aug 29)
Rousayan (IRE) 88 [2] (7f, Thir, GS, Aug 4)
Shanghai Glory (IRE) 88 [2] (7f, Newj, GS, Aug 11)
Snowy Winter (USA) 88 [1] (1m 1f 100y, Gowr, GF, Aug 15)
So Beloved 88 [2] (7f, Thir, GS, Apr 21)
Soldier In Action (FR) 88 [5] (2m 56y, York, GF, Aug 22)
St Brelades Bay (IRE) 88 [3] (6f, Naas, Gd, Sep 30)
Swift Approval (IRE) 88 [2] (7f, Newj, GF, Jul 13)
Tennessee Wildcat (IRE) 88 [1] (1m 1f, Tipp, Yld, Aug 30)
Threeandfourpence (USA) 88 [1] (1m, Naas, GF, Jul 25)
Uae Prince (IRE) 88 [2] (1m 4f, Newm, GF, May 6)
Victory Angel (IRE) 88 [4] (6f, Newm, GF, May 6)
Walk In The Sun (USA) 88 [6] (7f, Asco, GF, Jun 20)
Wuheida 88 [1] (1m 1f, Newm, GF, May 6)
Zac Brown (IRE) 88 [1] (6f, Chmf, SD, Apr 26)
Al Jellaby 87 [2] (1m, Asco, GF, May 11)
Almoghared (IRE) 87 (2m 110y, Newb, GF, Jul 21)
Ambassadorial (USA) 87 [2] (7f, Dunw, SD, Apr 6)
Auxerre (IRE) 87 [1] (1m, Kemw, SS, Oct 10)
Ayutthaya (IRE) 87 [2] (1m 1f 35y, Hami, GS, Aug 21)
Big Storm Coming 87 [1] (7f, Newj, GF, Aug 3)
Carlton Frankie 87 [1] (5f, Epso, Sft, Aug 27)
Cliffs Of Capri 87 [1] (7f, Asco, Gd, Oct 5)
Deauville (IRE) 87 [2] (1m 1f, Newm, Gd, Apr 18)
Desert Law (IRE) 87 [6] (5f, Epso, Gd, Apr 25)
Doctor Sardonicus 87 [8] (5f, Hayd, Gd, May 26)
Downdraft (IRE) 87 [1] (1m 2f, Nava, Gd, Jun 2)
Downforce (IRE) 87 [3] (7f, Leic, Hvy, Apr 28)
Dramatic Queen (USA) 87 [1] (1m 5f, Linw, SD, Nov 1)
Embour (IRE) 87 [1] (6f, Sali, GS, May 26)
Flying Pursuit 87 [3] (6f, Ayr, Hvy, Sep 22)
Gabrial The Saint (IRE) 87 [8] (6f, York, GF, Jun 16)
Global Applause 87 [1] (5f 10y, Sand, GS, Sep 1)
Grandee (IRE) 87 [2] (1m 4f 10y, Ripo, GS, Apr 28)

Happy Family 87 [1] (7f 1y, Linw, SD, Mar 3)
Harry Hurricane 87 [5] (5f, Epso, Gd, Apr 25)
Helvetian 87 [4] (5f, Good, Gd, Aug 2)
Henley 87 [1] (5f, Thir, GS, Aug 4)
Herculean 87 [2] (1m, Newm, GF, May 18)
Holmeswood 87 [3] (5f 89y, York, GF, Aug 22)
Horseplay 87 [4] (1m 3f 188y, York, GF, Aug 23)
Indianapolis (IRE) 87 [3] (1m 1f, Tipp, Yld, Aug 30)
Isomer (USA) 87 [3] (1m, Newm, GS, Apr 17)
Khafoo Shememi (IRE) 87 [3] (1m 31y, Wind, Gd, May 14)
King's Pavilion (IRE) 87 [1] (1m 37y, Hayd, GS, Sep 28)
Kloud Gate (FR) 87 [2] (2m 110y, Newb, GF, Jul 21)
Koeman 87 [1] (1m 3f 211y, Asco, GF, Jul 28)
Making Light (IRE) 87 [1] (1m, Cork, Gd, Aug 11)
Maverick Officer 87 [1] (7f 212y, Hayd, GF, Jun 13)
Missy Mischief (USA) 87 [2] (6f, Chmf, SD, Sep 10)
Mountain Angel (IRE) 87 [2] (1m 1f 209y, Sand, GS, Sep 1)
Move In Time 87 [1] (5f, Newm, GF, May 19)
Muscika 87 [5] (5f 143y, Donc, Gd, Sep 15)
Outrage 87 [1] (5f, Ncsw, SD, Nov 22)
Precious Ramotswe 87 [8] (2m 2f, Newm, GF, Oct 13)
Reckless Endeavour (IRE) 87 [3] (6f, Chmf, SD, Jan 25)
Rosina 87 [1] (5f, Ncsw, SD, Jan 2)
Scarlet Dragon 87 [3] (1m 4f, Newb, GS, Oct 27)
Smart Call (SAF) 87 [4] (1m 2f 56y, York, GS, Jul 28)
Surrounding (IRE) 87 [2] (1m, Curr, GF, Jul 22)
Tajaanus (IRE) 87 [2] (7f, Newb, GS, Apr 21)
Take The Helm 87 [2] (7f, Chmf, SD, May 10)
Tanasoq (IRE) 87 [1] (5f, Epso, Gd, Jun 2)
Theglasgowwarrior 87 [3] (1m 6f 115y, Donc, GS, Sep 14)
Tribute Act 87 [2] (1m, Asco, GF, May 12)
Tropics (USA) 87 [1] (5f, Chmf, SD, Jun 13)
West Coast Flyer 87 [1] (1m 3f 219y, Kemw, SS, Jun 6)
Xenobia (IRE) 87 [1] (7f, Fair, GF, Jul 8)
You're Hired 87 [2] (1m 1f 209y, Sand, GF, Jul 26)
Almodovar (IRE) 86 [4] (1m 1f 209y, Sand, GS, Apr 27)
Amazing Red (IRE) 86 (2m 110y, Newb, GF, Jul 21)
Anna Nerium 86 [1] (7f, Newm, Gd, Apr 18)
Ashpan Sam 86 [1] (4f 217y, Ling, GF, Jul 21)
Bartholomeu Dias 86 [2] (1m 3f 218y, Good, GF, Jun 15)
Blakeney Point 86 [4] (1m 3f 218y, Good, GF, Aug 3)
Bobby Wheeler (IRE) 86 [1] (7f, Kemw, SD, Feb 1)
Bowson Fred 86 [3] (5f, Catt, Sft, Oct 20)
Buridan (FR) 86 [1] (6f, Hayd, GF, Jul 7)
Casey Jones (IRE) 86 [3] (1m 2f, Chmf, SD, Aug 17)
Cecchini (IRE) 86 [2] (1m 3f 133y, Ling, GF, May 12)
Charles Molson 86 [2] (7f, Chmf, SD, Sep 22)
Cliffs Of Dooneen (IRE) 86 [7] (1m 4f 180y, Leop, GF, Sep 15)
Coeur De Lion 86 [3] (2m 110y, Newb, GF, Jul 21)
Count Otto (IRE) 86 [3] (6f, Chmf, SD, Sep 15)
Dance Diva 86 [3] (7f, Newb, GS, Apr 21)
Dathanna (IRE) 86 [1] (7f 213y, Asco, Sft, May 2)
Dawn Delivers 86 [4] (6f, Curr, GF, Jun 8)
De Medici (IRE) 86 [1] (1m 1f 209y, Sand, GF, Jul 7)
Desert Encounter (IRE) 86 [2] (1m 2f, Newb, GF, Jul 21)
Desert Path 86 [1] (1m 3f 44y, Good, GF, Aug 3)
Documenting 86 [1] (7f 36y, Wolw, SS, Jul 29)
Drapers Guild 86 [7] (1m 4f, Gowr, GF, Aug 15)
Equitant 86 [1] (1m, Dunw, SD, Nov 23)
Gabr 86 [6] (7f 213y, Asco, GF, Jun 19)
Gustavus Vassa 86 [3] (1m 6f, Kill, Gd, Aug 23)
Hakam (USA) 86 [4] (6f, Asco, GF, Jul 13)
Hydrangea (IRE) 86 [5] (1m 3f 211y, Asco, Sft, Oct 20)
Joegogo (IRE) 86 [2] (4f 214y, Souw, SD, Mar 21)
Just That Lord 86 [3] (5f, Epso, Gd, Apr 25)
Knight Errant (IRE) 86 [1] (1m 1f 209y, Sand, Gd, Sep 19)
Magnificent 86 [2] (1m, Donc, Gd, May 5)
Mazzini 86 [1] (6f, Chmf, SD, Aug 11)
Merry Banter 86 [1] (5f, Redc, Gd, Oct 6)
Mr Owen (USA) 86 [4] (1m 31y, Wind, Gd, May 14)
National Army 86 [1] (1m, Donc, GF, Jun 1)
Not So Sleepy 86 [2] (1m 3f 197y, Donc, Sft, Nov 10)
Pactolus (IRE) 86 [1] (1m, Kemw, SS, Oct 8)
Petticoat 86 [1] (7f, Curr, GF, Jun 30)
Pinnata (IRE) 86 [1] (1m, Kemw, SS, Dec 14)
Poyle Vinnie 86 [2] (5f, Thir, GF, May 8)
Presidential (IRE) 86 [1] (7f, Newm, Sft, Nov 3)
Qaffaal (USA) 86 [1] (7f, Chmf, SD, May 31)
Racing Country (IRE) 86 [1] (7f 213y, Asco, GF, Jul 13)
Raven's Lady 86 [4] (6f, Asco, Sft, Oct 6)
Repton (IRE) 86 [1] (6f, Kemw, SD, Mar 31)
Roman River 86 [4] (5f, Ripo, Gd, Jun 20)
Romanised (IRE) 86 [1] (1m, Curr, GF, May 26)
Saltonstall 86 [2] (1m, Naas, Hvy, Mar 25)
Shared Equity 86 [2] (6f 2y, Donc, Sft, Mar 25)
Shenanigans (IRE) 86 [2] (1m 2f 43y, Donc, Sft, Nov 10)
Sleeping Lion (USA) 86 [1] (1m 4f, Newb, GF, Jul 5)
Sovereign Debt (IRE) 86 [1] (7f 192y, York, GF, Jun 15)
Theobald (IRE) 86 [1] (1m, Dunw, SD, Nov 9)
Time Shanakill (IRE) 86 [3] (1m 3f 219y, Kemw, SS, Dec 5)
Time To Study (FR) 86 [9] (1m 6f 115y, Donc, GS, Sep 14)
Tuff Rock (USA) 86 [2] (1m 4f 8y, Thir, GS, Apr 21)
Ulshaw Bridge (IRE) 86 [2] (7f 212y, Hayd, GF, Jun 13)
Zylan (IRE) 86 [1] (6f 16y, Souw, SD, Apr 12)
Alemaratalyoum (IRE) 85 [2] (7f 50y, Ayr, Hvy, Sep 22)
Aljazzi 85 [1] (1m, Asco, GF, Jun 20)
Alwaysandforever (IRE) 85 [2] (1m 5f, Linw, SD, Nov 1)
Arcanada (IRE) 85 [1] (1m 1y, Linw, SD, Jan 6)
Baraweez (IRE) 85 [7] (7f 192y, York, GF, Aug 23)
Betty F 85 [3] (7f, York, GF, Aug 23)
Blue Laureate 85 [7] (1m 5f 188y, York, GF, Aug 25)
Blue Mist 85 [1] (1m, Asco, Gd, Oct 5)
Bona Fide 85 [3] (1m 2f 43y, Donc, Sft, Nov 10)
Brick By Brick (IRE) 85 [6] (5f, York, GF, May 17)
Classic Pursuit 85 [1] (5f 3y, Pont, GF, Aug 8)
Collide 85 [1] (1m 2f 50y, Nott, Sft, Oct 17)
Danzan (IRE) 85 [2] (6f, Newm, Sft, Nov 2)
Dutch Connection 85 [7] (7f, Good, Gd, Jul 31)
Erissimus Maximus (FR) 85 [2] (5f 3y, Donc, GS, Oct 27)
Escalator 85 [1] (1m 1f 197y, Good, Sft, Aug 26)
Flavius Titus 85 [4] (6f, Asco, Gd, Oct 5)
Full Moon (IRE) 85 [1] (7f, Curr, Gd, Aug 25)
Gallipoli (IRE) 85 [2] (7f 14y, Ncsw, SD, Feb 21)
Get Knotted (IRE) 85 [8] (7f 192y, York, GF, Aug 23)
Glencadam Glory 85 [5] (2m 5f 143y, Asco, GF, Jun 23)
Gold Chest (USA) 85 [1] (1m, Newj, GF, Jul 12)
Gold Filigree (IRE) 85 [1] (5f 15y, Ches, Gd, Jun 16)
Golden Apollo 85 [9] (5f 143y, Donc, Gd, Sep 15)
Gossip Column (IRE) 85 [1] (1m 2f 100y, Hayd, GF, Jul 7)
Hayadh 85 [4] (1m, Ripo, Gd, Aug 18)
Hence (IRE) 85 [2] (1m 1f 100y, Gowr, GF, Aug 15)
Indian Blessing 85 [3] (7f, Good, GF, Aug 3)
Infrastructure 85 [1] (1m 4f 5y, Sali, GF, Jun 27)
Knighted (IRE) 85 [1] (7f 219y, Redc, GF, Sep 18)
Laraaib (IRE) 85 [9] (1m 1f 212y, Asco, GF, Jun 19)
Lush Life (IRE) 85 [1] (7f, Asco, Gd, Oct 5)
Magnus Maximus 85 [2] (6f 1y, Linw, SD, Jan 19)
Makitorix (FR) 85 [3] (1m 4f, Curr, Yld, Aug 31)
Mickey (IRE) 85 [2] (7f 1y, Linw, SD, Feb 23)
Ming (IRE) 85 [1] (1m 2f 150y, Dunw, SD, Apr 11)
Mount Moriah 85 [5] (2m 50y, Sand, Gd, May 24)
Mount Tahan (IRE) 85 [6] (1m 4f 51y, Wolw, SD, Dec 8)
Mr Top Hat 85 [2] (1m 6y, Pont, GS, Oct 8)
Normandy Barriere (IRE) 85 [5] (6f, Asco, GF, Jul 13)
Pacify 85 [4] (1m 3f 188y, York, GF, Aug 24)
Parys Mountain (IRE) 85 [1] (7f, Redc, Sft, Nov 6)
Podemos (GER) 85 [3] (1m 3f 219y, Kemw, SS, Nov 5)
Raa Atoll 85 [2] (1m 2f, Newm, Gd, Apr 19)

INDEX OF HORSES

INDEX OF HORSES